OVER OUR DEAD BODIES
Port Arthur and Australia's fight for gun control

Simon Chapman

SYDNEY UNIVERSITY PRESS

Originally published in 1998 by Pluto Press (Annandale, Australia)
This reprint edition published in 2013 by SYDNEY UNIVERSITY PRESS

Sydney University Press
Fisher Library F03
University of Sydney NSW 2006
AUSTRALIA
Email: sup.info@sydney.edu.au

National Library of Australia Cataloguing-in-Publication entry

Author: Chapman, Simon
Title: Over our dead bodies : Port Arthur and Australia's fight for gun
         control / Simon Chapman.
ISBN: 9781743320310 (pbk.)
Notes: Includes bibliographical references.
Subjects: Gun control--Australia.
          Firearms ownership--Australia.
Dewey Number:
         363.330994

Cover design by Dushan Mrva-Montoya

Contents

Foreword to the reprint edition

The firearm massacre at a primary school in Sandy Hook, Connecticut on 14 December 2012 in which a lone gunman armed with three semi-automatic firearms killed 20 children, six teachers, his gun-owning mother and then himself, has stimulated unprecedented momentum for meaningful gun controls in the US.

In 2006, with colleagues, I published a report[1] that examined what had happened to gun deaths in Australia since the implementation of comprehensive gun law reforms in Australia, following the Port Arthur massacre in April 1996, where 35 people were killed by a single gunman.

On the day of the US massacre, I tweeted a link to that report, published in the *British Medical Journal*'s specialist journal *Injury Prevention*. In the six years since our paper had been published, it had been opened online 14,742 times. In the month of December 2012, it was opened a remarkable 84,542 times, quite easily the most opened paper I have ever published on any subject in 35 years of public health research.

Americans might value reflection on Australia's recent experience in reducing deaths from firearms. The US has 13.7 times Australia's

---

1 Chapman S, Alpers P, Agho K, Jones M. Australia's 1996 gun law reforms: faster falls in firearm deaths, firearm suicides, and a decade without mass shootings. *Injury Prevention* 2006, 12: 365–72. Available at: http://injuryprevention.bmj.com/content/12/6/365. full?sid=4d930b0a-0f5d-484a-8ad4-b5839c7d10c5.

population, 104 times its total firearm-caused deaths (32,163 in 2011 vs 236 in 2010), and 370 times Australia's firearm homicide rate (11,101 in 2011 vs 30 in 2010).

Importantly, in the 16 years since the law reforms, there have been no mass shootings. While the rate of firearm homicide was reducing by an average of 3% per year prior to the law reforms, this increased to 7.5% per year after the introduction of the new laws, although this failed to reach statistical significance because of the low power inherent in the small numbers involved. Our report showed that firearm-related suicides in males declined from 3.4 deaths per 100,000 person-years in 1997 to 1.3 per 100,000 person-years, representing a decline of 59.9%. The rate of all other suicides declined from 19.9 deaths per 100,000 person-years in 1997 to 15.0 per 100,000 person-years in 2005, representing a decline of 24.5%, and suggesting there was no substitution effect. The yearly change in firearm-related suicides in males was –8.7%, and the yearly change in other suicides was –4.1%, less than half the rate of fall in firearm suicide.

Plainly, there is great interest in Australia's experience in gun law reform.[2] I wrote this book after the Port Arthur massacre, to provide a record of the events leading up to the law reforms, and the reaction to them. The book quickly went out of print and has ever since been very hard to obtain, with the publisher Pluto Press, since closing. I am very thankful to Sydney University Press for agreeing to republish the book in its original form, less the cartoons which were contained in the first edition. Unfortunately many of the links are no longer active (being old) and cannot be recovered. We recommend that those inclined to do so, try their luck finding them in the Wayback Machine.[3]

---

2 See 'Australia – gun facts, figures and the law' for specific information and updates: http://www.gunpolicy.org/firearms/region/cp/australia.

3 http://archive.org/web/web.php.

My editor Agata Mrva-Montoya, who worked on my previous book with Sydney University Press,[4] turned this around in weeks. I am very grateful to her.

Simon Chapman
5 February 2013

---

4 Chapman S, Barratt A, Stockler M. *Let sleeping dogs lie? What men should know before being tested for prostate cancer.* Sydney: Sydney University Press, 2010, http://ses.library.usyd.edu.au/handle/2123/6835.

Preface and acknowledgments to the 1998 edition

This book was written for two main groups of readers. Foremost in my mind were Australians who were appalled by the Port Arthur gun massacre which killed 35 people and who want to understand more about the struggle to secure the historic reform of gun laws in the months after the incident. For millions, the massacre and the long overdue need for reform of gun laws became a major topic of conversation among family, friends and workmates. Tens of thousands of you demonstrated in support of the new laws, wrote letters to politicians and expressed yourselves in public media such as letters to newspapers and calls to radio stations. The wisdom and timing of many of these contributions were enormously powerful in advancing the debate and convincing politicians of the huge community support for gun control, and that further excuses for inaction were unacceptable. I wanted to pay a sort of homage to this support, which more than one commentator pointed out was a wonderful example of non-violent 'people power' influencing law reform.

I have also written the book for people working to promote gun control in other countries. As will become apparent, I believe that it was not by mere serendipity that a massacre translated into major law reform. There are many lessons for others in how such tragedies can be catalysts for radical change. Yet law reform following massacres is not inevitable; rather, it requires the planned, strategic use of media and other forms of advocacy to convert anger and outrage into action. A prerequisite for this change would appear to be a sustained period of public advocacy for gun law reform that keys up communities to define soft gun laws as a blight on political courage and an affront to a safe community. Gun massacres force politicians to confront an electorate outraged at political spinelessness in an area which demands nothing less than strong leadership. Much of this book is an attempt to distil some lessons out of the chaos that became the day to day of the lives of those pushing for gun law reform in the months after Port Arthur.

Along with Rebecca Peters (NSW), Roland Browne (Tasmania), Helen Gadsen (Queensland), Tim Costello (Victoria) and Charles Watson (NSW) I have been a spokesperson for the Coalition for Gun Control, a coalition of associations and individuals committed to tightening the regulation of guns in order to reduce gun violence in our community. The CGC became incorporated in 1995 in NSW and became a national group (thereafter, the National Coalition for Gun Control or NCGC) on 15 June 1996, when Rebecca was appointed national coordinator. Over 300 organisations from the fields of public health, medicine, law, domestic violence advocacy, women's, religious, ethnic and community groups have supported NCGC lobbying activities. While no longer active in the NCGC, between 1992 and 1996 I was one of its main members.

Despite this huge support and the overwhelming weight of public opinion in favour of gun control, the NCGC today remains an organisation run on the goodwill and dedication of volunteers, on the financial shoe-strings provided by public donations and on the occasional largesse of supportive organisations. Gun control has always been an immensely politicised issue. Despite an average of some 560 people who are killed by guns in Australia in each of the last six years, there has so far been no government with the courage or foresight to support the NCGC with little but pats on the back in times of mutual agreement. At one stage word was passed from the NSW Labor government that we would not be receiving funding because it was plain some of us were connected with the Liberal Party. We got the same news from the Federal (Liberal Coalition) government, being told that it was obvious the *same* people were Labor supporters. Frequently during the post–Port Arthur debate, people would contact us and make comments that implied we were a huge organisation with a fully equipped office, salaried staff and a lot of money in the bank. Nothing could have been further from the truth.

We were very honoured that the National Coalition for the Gun Control was awarded the Human Rights and Equal Opportunity Commission community award for 1996 (shared with ECPAT, the group working to end child prostitution in Asian tourism). Rebecca Peters shared the individual award, the 1996 Human Rights Medal, with Rob Riley, long-time Western Australian campaigner for Aboriginal rights who died during the year.

At the height of the debate and well after it peaked, Rebecca often worked 16 hours a day, seven days a week. She was supported by dozens of volunteers who helped in many invaluable ways. Roland Browne fitted gun control advocacy around his work as a lawyer, and my sabbatical leave plans were turned upside down. Julia Tsalis worked as the NCGC's Sydney office secretary from May until December 1996, and was supported by dozens of volunteers who helped in many invaluable ways.

There are countless people who should be thanked for their support throughout the months when the new gun laws were being secured. Here, I want to give special thanks to several people who assisted me in writing this book. The first draft of the book was written between August and Christmas 1996. Philip Alpers from New Zealand was invaluable in his support. His encyclopedic knowledge of shooting incidents and his expertise in technical matters about guns and the gun lobby was always just a phone call away. As drafts of chapters were finished, I sent them off to Rebecca and Philip for comment. My original hope was for Rebecca to coauthor the book, but her concern to give all her amazing energy to the implementation of the new laws, to forging links with gun control groups in other nations, to the visit of three Dunblane fathers in April 1997 and taking up a research position in the United States took precedence. I am certain that the book would have been far better with her further contribution. But I'm also certain that support for gun control has advanced still further by her decision to put advocacy for gun control before writing about it.

Roland Browne, Michael Dudley, Richard Harding, Satyanshu Mukherjee and Philip Alpers read and commented on early drafts. Roland helped out with Tasmanian material. The Advocacy Institute in Washington DC provided quiet space for me to write in July and August 1996. Thanks go to Michelle Scollo who clipped all gun stories from the Melbourne *Age* for me over five months. And thanks go especially to the cartoonists – Michael Leunig, Bruce Petty, Cathy Wilcox, Ron Tandberg and Alan Moir – who have allowed their work to be used in the book. Finally, I thank Penny O'Donnell, Tony Moore and Sean Kidney at Pluto for their calm steerage of the book through many months of unexpected difficulties.

Because I live in Sydney, the book reflects a perspective very much constrained by my experience of the events following Port Arthur, particularly as it unfolded through Sydney's mass media and political system. I make no pretence that this book is in any way a formal history of all that happened throughout Australia. Such a book would need to be massive. My main interest in writing the book was to capture the nature of the public discourse on gun control that the Port Arthur killings unleashed and which framed the way that the issue came to be defined by ordinary people throughout the country and by the politicians who were now forced to act. As all will recall, in 1996 gun control was to suddenly become one of the most discussed public issues in Australia's mass media. The 10,000 watt lights of the mass media turned on a situation focus the minds of politicians very quickly. This book is largely an attempt to peer into those lights and review the sort of light that they cast on gun control as a public issue.

I had only occasional contact with staff in the political offices of those politicians working to pass and implement the new gun laws. Their roles, particularly that of the Office of Law Enforcement Coordination (or as it was known during the Port Arthur Period, the Commonwealth Law Enforcement Board) in Canberra whose staff played a critical role in drafting the legislation and in briefing politicians, are unsung in this book. The behind-the-scenes work of those government officers and politicians' staff who worked to ensure the laws had the best chance of passing deserves the highest praise.

All royalties from the sale of this book will go to support an international internet-based network that is allowing the rapid communication of information and strategy among gun control advocates from many nations.

Simon Chapman
Department of Public Health and Community Medicine
University of Sydney
May 1998

Introduction

On the afternoon of 28 April 1996 a man armed with two military-style semi-automatic rifles shot dead 35 people and wounded 18 others in and around the historic tourist precinct of Port Arthur, about 100 kilometres from the Tasmanian capital city of Hobart.

Most of those killed were tourists on a Sunday visit to Tasmania's busiest tourist site, ruins of a notoriously cruel prison established in 1830. Twenty of the 35 were killed inside the Broad Arrow Café after the gunman entered, took a semi-automatic weapon from a sports bag and began shooting at people eating their lunch. The shooting rampage lasted about two minutes, during which time the killer laughed aggressively. Most of the remaining victims were shot at an approach to the site. A further 18 were injured by bullet wounds, some suffering horrific injuries. The gunman was captured the next day and identified as Martin Bryant, a 28-year-old from a Hobart suburb who had no previous criminal record of violence nor any history of diagnosed mental illness. The event generated huge media attention, and for the next three months the nation witnessed an impassioned debate between those who argued that it was unconscionable to allow Australia to continue to 'go down the American path' and those opposed to virtually any form of gun control.

The death toll of 35 was almost half the total of all gun homicides for the entire country in an average year and equal to Tasmania's total annual gun death rate. The Australian media described the massacre as 'the worst massacre by a single gunman in Australian history'[1] and Bryant as 'the world's worst lone mass killer'.[2] (Note, however, that the wholesale slaughter of Aborigines in the 19th century often involved far more deaths. For example, about 170 Aborigines were slaughtered in the Medway Ranges, Queensland, in October and November 1861. There are no records of how many were killed by single individuals.)[3]

The day after the murders, Australia's Prime Minister, John Howard, who had been in office only 57 days following his party's 13 years in Opposition, announced his intention to introduce the most sweeping gun control reforms ever contemplated by any Australian government. These reforms were drafted by Attorney General Daryl Williams and the Commonwealth Law Enforcement Board, based on the recommendations of the 1990 report by the National Committee on Violence. The reforms were detailed in an historic agreement between all nine state, territory and Commonwealth governments, announced at an emergency meeting of the Australasian Police Ministers' Council (APMC) on 10 May.

The resolutions committed every state and territory to pass laws requiring the following:

1. A ban on the importation, ownership, sale, resale, transfer, possession, manufacture or use of:

-   all self-loading centre-fire rifles, whether military-style or not
-   all self-loading and pump-action shotguns
-   all self-loading rim-fire rifles.

    Exemptions for low-powered (rim-fire) self-loading .22s and pump-action shotguns would be available to primary producers

---

1 Simpson L, Hayes B. 'Sunday slaughter', *Sydney Morning Herald (SMH)*, 29 April 1996: 1.

2 Sutton C, Gilmore H, Kent S. 'He could have been stopped', *Sun Herald*, 5 May 1996: 1.

3 Elder B. *Blood on the wattle: massacres and maltreatment of Australian Aborigines since 1788.* Sydney: Child & Associates, 1988: 167.

(farmers) who could satisfy police that they had a 'genuine need' which could not be achieved by some other means, or by non-prohibited weapons. A further exemption was added later to permit some clay target shooters to own a semi-automatic shotgun. No other 'sporting' or competitive use of semi-automatic long-arms was to be allowed.

2. A compensatory 'buyback' scheme funded through an increase in the Medicare levy, whereby gun owners would be paid the market value of any prohibited guns they handed in. Owners of prohibited weapons would have 12 months to surrender their guns. After this amnesty, penalties for illegal ownership would be severe.

3. The registration of all firearms as part of an integrated shooter licensing scheme, maintained through the computerised National Exchange of Police Information (NEPI).

4. Shooter licensing based on a requirement to prove a 'genuine reason' for owning a firearm. Genuine reason could include occupational uses such as stock and vermin control on farms; demonstrated membership of an authorised target shooting club; or hunting when the applicant could provide permission from a rural landowner. The APMC agreement explicitly ruled out 'personal protection' or self-defence as a genuine reason to own a gun.

5. A licensing scheme based on five categories of firearms (A, B, C, D, H), minimum age of 18, and criteria for a 'fit and proper person'. These criteria would include compulsory cancellation or refusal of licences to people who have been convicted for violence or subject to a domestic violence restraining order within the past five years.

6. New licence applicants would need to undertake an accredited training course in gun safety.

7. As well as a licence to own firearms, a separate permit would be required for each purchase of a gun. Permit applications would be subject to a 28-day waiting period to allow the licensee's genuine reason to be checked.

8. Uniform and strict gun storage requirements.

9. Firearm sales could be conducted only by or through licensed fire-arms dealers, thus ending private and mail order gun sales. Detailed records of all sales would have to be provided to police.

10. The sale of ammunition would be allowed only for firearms for which the purchaser is licensed and limits would be placed on the quantity of ammunition that may be purchased in a given period.

This agreement represented the single biggest advance in gun control in Australian history – and possibly anywhere in the world. When enacted in the weeks and months ahead by Australia's six state and two territory governments, these measures placed Australian gun laws among the most strict in the world. To gun control activists, the Police Ministers' agreement was an advance of unprecedented proportions, surpassing even the most remote expectations of what might be achieved in a single package of reforms.

To Australia's gun lobby, the resolutions were an unrivalled catastrophe. Besides the restrictions brought by the new laws, the killings unleashed a conflagration of almost wholly negative media attention onto the gun lobby, and especially onto a handful of its key spokesmen, who strove relentlessly to block the new gun laws. Never before had shooters been subject to such prolonged and overwhelmingly negative public examination. Night after night on their televisions, Australians saw and heard embittered, belligerent men whose main purpose in life appeared to be ensuring that they could keep military-style and rapid-fire weaponry capable of blowing apart all in its path. This was a far cry from any sentimental notions of rustic farmers bagging a few ducks, rabbits or kangaroos that many Australians might have visualised when the subject of shooting had arisen in the past. At worst, many of these men rapidly came to signify a subterranean, angry and potentially dangerous side of Australian life.

Bryant's short rampage at Port Arthur marked a change in the gun lobby's smug and wholly disproportionate political power in Australia. It irrevocably changed the way the great majority of the community saw the gun lobby. These men (there were very few women – see Chapter 5) were seen to be more determined than ever to maintain their self-styled 'right' to own semi-automatic weapons, without providing the police with any record of how many of these or other guns they might be holding. The contrast between those fixated on this 'right' and the horror and outrage felt by millions of Australians wanting a safer community could not have been more stark. As will be shown, Australia's politicians united in a rare show of support and responded to the will of the great majority of community that action, unprecedented in the history of national gun control, should be taken.

Throughout the debate the gun lobby repeatedly claimed that it was not to 'blame' for the events at Port Arthur; that its members were decent, law-abiding citizens who had and would not harm anyone; and that attempts to control guns were 'attacking the wrong end of the problem' while ignoring the 'real causes of violence', such as media glorification of violence and the breakdown of 'the family'. 'Legitimate' gun owners, they argued, were being punished and made to feel guilty for the actions of a madman. 'Ordinary shooters' repeatedly stated that they were highly affronted at being considered a potential danger to themselves and the community. The gun lobby insisted that the only people who should be denied firearms were those who could be predicted to commit violence (see Chapter 6). Everyone else – all 'ordinary shooters' – should be allowed open access to guns. On Monday 29 April, while the Port Arthur emergency was still in progress – with Martin Bryant keeping police at bay at the Seascape Guesthouse – a Tasmanian gun lobby representative spoke on national radio defending the free availability of military weapons in Tasmania.

Gun control reform

This book has two main and closely related goals. The first is an attempt to answer the question: 'Why did politicians from all main parties, many of whom had previously opposed gun law reform, suddenly come to unite behind the Prime Minister's determination to reform Australia's gun laws?' A short and superficial answer to this question would be to conclude simply that Port Arthur alone justified Howard's conviction: that 'it took an act of savagery unprecedented in peacetime to produce a coalition of interest unprecedented in peacetime – in its breadth, its depth and its strength of resolve.'[4] Quite obviously, the special APMC meeting would not have been convened, nor its task made so urgent, had Port Arthur not occurred.

The second goal is to give a detailed account of the ways the discourse on gun control was conducted in the mass media across Australia during the main advocacy period, lasting three months after the massacre. The main question addressed here is: 'How did protagonists and opponents of gun control seek to frame or define the debate on gun control?' Port Arthur made gun control almost undeniable as a political response because the preceding years of advocacy for gun law reforms had succeeded in positioning them as sensible, easily understood and above all the course that any *decent* society committed to public safety should adopt. When Port Arthur occurred, the seeds sown during these years of advocacy erupted out of an angry community who made it plain they would countenance no more of the political equivocation that had characterised gun control in the past. Suddenly, the debating frames that had been set and continually repeated throughout the preceding years became politically compelling, entering into countless public statements made by citizens and by politicians now keen to side with gun control. The core success of gun control arguments having seized the dominant debating frames, the gun control position was sustained in the face of many and prolonged attempts by the gun lobby to recapture the debate by defining it according to the catalogue of gun lobby arguments about the desirability of an armed society.

Certainly there were some signs of hope before Port Arthur. The Federal Government had banned the importation of military style semi-automatic weapons in 1991, but tens and possibly hundreds of thousands of these guns remained in circulation. In the absence of gun

---

4 Gordon M. 'Savagery unites an unlikely coalition', *The Australian*, 11 May 1996.

registration in three states, no-one knew where they were. A month before Port Arthur – and only 33 days after his election – Federal Attorney General Daryl Williams told *The Australian*, 'I intend to pursue [uniform gun laws. These are] really very important. You can't have one part of Australia tightly controlled only to have another part with lax controls.'[5] Williams had previously advocated tighter gun control in his home State of Western Australia, with particular reference to the problem of rural youth firearm suicide. Williams may well have vigorously pursued national gun law reform as an early priority, but he would not have been the first politician to do so. Nor, most likely, the first to fail.

The massacre then, was almost certainly a *necessary* condition enabling Howard and Williams to smash through the political timidity about gun lobby backlash that had long infected Australian politics. But a massacre is rarely if ever *sufficient* cause for wholesale legislative reform – as government responses to previous massacres in Australia and elsewhere have shown. There is a great deal of advocacy work that must take place before, immediately after and then well into the critical post-massacre period to ensure that community and political grief, outrage and anger translate into policy and law reform.

Some commentators suggested that the sheer magnitude of the Port Arthur slaughter tipped it over a critical edge and made law reform inevitable. By this argument, massacres involving say, four, eight or ten people may be horrifying and highly newsworthy, but not cataclysmic enough to prompt major law reform. By this view, 35 deaths lie beyond some macabre number that marks the boundary between political inertia and action.

I reject this idea. Each year there are dozens of avoidable tragedies in different parts of the world involving the deaths of many people. These often involve airline, rail, boat or road safety; fires or building collapses; major industrial explosions or mining disasters. Often the death toll from such events surpasses the number killed at Port Arthur, or previous records for numbers killed in particular circumstances. And

---

5 Taylor L. 'Uniform gun laws pursued', *The Australian*, 28 March 1996.

in many such cases, little if any real change in law or policy is made afterwards to reduce the chances of these events reoccurring. Where change does occur, it is often precipitated by such disasters. But a more penetrating analysis has to ask what distinguishes the social and political climate around a disaster that leads to law or policy reform from the far more usual outcome: disasters leading to little or only superficial change.

All over the world annual death tolls caused by firearms owe little to mass killings. The overwhelming majority of deaths are single suicides and homicides, followed by dual murder-suicides and homicides. For example, in NSW between 1968 and 1992, there were 2,321 homicide incidents involving 2,544 victims – an average of 1.09 victims per incident.[6] Yet internationally, major advances in gun control depend largely on relatively uncommon but more dramatic killings, particularly when these occur in public places and the victims are unknown to the perpetrator. These infrequent events can therefore be considered critically important to possible advances in gun control policies. They raise questions about how gun control advocates should prepare for the dreadful inevitability of such incidents and, when they do occur, how advocates should respond to achieve a positive outcome.

Disaster plans advocacy

Hospitals and public health agencies routinely develop plans that allow them to respond effectively to major disasters involving large numbers of victims or where there is imminent threat to communities. Hospitals have disaster plans for contingencies such as transport crashes, major fires, and warfare. In public health, the disaster plan concept has been extended to cover hazardous events such as exposure to pathogenic agents, major chemical spills and leaks, the emission of toxic industrial gases and the inadvertent release of biologically or chemically contaminated food.

---

6 Gallagher P, Huong MTND, Bonney R. 'Trends in homicide 1968 to 1992', *Crime and Justice Bulletin*, 1994, 21: 1.

I have been intrigued at the possibilities for applying the notion of a disaster plan in the area of advocacy, as well as in its present application in treatment and early intervention. Major, potentially preventable disasters, whether they be chemical spills, vehicle pile-ups at black spots on the roads, building fires or collapses or – as here – violent gun incidents, should be anticipated and planned for by those advocating preventive measures. The question is, how can advocates exploit to advantage the huge public and political interest these disasters generate when they occur? How can they move the discourse on gun massacres beyond community outrage and on to how such massacres might be made less likely to occur? In the jargon of public health, how can the debate be moved from 'downstream', where the community expresses its grief, anger and outrage and desire to comfort victims, to 'upstream', where those so grieved and angered can feel assured that real efforts at prevention are being made?

From 29 April 1996 to the passage of the last new gun law in the Northern Territory, advocacy both supporting and attacking the proposed new laws was often unrelenting. This was a critical period when both sides realised that enormous gains or losses were within their grasp. The NCGC's efforts to harness advocacy opportunities as they arose became concentrated like never before – as did those of the gun lobby.

To some, the word 'harness' might connote a vulture-like attitude to human tragedy, with advocates waiting patiently for disasters or gun massacres so they might climb aboard community outrage and opportunistically capitalise on the misfortune of others. Some in the gun lobby might have even suggested that the appropriate word here is waiting 'hopefully'. Gun lobbyist Roy Smith, of the Sporting Shooters Association of NSW, was one who took this view of gun control advocates:

> We are sickened by the way these do-gooders will capitalise on other people's tragedies to push their own agenda. As long as these anti-gun academics and bureaucrats are prepared to use any tragedy involving firearms as a platform from which

to chant their anti-gun mantras, we have no chance of dealing with the real problem.'[7]

But only those opposing gun law reform or the most politically
myopic could take this view. If we are to learn preventive lessons from
past disasters, there can be no place for overly respectful meekness by
advocates when the community is most angered and demanding of
change. Such times are simply critical to the gun control advocacy process and require contingency plans.

The typical pattern of community and political outrage about disasters follows a pattern of shock, anger, condolence to the victims and talk
of remedial actions, culminating in referral of such plans to bureaucrats and experts for consideration. As a *7.30 Report* journalist put it:
'Australian massacres have a dulling familiarity. Public shock and outrage is soothed by assurances of tougher gun laws. But as public outcry
dissipates, often so does political will in the face of the gun lobby.'[8] In
the period between referral to committees and special inquiries and
the time taken for them to make their recommendations, two things
almost invariably happen: the passage of time fades the community's
memory of how outraged they felt about the incident; and those opposing change do all they can to lobby governments against taking action.
Opponents of change also seek to reframe public discourse about the
way the massacre is defined and talked about, who should be blamed
for it and what might be a reasonable response. As will be discussed at
length (see particularly Chapter 6), the Australian gun lobby worked
strenuously to define what happened in Port Arthur as being wholly
irrelevant to gun laws. The blame, according to the gun lobby, lay with
the authorities who had failed to recognise and control Bryant before-
hand. Plans to reform gun laws were, by this definition, entirely unjust
and misguided. In this and many other respects, its strategy mirrored
that of the US gun lobby, from which it derives considerable counsel.

---

7 SSAA. Press release. 'Shooters slam health department survey', 22 March
1996.

8 McGuire F. *7.30 Report*, ABC TV, 9 May 1996.

Community voices

The sheer immensity of what happened at Port Arthur ensured that the volume of political and community participation in this discourse quite easily surpassed that emanating from the various groups in the organised gun control lobby. This was never going to be a routine media joust between two single-issue lobby groups. The role played by groups like the National Coalition for Gun Control (NCGC), the Australian Medical Association (AMA) and the Melbourne-based Gun Control Australia (GCA) was greatly overshadowed by the role of ordinary Australian citizens and the politicians who climbed out of their closets to become strong advocates for gun law reform. The task for the NCGC changed: from being virtually the only regular public commentators on the need for law reform, it now had to strategically maintain the nation's outrage over what had happened and challenge any possibility of inadequate reform.

In the three months after the massacre, the volume of anger against the gun lobby remained so intense that whenever a gun lobby initiative needed a response, the public was more than obliging. This response included everything from ordinary people expressing their heartfelt, untutored reactions to gun lobby rhetoric, to those who had particular personal experiences relevant to the argument. On many occasions we read and heard arguments, analogies, and factual perspectives on gun control from people who had no connection with the NCGC. Frequently, we recognised these as identical to arguments and analogies that we and others in gun control had sown in the media in preceding years on issues like gun registration, safe storage and international comparisons. Our past media advocacy efforts were bearing fruit in the form of articulate and informed public comment.

The NCGC itself was often able to play a key role in the discourse on gun control because we were constantly contacted by journalists to comment or to participate in debates. From the day of the Port Arthur massacre, our lives were dominated for weeks that for some grew into months by the media seeking comment and information. We also initiated countless interviews by phoning radio and television stations and the press with comments on news, issuing press releases and trying to make ourselves constantly accessible to the media. Throughout the book I provide accounts of some of the ways we tried to take part in these discussions.

The second aim of the book, then, is to provide a detailed analysis of how guns, shooters and gun control were talked about in Australia during the three months at the height of the debate, when the political events on gun control were most acute. This public discourse was conducted in the mass media between two broad camps: those who supported the changes John Howard sought to introduce, and those who were (mostly virulently) opposed to them.

The former group comprised politicians in charge of introducing and supporting the changes; the various lobby groups advocating gun law reform; editors, columnists, broadcasters and cartoonists who covered the events; and without doubt, the most powerful group of all – the huge section of the public who wrote into newspapers, called up radio discussion programs and phoned, faxed and wrote to politicians. Among this group were many gun owners who demonstrated either their indifference to or support for the new laws by their answers to opinion polls, their absence from the gun lobby's protests and demonstrations, and their eagerness to surrender their prohibited and other guns from the day the buyback schemes began.

Those opposed to change comprised the organised gun lobby in Australia, and those who belonged to its various associations or supported its objectives. Several diverse groups can be loosely grouped together as the collective voice seeking to oppose tough gun laws in Australia. Chief among these are the Sporting Shooters Association of Australia (SSAA) and the NSW-based Shooters' Party. Both claim to be well resourced and to have large constituencies for whom guns are plainly a major focus of their lives. Consequently, they have an impassioned and willing network of people who are very determined to safeguard their interests. It was these interests which had so successfully prevented gun law reform from proceeding after previous Australian massacres. So a major task for gun control advocacy became not only advancing support for gun control, but also systematically eroding community and political support for the gun lobby and its arguments.

Structure of the book

Chapter 1 examines the Port Arthur massacre and its immediate impact on the Australian community, as reported in the mass media. It describes how the massacre was reported and what was said about its perpetrator in an attempt to place the enormity of this massacre in the context of reports of other Australian gun violence of recent times. Aspects of the Port Arthur reportage, and particularly of Bryant's alleged mental state, held major implications for the gun control debate which followed in the next few months.

Chapter 1 also looks at the role of political leadership in securing gun control reforms. National reform of gun laws became the unplanned first major test of Prime Minister John Howard's leadership. Had Howard followed the example of previous political leaders in their dealings with gun massacres, he could have dropped the matter into the abyss of the parliamentary committee process or, more predictably, responded that gun control was a matter for the state governments. In other words, he could have washed his hands of a political controversy and left eight state and territory governments to continue to fail to reach consensus on gun law reforms. Howard's position and his determination to see it fulfilled became one of the most enduring and important political narratives in the months after Port Arthur. Chapter 1 reviews Howard's role, and those of other political forces across Australia, examining particularly the U-turns taken by some who had previously opposed gun law reform.

Chapter 2 briefly reviews the evidence about gun violence in Australia and overseas. It examines the two core propositions in gun control: that there is a relationship between the number of guns in a community and the degree of gun violence in a community; and that governments concerned to reduce violence are therefore justified in controlling access to guns. These propositions provided the bedrock on which the reforms rested.

Chapter 3 gives a brief history of gun control advocacy in Australia, describing the debate in the months prior to Port Arthur.

Chapter 4 examines the reforms agreed on in 1996 by the Police Ministers, which mostly passed into law as planned. It first explores the reasons each reform was proposed, the gun lobby's case against each of them, and the ways the NCGC, the public and political supporters of the changes sought to promote and defend these reforms in the face of gun lobby opposition.

Chapters 5 and 6 examine the gun lobby in Australia and its public arguments about the folly of gun control. They examine their response to the massacre and their repertoire of arguments against gun control.

Chapter 6 analyses the key arguments the gun lobby used to oppose the public demand for tighter gun laws. This shows how the gun lobby attempted to frame the discourse about gun control, and the alternative frames gun control advocates sought to promote. I hope this chapter of the book will be most useful to people elsewhere in the world who face the task of gaining public and political support for gun control. I have set out to document the advocates' efforts to counter the gun lobby and to reflect on how we might have done better.

Chapter 7 reviews examples of how the original APMC resolutions were toned down as the states and territories introduced and then amended their legislation. It discusses several cases where state law reform fell disturbingly short of the original Howard plan. Finally, the chapter reviews two issues for future gun law reform in Australia: the storage of guns outside urban homes, and the need for tighter controls on semi-automatic handguns.

A note on source material

As mentioned above, one of the main interests in this book is how the media contributed to the gun control debate. I obtained a complete set of all press coverage on guns for the three months after the massacre from: *The Australian*, the *Bulletin*, four Sydney metropolitan news-papers (*Sydney Morning Herald, Daily Telegraph, Sun Herald, Sunday Telegraph*) and the Melbourne *Age*. I also obtained a three-month set of clips from the *West Australian*. When possible, I videotaped news reports and current affairs programs on the massacre and gun control. The collection here is incomplete, but contains some of the key inter-views and reports. I could not afford even samples of the massive radio coverage the issue generated.

I have not attempted an exhaustive analysis. I was not interested in formally cataloguing the huge press coverage of the events, but set out to chart the dominant themes that unfolded in the discourse on gun control. There was a great deal of repetition of many themes and argu-ments, and I have indicated the range of these with examples. I hope the analysis of the factors driving and retarding proposals for gun control in Australia will assist in the development of successful strategies in other countries.

1

The massacre

History is dotted with decisive events that leave indelible marks on nearly everyone's memory. The day wars are declared or end are such events, as are the assassinations of major world figures. Most people over 40 can recall exactly where they were and what they were doing when the news of President John Kennedy's assassination was first broadcast. So momentous was that event, and so intense and prolonged was much of the Western world's attempt to come to terms with the meaning of his murder, that it marks a special point in the memories of millions. The Port Arthur shootings seem destined to become another such event for most Australians. As one newspaper expressed it, 'The cloth of our nation was torn across.'[1]

About 3pm on 28 April 1996, radio and television programs were interrupted by news flashes of a man running amok with a gun at Tasmania's Port Arthur tourist site. Ironically, Roland Browne was at home in Hobart holding a meeting of the Tasmanian Coalition for Gun Control (TCGC). They were developing a strategy for gun law reform including semi-automatic weapons ahead of a meeting scheduled for the following Wednesday with the Tasmanian Police Minister. Even more ironically, just one month earlier the Hobart *Mercury* had published a letter from Roland Browne pointing out that the Dunblane massacre could easily be repeated in Tasmania, because semi-automatic weapons were so easily obtainable in that state.

---

1 Anon. 'Out of the shadow of the gun' (editorial), *Daily Telegraph*, 11 May 1996.

I learned of the killings while at home in Sydney, reading and listening to a radio broadcast of a football match. The early radio reports said that several, then ten or more, had been killed. Subsequent reports added three, four or five more, with speculation mounting that the toll could go as high as 20. As the afternoon progressed, the death toll rapidly passed 20, rising to unbelievable levels which could only be compared with major bus or train crash figures. By early evening, the number of dead was 32. Three more bodies were discovered in the next two days at the burnt-out guesthouse which Martin Bryant set alight, and where he was arrested.

I sent the following release to all main media outlets at 4.39pm that day. The next day, the Coalition for Gun Control did little else but give interviews to the Australian and international media.

Media release

PORT ARTHUR MASSACRE

Please feel free to use the following comment regarding the Port Arthur massacre.

'The Coalition for Gun Control has called on the Prime Minister to take immediate action and show leadership to prevent Australia going further down the American road of increasing levels of gun violence. Mr Howard must act tomorrow to announce national uniform gun registration; a ban on private ownership of semi-automatics; steep annual licence and registration fees; and far tougher guidelines on who can own firearms.

State governments like Tasmania, New South Wales and Queensland which have no gun registration are cowering in political fear of the gun lobby while the whole community waits anxiously for the inevitable incidents like today's. Bi-partisan political support for uniform strong gun laws is long overdue but unlikely while gutless state politicians keep on referring gun slaughter to backroom committees.

Opinion poll data show that over 90% of the community will applaud Mr Howard if he were to act decisively.'

For comment:
Assoc. Prof. Simon Chapman (phone) Rebecca Peters (phone)
28 April 1996

It is difficult to describe the frenzied interest of the media over the following weeks. Those who had been active in gun control were besieged with requests for interviews, fielding incessant calls on our mobile phones. During the occasional lull, the message bank would call and for me, instead of the usual few messages stored, there would be up to 20. For several weeks after the massacre, Rebecca was getting virtually non-stop calls on two mobile phones, a pager and three phone lines. Most of these were from journalists seeking information for articles and features. On the spot in Tasmania, Roland Browne was inundated with calls up to midnight on the day of the massacre, with calls starting again with the BBC at 6am the next day.

In the days, weeks and months which followed, the Australian mass media devoted unprecedented time and space to the incident and to the many aspects of its aftermath. For days afterwards, nearly every major newspaper devoted several full pages to the story. The event dominated radio and television news bulletins, with current affairs programs devoted entirely to news, background and analysis of the massacre, not once but several times.

It was repeatedly stated that the killings represented the worst and largest civilian death toll involving a single gunman anywhere in the world this century ('the worst mass murder of civilians in modern times', 'a grotesque world record'). Comparisons were made with highly publicised massacres in the US in recent years and at Hebron, Israel, in 1994 when Baruch Goldstein shot dead 29 Palestinians.

This massacre was larger, and of all places it happened in the sleepy, sylvan backwater of Tasmania, a place psychiatrist Professor Beverley Raphael described as an 'innocent part of Australia'. Because Tasmania seemed such an unlikely location, it lent a special sub-text to the phrase, 'these things can happen in the most ordinary of places'. As one newspaper put it, 'This is the State where nothing happens . . . this hideaway from the worst of the world.'[2] Ironically, Tasmania had the worst record of gun deaths in Australia and, significantly, the weakest gun laws in the country (see Chapter 3).

The perpetrator

From the outset, there was immense interest in the man who had committed this atrocity. In the days after the murders, dozens of articles appeared in the media purporting to provide scoops on Martin Bryant, the man accused and later convicted. Elements in the portrait painted repeatedly by the media included the claim that he had been left a large inheritance by a woman who had herself inherited a fortune; allegations of his extravagant and idiosyncratic expenditure and lifestyle; and comments on his upbringing and his relationships.[3] Neighbours repeatedly described him as variously lonely, quiet or 'like a normal person'. The *West Australian*'s page 1 summarised these descriptions in its opening paragraph: 'Australia's worst mass murderer is a rich, lonely, deluded 29-year-old social outcast, haunted by the memory of his dead father.'[4] On the front page of *The Australian* on 30 April, a full-colour photograph of Bryant accompanied an article claiming he slept with a pig in his bed and that he 'spooked' people who knew him.[5] *The Australian* subsequently admitted to re-touching Bryant's eyes in the photograph to create an intense, glaring look.

---

2 Darby A. 'Nightmare shatters the island of dreams', *Sydney Morning Herald (SMH)*, 30 April 1996.

3 McGeough P, Simpson L. 'Young, rich and out of control: the portrait of a lone gunman', *SMH*, 30 April 1996: 1; Sutton C, Condon M, Gilmore H. 'Silly Martin, the boy a town hated', *Sun Herald*, 5 May 1996: 14–15; Gora B. 'How to spend a fortune . . .' *Sunday Telegraph*, 5 May 1996: 4.

4 Barrass T. Killer. 'The misfit who had no pity', *West Australian*, 30 April 1996: 1.

5 Fife-Yeomans J. 'Violent loner spooked locals', *The Australian*, 30 April 1996: 1.

Any perpetrator of such a crime could have scarcely avoided the glare of those parts of the media intent on demonising the killer. But journalists seized on particular elements of Bryant's alleged biography in an attempt to match the killer with the enormity of the outrage. Anyone who had even the slightest acquaintance with Bryant became an unquestionable witness to his character. Dozens of people were interviewed, ranging from ex-girlfriends to neighbours and even the proprietor of a coffee shop he frequented.

For the purposes of a main focus of this book – analysing media discourse on gun control – the picture of Bryant that became the subject of countless discussions across the country was that he was insane, had given the community many opportunities to notice his eccentricities, and could have been 'stopped'. This theme is taken up in greater detail in Chapter 6.

Repeated allegations were made about Bryant's mental health. The *Sun Herald* claimed Martin Bryant 'had slipped through the net of health authorities and police at least three times before he embarked on his killing orgy . . .' The paper alleged he had a record of 'known criminal or anti-social acts . . . stealing, violent mood swings and one attempt at self-immolation'. It suggested that Bryant was now suspected in previous unsolved and suspicious deaths[6] and that a series of complaints about his violent nature had been ignored.[7] A *Daily Telegraph* 'investigation' reported that Bryant had been 'examined by doctors from Tasmania's Health and Community Services and found to be suffering from a personality disorder and schizophrenia'.[8] This diagnosis was repeated in a *Bulletin* article.[9] These reports allegedly concluded that he was 'unable to handle his own affairs and would need continuing

---

6 Sutton C, Gilmore H, Kent S. 'He could have been stopped', *Sun Herald*, 5 May 1996: 1–3.

7 McGeough P. 'Neighbours' complaints were not recorded', *SMH*, 1 May 1996: 5.

8 Jones W. Bryant 'Unable to handle affairs', *Sunday Telegraph*, 5 May 1996: 3.

9 Murphy D. 'Terror Australis', *The Bulletin*, 7 May 1996: 18–21.

medical treatment'[10] and that the Tasmanian Supreme Court had ordered a trustee company to administer his inheritance lest he squander it. As described in Chapter 6, it emerged at Bryant's sentencing that he was not considered unfit to plead, and no details of any previous diagnoses of mental illness were revealed.

An illustration of the extraordinary effort the media made to portray Bryant as a disaster waiting to happen was the ABC's *Four Corners* program on the question of whether psychiatry can predict violence in children and young adults. The program had located archival television footage of Bryant as a 12-year-old in a hospital bed, having been burnt while using fireworks. The program included the following dialogue:

Archive footage of 12-year-old Bryant

Bryant: I had this lighter and I had this coloured sky rocket and I wanted to see if the wick went quick so I lit it and it went fast and I tried to make it go out but I couldn't and I . . . I . . . broke the stick trying to get out but I couldn't and it made a hole through my jeans.

Interviewer: Do you think you'll be playing with fire crackers anymore?

Bryant: Yeah.

Interviewer: Don't you think you've learned a lesson from this?

Bryant: Yes . . . but I'm still playing with them.

Four Corners journalist: Psychiatrist Dr Rod Milton sees the classic signs of a psychopathic or anti-social personality disorder even in this short video from when Bryant was 12 years old.

Milton: Risk-taking behaviour and not being of much concern over having taken those risks. He didn't show much concern at all . . . no suffering . . . anything like that. And firm determination that he was going to go on and do the same thing again.

---

10 Ibid.

Four Corners journalist: Fire-setting as a child is one of the
key indicators Milton looks for when he's assessing the make-
up of brutal killers.

This brief, commonplace response from a young boy that he would not
be deterred from using fireworks again by this one incident was thus
decoded into an 'obvious' sign of future psychopathology and brutality.
If the young Bryant was asked about any pain and trauma he suffered,
it was not broadcast. *Four Corners* saw a single reply to one question
as sufficient material to formulate a diagnosis. In the rush to satisfy
its line that Bryant's actions might have been predicted, the program
did not consider that the 12-year-old's words might indicate he had
in fact learnt from the incident and would be more careful in future.
Apparently only a total swearing away from ever using fireworks again
would have sufficed as a sign of normality.

This discourse assisted the gun lobby's argument that those
involved in gun massacres were mentally unstable, and that authorities should establish a register of such people who should be prohibited
from owning or using guns (see Chapter 6). The gun lobby also focused
on the culpability of doctors and the police in not controlling people
like Bryant: 'They are going to punish everybody over the actions of
one man who, if the Tasmanian authorities had done their job properly,
would not have been on the loose,' said one Queensland shooter.[11]

Angry scenes were reported outside the Royal Hobart Hospital
where Bryant was first treated for burns, as well as failed attempts by
people to enter the hospital with the presumed intent of harming or
killing him. The editor of *Australian Gun Sports* had no patience for
legal process and invited his readers to: 'Write in and describe your pre-
ferred method of punishment to be meted out to the accused massacrer
at Port Arthur.'[12] Reporters noted that police sharpshooters had been
'prevented' from shooting Bryant because he had not made any attempt

---

11 Barker G. 'Rural rebels have Coalition on the run', *Financial Review*, 11
June 1996.

12 Galea R. 'Howard's hidden agendas?', *Australian Gun Sports*, 2 June 1996: 6.

to escape or avoid arrest.[13] These remarks were enthusiastically taken up by several talkback radio callers, who argued that in a decent, sensible society it would have been natural to shoot such a person.

Advocacy lessons

A 'wise after the event' phenomenon frequently follows gun massacres. Acquaintances and neighbours of these gunmen often report that they had always thought the person 'acted strangely' or displayed anger or odd behaviour. Reportage of these accounts rarely questions whether this behaviour was within the normal range of human behaviour or why little was ever done if it was so obviously remarkable. The gun lobby will seek to fully exploit the slightest rumour about a perpetrator's mental health, seizing on such reports as if they were credible and official diagnoses. It is in their interests to promote the view that anyone who acts violently with a gun could have been prevented from doing so by the vigilance of the community or, more particularly, by doctors and the police. This argument attacks solutions to gun violence directed toward reducing guns in the community as inappropriate, suggesting that authorities are using a sledgehammer to crack a walnut.

Gun control advocates should come to expect reportage that describes gunmen as mentally unstable, followed by attempts by the gun lobby to fan this into an accepted explanation of the events. While some high profile killers have histories of mental illness, it is far more common that they do not. Advocates need to be thoroughly acquainted with the facts on the relationship between mental health and violence. Chapter 6 explores this issue in further detail.

The victims

In the few days after the killings, newspapers began to publish the names and biographical sketches of the victims. Most newspapers published

---

13 Snell S. 'The law stopped police from shooting gunman', *Sunday Telegraph*, 5 May 1996: 5.

whole pages showing photographs of all the victims, or their names beneath photographs of bullets.[14] In every respect, those killed were a cross-section of normal, ordinary citizens. Many articles reviewed the impact of the shootings on the victims' families and friends,[15] the local Tasmanian community,[16] the Tasmanian tourist industry,[17] health workers and counsellors,[18] and Bryant's mother.[19]

The Mikac family

Of all the victims at Port Arthur, three were profiled more than any others. These were Nanette Mikac and her two daughters, Alannah (aged 6) and Madeline (aged 3). They had been killed while hurrying away from the main site of the shootings. Bryant first shot Nanette Mikac and Madeline and then chased Alannah behind a tree and shot her at point-blank range. The pastor at their funeral said Nanette Mikac had 'died trying to protect her children against impossible odds.'[20] The death of the two children and the circumstances of their murder carried a particular poignancy.

Their husband and father, Walter Mikac, who had been playing golf nearby when the shootings occurred, came 'to symbolise the tragedy at

14 Staff Reporters. 'They never had a chance', *SMH*, 1 May 1196: 1; Anon. '35 reasons why our leaders must act', *Daily Telegraph*, 2 May 1996: 1

15 Wainwright R, Connolly E. 'Dream dies with "gentleman"', *SMH*, 1 May 1996: 6; Hatfield L, Simpson L. 'Maybe that is the only blessing . . . they have both gone together', *SMH*, 1 May 1996: 6; Anon. 'Birthday party was a date with death', *Daily Telegraph*, 2 May 1996: 5.

16 McMillan S. 'Heartbreak in paradise', *Sunday Telegraph*, 5 May 1996: 9. Condon M. 'A city cries for the dead', *Sun Herald*, 5 May 1996: 2–3.

17 Darby A. 'Tasmanian tourism dives', *The Age*, 1 June 1996: A10.

18 Vass N, Harvey A. 'Disaster services extended to the limit', *SMH*, 29 April 1996: 5; Overington C. 'Silence masks the full scale of the horror', *SMH*, 29 April 1996: 5; Kennedy H. 'Nothing will be the same', *Sunday Telegraph*, 5 May 1996: 5; Snell S. 'Grieving family forgives', *Sunday Telegraph*, 5 May 1996: 5.

19 Jones M, Vincent N. 'Killer's mother says I'm so sorry', *Daily Telegraph*, 2 May 1996: 5.

20 Freeman J. '1,000 mourn as tragic family is laid to rest', *SMH*, 10 May 1996.

Port Arthur,[21] with his grief at the memorial service the subject of most press photographers who attended.[22] 'Don't let Walter weep in vain,' wrote one woman, describing her own grief.[23]

Many reports covered the Mikac funeral,[24] giving detailed descriptions of the family and its life together. *A Current Affair*, the highest-rating TV current affairs program in Australia, sent its anchor Ray Martin to the funeral, thus allowing the nation to attend. The words of those at the service were repeated in editorials:

> Hold onto your resolve to deal with this menace of unnecessary firearms in our society. Listen not to the loud calls of the few who want to selfishly keep their weapons, but instead hear the cries of those who have died, listen to the quiet sobs of those who love, see the majority and stand with them. Deliver to us uniform laws that will give our children the best possible chance to live without the fear of someone having access to violent power that maims and kills.[25]

Gun law reform thus became a form of community prayer – a form of absolution that the community demanded from politicians. One report published on the morning of the Police Ministers' meeting opened with: 'Police Ministers searching for a compelling reason to support Prime Minister Howard's call for stronger gun control laws need look only at this haunting image of the Mikac family.'[26] The illustration showed a drawing made by one of the dead girls. Weeks later Walter Mikac told the media at a NCGC press conference that after he saw the bodies of his family on the roadside, 'I sometimes feel that maybe I should have taken a photo and sent that to [the gun lobby's leaders] to

21 Bearup G. 'How can I keep living without them?', *SMH*, 1 May 1996: 7; Nolan S. 'Grief of one spoke for all', *The Age*, 10 May 1996: A6.

22 For example: 'Jones M. 'Sorrow we've never known', *Daily Telegraph*, 2 May 1996: 2–3.

23 Mitchell DE. 'Paradise lost' (letter), *SMH*, 8 May 1996: 16.

24 For example: Freeman J, *op. cit.*

25 Anon. 'A victory for the PM and the people', *The Age*, 11 May 1996: A24.

26 Dunleavy S. 'For their sake', *Daily Telegraph*, 10 May 1996.

see if that made any difference. But with their methods of thinking, I somehow doubt it.'[27]

An *Age* editorial praising the 10 May Police Ministers' agreement concluded: 'Yesterday our political leaders honoured the wishes of the Australian people – and the memory of Nanette Mikac, her daughters, and all the other victims of the Port Arthur massacre.'[28]

Victims and witnesses speak up

Eyewitnesses to the shootings and those injured were also prominent in the reportage. Some survivors gave graphic accounts of the shootings.[29] A woman who had much of one arm shot away discharged herself from hospital to join a Melbourne gun control march. Her photo accompanied a page 1 story in the *Age*.[30] Relatives of the dead spoke to gun control rallies in Melbourne,[31] Brisbane and Adelaide.

One of the most memorable accounts was from a middle-aged nurse, Lynne, who had attended those still barely alive in the devastation of the Broad Arrow Café.[32] ABC TV's *7.30 Report* ran a lengthy interview with Lynne which was replayed many times and later won an award for excellence in current affairs TV. The interview was intensely moving and generated many letters to newspapers and extensive radio discussion.

---

27 Darby A. 'The father who lost all warns of betrayal', *The Age*, 20 July 1996: A7.

28 Anon. 'A victory for the PM and the people', *The Age*, 11 May 1996: A24.

29 Wainwright R, Freeman J, Pitt H. 'Man played dead to save two women', *SMH*, 1 May 1996: 7; Tippet G, Rule A. 'I felt guilty because I still had my man', *Sun Herald*, 5 May 1996: 16–17; 'Gora B. Family's night of fear', *Sunday Telegraph*, 5 May 1996: 7; Barrass T. 'Witness tells of his terror', *West Australian*, 30 April 1996: 7.

30 Winkler T. 'Survivor leaves hospital to make her point', *The Age*, 3 June 1996: 1.

31 Dow S. 'A sister in pain fights the guns', *The Age*, 3 June 1996: A4.

32 Anon. 'Nurse tells of terror', *SMH*, 1 May 1996: 6.

In what were called instances of 'searing intensity' and 'unpractised but touching speeches',[33] some of those most personally affected by the massacre spoke publicly in support of gun control, against the gun lobby[34] and commented despairingly about the wavering that took place in some states after the 10 May Police Ministers' agreement.[35] After a Tasmanian politician joked in the Tasmanian Parliament about burying guns, speaking about 'holes all around my garden', Nanette Mikac's father wrote to a Tasmanian newspaper: 'I dearly wish that a certain gun, used at Port Arthur, had been placed under the ground long before we had to place my daughter and two granddaughters in that position.' Not surprisingly, the gun lobby always failed to respond directly to the statements of victims and their loved ones, allowing the weight of their words to resonate unchallenged.

Virginia Handmer, mother of 15-year-old Dali Handmer-Pleshet, who had been shot dead by a bullet from a semi-automatic rifle in 1993, near Mudgee in New South Wales, spoke about her daughter's killing at a CGC rally on 4 May at Hyde Park, Sydney. On the three-month anniversary of the Port Arthur killings on 28 July, survivors and relatives of the dead laid flowers on the steps of the Victorian Parliament[36] and spoke at another gun control rally in Sydney. Walter Mikac spoke at the Sydney rally. Earlier in July, at his initiative, he supported the Tasmanian CGC by speaking at a press conference in Hobart when the TCGC called for a referendum should the states fail to carry out the Police Ministers' resolutions.[37] He later laid roses on the steps of the Tasmanian Parliament, while inside some conservative parliamentarians argued for loopholes in the new gun laws.[38]

---

33 Darby A. 'One hundred days of controversy', *SMH*, 6 August 1996: 13.

34 Anon. 'For survivors,friends the pain is still there', *The Age*, 10 May 1996: A6.

35 Anon. 'Mixed emotions and opinions from those close to Port Arthur', *The Age*, 19 July 1996: A7.

36 Pegler T, Faulkner J. 'Three months on, the grief of Port Arthur endures', *The Age*, 29 July 1996: A4.

37 Darby A. 'The father who lost all warns of betrayal', *The Age*, 20 July 1996: A7.

38 Farouque F, Darby A. 'Owners able to sell guns overseas', *The Age*, 24 July

Survivors of previous massacres were reported to be distressed by the Port Arthur massacre, phoning mental health hotlines at rates of up to 30 a day.[39] Some were contacted for media statements. For example, Frank Carmody, who was shot five times in Melbourne's 1987 Queen Street massacre, said of the new gun laws: 'I think it's really wonderful. It's taken a long time, but at least they've got it all together.'[40]

Among the thousands who wrote to newspapers and called talkback radio programs were many who had personally suffered from gun violence in domestic situations, bank robberies and sieges.[41] Typical of these was the story of a young man whose mother had been shot dead by an armed robber.[42] The *Sydney Morning Herald* was so inundated with such letters that as well as publishing several, it ran a feature article profiling three of the writers. These included people who had been held hostage, women threatened over many years by violent husbands who menaced them with threats such as, 'I'm leaving . . . I'll shoot the lot of you', and a teacher whose class included a girl shot in the Strathfield massacre.[43] Doctors wrote about attending gunshot victims[44] and about patients who had told them of threats of violence from men with guns.[45] Such letters lent not only authenticity to the public debate but also a sense that gun violence was not something bizarre that happened only to 'others'.

1996: A3.

39 Anon. 'Hotlines busy', *Sunday Telegraph*, 5 May 1996: 5.

40 Farouque F, McKay S. 'Angry shooters plan a $1 million protest', *The Age*, 11 May 1996: A6.

41 Maurice S. 'Lobby defies logic' (letter), *Daily Telegraph*, 18 May: 12; Mulligan BL. 'Average lunatic' (letter), *Sunday Telegraph*, 19 May 1996: 134.

42 Ryan R. 'A "silent" majority', *Daily Telegraph*, 3 June 1996: 5.

43 Gripper A. 'The legacy of fear', *SMH*, 10 May 1996.

44 Gotis-Graham I. 'Memories of Strathfield revived' (letter), *SMH*, 11 May 1996: 36.

45 Beveridge H. 'Police should act on acts of violence' (letter), *The Age*, 7 May 1996: A14

Advocacy lessons

Politicians, gun control lobbyists and the general public have a great deal to say about gun control after massacres. But people who have been injured, who lose loved ones and who survive or witness violent incidents can bring an invaluable authenticity to such comments. Journalists will do all they can to seek out such people. As one said, 'Experts are fine, but they're not actually a living thing.' Gun control advocates should seek to contact survivors of shootings and relatives and friends of those who died. Through their personal tragedies, many of these people become passionate advocates for gun control. The Dunblane Snowdrop group in Scotland was formed by a group of people including some who had friends in and associations with the town of Dunblane. They collected more than 700,000 signatures after the Dunblane massacre, and are perhaps the best example of this. The views of such people on gun control will be eagerly sought by the media after public shootings or for policy debates. Advocacy groups should keep contact details of such people, noting their willingness to speak to the media.

Of course, the gun lobby occasionally convinces victims to support its cause, calling for retribution against criminals as the best solution to violence. One memorable speaker in support of the gun lobby was a former security guard, confined to a wheelchair by spinal injuries incurred when he was shot during a robbery. He proclaimed at a Sydney rally and on *60 Minutes*: 'I don't blame the gun – the gun had nothing to do with this! I've never seen a gun that loaded itself!' Gun control advocates should not therefore assume all victims of gun violence will automatically support stricter laws. Many people who have been personally affected are understandably angry about their loss and suffering and become strong advocates for capital punishment and other punitive responses. In an arena where clarity of communication is at a premium, there is a risk that their hopes for retribution can come to dominate their concern for gun control. This can place them in unwitting partnerships with the demands of the gun lobby who may seek to build explicit or implied alliances with such victims to the detriment of a gun control agenda.

The gun laws

The Port Arthur massacre focused the national and international spotlight on Australia's weak gun laws. This went way beyond an examination of only Tasmania's feeble gun laws. In a country where the laws are different in every state, the system of gun control is only as strong as the weakest link. Two days after the massacre *The Australian* published an article by Rebecca Peters describing the problem: [46]

> Here's how weak our weakest guns laws are. In Tasmania if you're an adult without major criminal convictions in the past eight years, you qualify for a licence to buy or own as many guns as you like. No need to prove you've got a legitimate reason to own a gun. No need to show police that you have appropriate storage facilities. And your licence lasts for life, as long as you update the photograph every 10 years.
>
> Down at the local gun shop, your plain, ordinary gun licence entitles you to buy military-style semi-automatic weapons designed to mow down enemy soldiers on the battlefield. Remember, there's no limit on the number you can buy.
>
> When you make your purchase, no record is kept by any government department. So if you later had a mind to sell one of your guns to a mate who didn't happen to hold a licence, no government department would ever be the wiser. Once you leave the gun shop, you can also leave the State. Take your gun to the mainland and expose the rest of Australia to the danger created by Tasmania's half-hearted pretence of regulation.
>
> Those of us who live in other parts of Australia cannot derive much comfort from local ministerial reassurances that their States' gun laws are stricter than Tasmania's. The fact is we're one country, we travel a lot, guns are easily transportable, and bullets rip apart human bodies just as easily, regardless of postcode.

46 Peters R. 'Half-hearted pretence of conflicting gun laws', *The Australian*, 30 April 1996: 15.

The article outlined three cardinal points needed to improve Australia's gun laws: registration of all guns; proof of reason for gun ownership; and a ban on semi-automatics. Ten days later this was the core of what was delivered through the Police Ministers' national agreement. This newspaper article was photocopied and circulated widely among journalists and political advisers because it summarised briefly, and in plain English, what the legal problem was and how it could be solved.

The political response

The Port Arthur massacre presented John Howard – a newly elected leader barely settled into the prime ministerial role – with his first serious challenge. It was one that had been merely hinted at in the electoral promises made only weeks before: in Howard's pre-election televised debate with then Prime Minister Paul Keating, Howard had declared his wish to control military firearms. There were many political options available to Howard, including those taken by previous national and state political leaders responding to gun massacres. As all aspects of gun law (except importation) are state rather than federal responsibilities, Howard could have followed the example of previous prime ministers such as Bob Hawke, electing to express outrage, offer condolence and predictably urging the states to reform *their* laws.

In the decade before the Port Arthur killings, there had been 13 gun massacres in Australia and New Zealand which involved the death of five or more people.[47] With the exception of the Hawke Labor Government's ban on imports of military-style semi-automatics (MSSAs), prime ministers and their governments had taken little action beyond urging state reviews of laws and placing gun law reform on the agenda of various federal/state committees for discussion. For example,

---

47 For full details see http://www.health.su.oz.au/cgc/fp_6_2_2.htm [no longer active, 2013; 'Australia – gun facts, figures and the law' is a useful source of statistical data: http://www.gunpolicy.org/firearms/region/cp/australia].

the Hawke Labor Government established the National Committee on Violence in response to the Hoddle and Queen Street massacres. The 1990 report from this committee[48] recommended 25 reforms, very few of which had been taken up by any state or territory by the time of the Port Arthur shootings. By late 1995, six months before Port Arthur, the Australasian Police Ministers Council had drafted a set of resolutions for uniform gun laws which were barely stronger than the existing laws in the weakest jurisdictions.[49] The resolutions had been decided after consultation with relevant 'interest groups', namely the gun lobby. No consultation had occurred with the public health community or any group representing the 80–90% of Australians who have consistently supported tighter gun laws.

Not down the American path . . .

Prime Minister Howard convened a press conference the morning after the massacre and gave strong hints that his own performance would be markedly different to previous gun law reform rhetoric. His personal commitment to overseeing gun law reform became explicit within days when he announced the emergency meeting of the Australasian Police Ministers Council.[50] Howard had signalled his interest in gun law reform in one of his 'headland' speeches, made as Leader of the Opposition on 6 June 1995. In that speech he referred to gun violence in the United States, saying that Australia needed to 'learn the bitter lesson of the United States regarding guns . . . Whilst making proper allowance for legitimate sporting and recreational activities and the needs of our rural community, every effort should be made to limit the carrying of guns in Australia.'

---

48 National Committee on Violence. *Violence: directions for Australia* (Duncan Chappell, Chair). Canberra: Australian Institute of Criminology, 1990.

49 Australasian Police Ministers Council. National Uniformity in Firearms Legislation. Draft APMC Resolutions (Final Draft), 26 September 1995.

50 Farr M. 'PM vows a nation wide ban on rifles', *Daily Telegraph*, 2 May 1996: 4.

This reference to the United States became a central element of all advocacy for the new gun laws: again and again, political leaders, media commentators and ordinary people said that Australia 'must not to go down the American path' of gun culture and violence. Years of news reports detailing the US homicide rate, muggings, a seemingly interminable series of gun massacres, and frequent TV documentaries on American gun culture had given Australians a strong sense of America going down a violent road of no return. People who had lived and worked in the US wrote to newspapers describing the mayhem of street gunfights they had witnessed.[51]

The 'down the American path' catchcry had been used for many years by gun control groups in Australia and now it was picked up again by the Prime Minister who, along with editorial writers, made it the core explanation of his actions, repeating it many times:

> [This decision] means that this country through its governments has decided not to go down the American path, but this country has decided to go down another path.[52]

> The governments of Australia decided that this country was not to go down the American path, that we would strike a great blow for the future safety of our suburbs, our provincial towns and our cities.[53]

> There is a deep feeling within the Australian community that we have a historic opportunity to ensure that this nation does not go down the American path and we have an opportunity to deliver on that hope and aspiration.[54]

> In the United States a culture in favour of gun ownership has allowed firearms to spread out of all proportion to real

51 Townsend S. 'Reducing firepower will make us safer' (letter), *SMH*, 9 May 1996: 14.

52 Howard J. 'Statement at press conference', *ABC TV News*, 10 May 1996.

53 Chan G, Gordon M. 'Howard victory on gun bans', *The Australian*, 11 May 1996: 1; Rees P. 'Shooters call crisis talks', *Sunday Telegraph*, 12 May 1996.

54 Riley M. 'Howard set for victory on guns', *SMH*, 22 July 1996: 1.

need, putting American society more or less at ransom to the menace of the destructive power of . . .[55]

We were echoing the path of American society and we have now turned back on that.[56]

Australia has taken a far-reaching decision to reject the United States' approach to gun control.[57]

The main task is to make sure Australia does not go down the route taken by the United States, where the proliferation of guns has reached extreme and frightening levels under the auspices of a gun lobby that has intimidated many legislators into virtual impotence on this issue.[58]

We're moving away from the US-style gun culture in our community.[59]

In the USA, we see the consequences of the lack of proper gun laws in a 14-in-100,000 murder rate, seven times the UK rate. Mr Howard has said he will not tolerate US-style intimidation by a too-powerful gun lobby.[60]

There was perhaps no better sign of just how out of touch the gun lobby was with the mood of the Australian people than when it lamely sought to turn the tables on the 'down the American path' reference in December 1996. In an SSAA recruitment pamphlet letterboxed throughout Australia, the opening line was: 'It's John Howard's gun laws that are taking Australia down the American path.'[61] The pamphlet

55 Anon. 'Making gun laws work' (editorial), *SMH*, 23 July 1996: 12.

56 McLean L. 'Bans opposition turns to support', *The Australian*, 11 May 1996.

57 Anon. 'Historic pact on gun reforms', *SMH*, 11 May 1996.

58 Anon. 'The people expect new gun laws' (editorial), *Weekend Australian*, 22–23 June 1996: 20.

59 Dunleavy S. 'Lobby warns of black market', *Daily Telegraph*, 11 May 1996.

60 Anon. 'Holding the line on guns', (editorial) *The Age*, 4 June 1996: A12.

61 SSAA. *Gun control: the facts. Is Australian going down the American path?* Pamphlet, December 1996.

stated, 'over 20,000 gun laws in the USA . . . have not worked in reducing crime there.' Curiously, the SSAA failed to mention the primary reason why the American laws have failed: they are not uniform between states or even between local council areas.

As senior *Australian* journalist Mike Steketee wrote: 'The greatest achievement that can flow from Port Arthur . . . is that the American gun culture which is nascent in this country is eradicated; that owning a gun is a privilege, not a right; and that reducing the murder rate is more important than the contrived objections to disarming the civilian population.'[62] Chapter 2 describes the extent of gun violence in the US, contrasting it with nations like the United Kingdom and Japan, which have different policies on gun control.

Leadership

From the day after the Port Arthur massacre, Howard and his Attorney-General, Daryl Williams, became the central figures advocating gun law reform. As an *Age* editorial expressed it, Howard began by 'appointing himself chief spokesman for the anti-gun lobby'.[63] Daryl Williams – described as 'studious-looking and quietly spoken . . . not a bar room brawler', 'too legal, too logical, too polite, too right' and having the gently deprecating nickname of 'Rowdy' – had been 'catapulted into an alien world of pump-action shotguns, rim-fire .22s and heavy assault weapons'.[64] Together, the two men stood like principled and determined Davids against the angry and threatening Goliath of the gun lobby.

With immediate and unequivocal support from the Labor party ('The Federal Opposition will do everything it can to support the measures'[65]), the Greens and the Australian Democrats (which had both

62 Steketee M. 'Culture of violence demands tight controls', *The Australian*, 11 May 1996.

63 Anon. 'A victory for the PM and the people', *The Age*, 11 May 1996: A24.

64 M. 'Howard's gun gamble', *SMH*, 11 May 1996; Chan G. 'Pragmatist prepares to convince the states on gun control', *The Australian*, 10 May 1996.

65 McLean L. 'Bans opposition turns to support', *The Australian*, 11 May 1996.

always advocated tougher gun laws), gun control in Australia suddenly became a mainstream political priority.

The near-unanimous political support extended well into the heartland of the electorate. Many non-Liberal voters expressed their admiration for Howard and for the rare political maturity the issue had generated: 'I have voted Labor all my life, but at this time, I have nothing but admiration for Prime Minister Howard . . . for once, political differences are buried by concern for the safety of Australia.'[66]

It is impossible to overestimate how much the leadership of Howard and Williams contributed to the successful outcome. On the night of the 10 May Police Ministers' meeting, Howard reflected: 'This is an agreement I don't think that anybody would have thought remotely achievable three weeks ago or even a few days ago.' But as his first significant political challenge, gun control became a test he could not afford to lose. This point was repeatedly noted by the media: 'Mr Howard has staked his leadership authority on achieving nationwide gun control . . .'[67] Equally noteworthy was his dogged resolve to see through the reforms he demanded in the face of the political risks involved. Howard's language, and commentary describing his leadership, were spiked with aggressive and militaristic turns of phrase:

> I will not retreat an inch from the national responsibilities I have in this issue. Not an inch.[68]

> [Howard had] drawn a line in the sand.[69]

> There was no question Howard had to strike fast.[70]

> It was John Howard's plan and he dared anyone to reject it.[71]

66 Daniel H. 'Admiration for PM's lead' (letter), *The Age*, 10 May 1996.

67 Dunleavy S. 'For their sake', *Daily Telegraph*, 10 May 1996.

68 Howard J. *Channel 7 News*, 30 April 1996.

69 Millett M. 'Howard's gun gamble', *SMH*, 11 May 1996.

70 Ibid.

71 Kitney G. 'PM's personal triumph becomes his symbol of authority', *SMH*, 11 May 1996.

> Howard vowed to 'bury' any State which blocked the push
> for a national gun control code.[72]

His performance evoked the quietly spoken schoolboy who is being cajoled and bullied but has the courage to defy all threats. The media were intrigued by Howard's obvious personal dedication to the issue. Many reports noted his grief at the massacre: 'Colleagues say he was clearly distraught . . . his eyes red-rimmed, his face still registering shock . . .'[73] The television pictures of a plainly moved Howard confirmed his persona as an 'ordinary Australian'. An intriguing juxtaposition was created between his reputation as a somewhat grey character and the force of his convictions on gun law reform:

> Howard, portrayed as weak and an ideologue as Opposition Leader, has displayed authority and pragmatism as Prime Minister.[74]

> His style is rarely frightening, dramatic or spectacular. In time it may even come to be considered boring. But for the moment at least, Mr Howard is seen to be honest, workman-like . . .[75]

> For his political bravery . . . the Prime Minister deserves congratulations.[76]

Howard repeatedly claimed his demands for gun law reform came from the heartland of 'middle Australia'. He did not hector or adopt an overt campaigning mode. Rather, his style embodied a dignified determination to see his reforms through. He avoided framing the changes he was attempting to enact as in any way radical, world-beating or pioneering. Instead, he presented them as changes any ordinary, decent

---

72 Millett M. 'Howard's gun gamble', *SMH*, 11 May 1996.

73 Ibid.

74 Steketee M. 'Culture of violence demands tight controls', *The Australian*, 11 May 1996.

75 Anon. 'Mr Howard's first hundred days', *The Age*, 8 June 1996: A22.

76 Anon. 'A worthwhile victory on guns' (editorial), *The Age*, 24 July 1996: A12.

person would see as necessary. On the eve of the Police Ministers' meeting, Howard stated in Parliament that his radical reform position was not 'an ambit claim. It represents what we believe to be the collective aspiration of the Australian people . . .'[77] In his speech on the night of the 10 May agreement, Howard stated: 'I think we have done good work for the future of Australia today . . . We have done something that will send a signal to people all around this country that ours is not a gun culture, ours is a culture of peaceful cooperation.'[78]

As Geoff Kitney, a senior writer for the *Sydney Morning Herald* suggested: 'Any backlash from gun owners will be overwhelmed by the gratitude of ordinary people who will be hopeful that the Howard reforms will give them a safer future.'[79] Howard, he wrote, was 'the ordinary people's leader' who had been able to achieve the agreement because he had 'effectively mobilis[ed] the ordinary people's power.'

Another ironic aspect of Howard's stance was that he was first and always a conservative, anti-regulatory politician in matters of social policy. An unnamed politician said,

> The fact is no-one could have ever believed that a conservative government could have ever come this far in reforming gun control laws. Even if there is still some dispute at the margin, we are still going to come out with Australia's first comprehensive set of national gun laws.[80]

Howard 'believes in deregulation and getting government out of the lives of people; yet he has just imposed some of the most restrictive and intrusive regulations ever imposed on hundreds of thousands of Australians.'[81] This irony underscored the exceptional nature of the event

---

77 Millett M, Lagan B. 'PM's final plea on guns', *SMH*, 10 May 1996; Millett M. 'Howard's gun gamble', *SMH*, 11 May 1996.

78 Millett M. 'A victory for sanity.' *SMH*, 11 May 1996: 1.

79 Kitney G. 'PM's personal triumph becomes his symbol of authority', *SMH*, 11 May 1996.

80 Millett M. 'Howard's gun gamble', *SMH*, 11 May 1996.

81 Steketee M. 'Culture of violence demands tight controls', *The Australian*, 11 May 1996.

and the corresponding need for an exceptional policy response which married 'decency' with uniqueness. Mike Steketee in *The Australian* suggested: 'This is Howard's version of Richard Nixon's trip to China – a pragmatic response, taken in the national interest but contrary to normal expectations.'[82]

This decisive action by a conservative politician caused some great amusement:

> You've got to laugh! Just thinking about all those flak-jack-eted weekend Rambos stockpiling their weapons to protect their freedom from that homosexual, drug-taking, god-less, pinko, long-haired, commie, Hawke-Keating Socialist, Zionist, nigger-lovin', dole-bludging, fat-arsed excuse-for-a-government, and then whoa! Lo and behold, it's the Howard Government which takes away their guns! It's exquisite![83]

But Howard did not convince the Shooters Party's John Tingle of his sincerity. Tingle tried to explain to shooters that Howard was in fact a far left-wing ideologue, telling the Sydney pro-gun rally on 15 June: 'Understand this has nothing to do with guns. This is not about public health or public safety or guns. It's a political agenda from the far left outfield. What it's about is control!'[84]

Howard was not alone in abandoning his non-interventionist principles. Media personalities more commonly aligned with the political right – radio hosts like Stan Zemanek, Alan Jones, John Laws, Howard Sattler and the journalist Piers Akerman – all took a strong anti-gun position and most of them maintained it throughout the months-long aftermath of the first APMC meeting. John Laws, with Australia's largest radio audience broadcasting to more than 2.5 million people a day, was particularly tenacious in his support and apparently received several threats from shooters.[85] The rabid gun magazine *Lock, Stock and*

82 Ibid.

83 Ellis G. Letter, *The Australian*, 18–19 May 1996: 20.

84 *Channel 9 TV News*, 15 June 1996.

85 Safe M. 'Laws and order', *The Australian* Magazine, 7–8 December 1996: 12–19.

Barrel paid Laws the ultimate tribute by caricaturing him in Nazi uniform along with Hitler and Howard on the cover of their first post–Port Arthur issue, above the caption 'Tyrants comparing notes'.

Journalist Geoff Kitney wrote that the leadership Howard displayed over the issue was unprecedented in Australian political history: 'John Howard yesterday marked himself as the leader who has probably changed the nation's future more decisively, more quickly than any prime minister before him.' He said gun control would henceforth 'be long regarded as the symbol of John Howard's prime ministerial authority'.[86] *The Age* declared, 'Beyond question, the finest hour in the Prime Minister's first three months in office coincided with the nation's darkest hour.'[87] These comments were mirrored in the *Daily Telegraph*'s editorial: 'No matter what he does in the remainder of his term as Prime Minister, he will do no more important work than this.'[88]

To the *Sydney Morning Herald*, the decision was 'historic' because it 'put public safety ahead of political self-interest'.[89] It was compared to 'the introduction of seat belts, public sewerage systems and hygiene education'.[90] On 11 May *The Age* ran a banner headline, 'The historic bans', over its pages reviewing the agreement. Other comments on the portent of the decision included: 'To the credit of the Prime Minister, Premiers and police ministers, there was no back down yesterday, no kowtowing to the noisy protests of the gun lobby . . .'[91]

'The days of licensed gun owners assiduously assembling arsenals of weapons without any hindrance are gone.'[92]

---

86 Kitney G. 'PM's personal triumph becomes his symbol of authority', *SMH*, 11 May 1996.

87 Anon. 'Mr Howard's first hundred days' (editorial), *The Age*, 8 June 1996: A22.

88 Anon. 'Out of the shadow of the gun', (editorial), *Daily Telegraph*, 11 May 1996.

89 Anon. 'Historic pact on gun reforms', *SMH*, 11 May 1996.

90 Chatterton P. 'Show a bit of courage' (letter), *SMH*, 21 July 1996: 12.

91 Anon. 'Out of the shadow of the gun' (editorial), *Daily Telegraph*, 11 May 1996.

92 Ibid.

Over our dead bodies

Threat of a referendum

After the 10 May Police Ministers' meeting, three states (Queensland, South Australia and Western Australia) and the Northern Territory became the sites of prolonged debates and lobbying that sought to weaken and relax several of the resolutions, broaden definitions and amend provisions. The proposal to allow 'crimping' of whole categories of guns listed for banning (see Chapter 4), became a particular point of pressure on the Federal Government.

Fearing disintegration of the national resolve, the Prime Minister threatened to hold a national referendum if all parties to the agreement failed to introduce the laws they had promised on 10 May.[93] He set a deadline of 22 July for all states and territories to fall into line on the crimping issue, threatening a referendum if they failed to agree. The referendum question would have sought the electorate's permission to alter the constitution so as to transfer the power to make gun laws from the states to the Commonwealth Government. All opinion polls indicated that in each state the majority support required for this would have been very easily obtained, particularly since the reforms had the full support of the Federal Labor Opposition. Howard thus held a very powerful card, and was volubly supported by NSW Premier Bob Carr[94] who had earlier sought to transfer all gun control powers to the Federal Government. One commentator described the referendum threat as Howard 'arming himself with the political equivalent of a nuclear weapon'.[95] Knowing that a referendum would be easily won and that it would cost the community $50 million, the Northern Territory's chief minister admitted that it would have been 'reckless and irresponsible' for any state or territory government to force a referendum. Howard got his way before the deadline he set.[96]

---

93 Millett M. 'Referendum threat over gun deadlock', *SMH*, 18 July 1996: 1.

94 Humphries D. 'Carr to support people's gun vote', *SMH*, 16 July 1996: 9.

95 Millett M. 'PM's gun ploy may backfire', *SMH*, July 19 1996: 17.

96 Millett M, Roberts G, Graham D. 'Official: guns victory to PM', *SMH*, 23 July 1996: 1.

A *Sydney Morning Herald* editorial nonetheless suggested bluntly: 'In some ways it will be a pity if Australians are denied the opportunity of voting . . . A referendum would destroy the political power of the gun lobby in this country once and for all.'[97]

Prime Minister in bullet-proof vest

Howard's strong leadership on the issue was maintained throughout the months after the Police Ministers' agreement, before the states and territories introduced their legislation. On 15 June, as the first stop on a much-publicised tour of Australia's rural heartlands to sell the gun reforms,[98] Howard spoke at a 3000-strong pro-gun rally at Sale in rural Victoria.[99] On security advice he wore a bullet-proof vest underneath his suit. As he faced the crowd, who jeered and taunted him with cries of 'Nazi', 'Fascist' and 'Heil Hitler!', and signs reading 'Gun Culture Safer than Canberra Poofter Culture – Only Woosies Hand in Guns', the contours of the bullet-proof vest were plainly visible to TV and press cameras. Much was made about this being the first occasion that any Australian politician had taken such precautions and what this implied about the violent propensities of some gun owners.

The Prime Minister's appearance in the vest inspired many letters to the press, debating whether it was a symbol of his courage, cowardice or folly.[100] While the SSAA's Ted Drane predictably described the vest as 'an insult',[101] all editorials described his visit as 'courageous' and once again

---

97 Anon. 'Referendum on gun laws', *SMH*, 19 July 1996: 16.

98 Grattan M, Savva N. 'Howard to tour rural areas to sell gun laws', *The Age*, 6 June 1996: A5.

99 Farr M, Miranda C. 'Why he wore it', *Daily Telegraph*, 18 June 1996: 1; Wright T. 'PM dons anti-shrapnel jacket to face gun protesters', *SMH*, 17 June 1996: 1; Gordon M. 'PM braves angry gun crowd', *The Australian*, 17 June 1996.

100 Bennett C. 'A hysterical reaction' (letter), *The Age*, 19 June 1996: 14; Graham M. 'Sad to see PM in a bullet-proof vest' (letter), *The Age*, 19 June 1996: 14.

101 Anon. 'What they said about Mr Howard', *Daily Telegraph*, 18 June 1996: 4.

focused on the 'lunatic fringe' among the gun lobby[102] (see Chapter 5). One journalist observed that the incident provided a new type of courageous role model: 'At a time when courage is in short supply and we lament the lack of role models for our young, the sight of John Howard, hands outstretched in front of a hostile crowd, was inspiring. Shortish, balding, bespectacled and physically unimposing, he didn't look like a classic hero. But hero he is.'[103] This writer also described a farmer who attended the rally on 15 June and defied the crowd by shouting support for Howard.

A public opinion poll conducted on the same weekend found that Howard's personal popularity in country regions had risen to 66%, up six percentage points from May (also after Port Arthur) and higher than his 63% city rating.[104] The next day in Federal Parliament, Howard said he would visit other rural areas:

> I intend to undertake a number of other visits to do what I endeavoured to do yesterday, and that is to explain in direct and simple terms the reasons why the Government has taken this decision. I think it is part and parcel of the role of a political leader not to be deskbound on issues such as this. You do have an obligation to go around the country, particularly to regional and rural areas.[105]

But Howard did not undertake any more of these visits – perhaps because his advisers suggested they were unnecessary in the face of the huge public support he enjoyed.

---

102 Anon. 'The PM in armour' (editorial), *SMH*, 18 June 1996: 16; Anon. 'Democracy at work' (editorial), *The Age*, 18 June 1996: A14.

103 Devine M. 'Modest heroes defy the bullies', *Daily Telegraph*, 18 June 1996: 4.

104 Wright T, Roberts G, Lagan B. 'Qld breaks ranks on gun control', *SMH*, 18 June 1996: 1.

105 http://hansard.aph.gov.au/reps/dailys/dr170696.pdf [no longer active, 2013].

They did not die in vain . . .

Along with 'not down the American road', the declaration that the Port Arthur victims 'must not be seen to have died in vain' became one of the most enduring clichés of the period. It captured a redemptive morality fuelled by horror at the event, anger at collusive political inertia, and the long-standing Judeo-Christian tradition of atoning for wrong-doing. The *Sydney Morning Herald*'s editorial on the morning of the Police Ministers' meeting listed the moral choices facing the ministers that day: 'The nation looks today to Canberra for statesmanship, not opportunism; for wisdom, not ignorance; for cooperation, not petty squabbling; for courage, not intimidation. Those who were slain at Port Arthur must not be allowed to die in vain.'[106] An *Age* editorial used the same expression: 'The 35 victims may not have died completely in vain.'[107] By mid-July when there was anxiety that some states would renege on the changes, NSW Premier Bob Carr again repeated this appeal: 'It would be simply unforgivable in the wake of Port Arthur if we don't go for tighter gun laws. It will mean those lives were lost in vain. It's as simple as that.'[108] The Tasmanian CGC called a press conference in Hobart and Walter Mikac, the husband and father of three victims, invoked the reference too, saying, 'To do anything else would be a betrayal of those 35 people who died that day.'[109]

A less sentimental comment on the cliché was run by the *Daily Telegraph* on the day after the Police Ministers' meeting:

> It would be a travesty and an insult to the memory of the Port Arthur 35 to declare now that 'they did not die in vain'. Their lives *were* spent for nothing . . . They died because we allowed lax gun laws . . . we should remember not only the 35 victims of Port Arthur but also the hundreds of others who have died unnecessarily by gunfire.[110]

106 Anon. 'Deaths can't be in vain' (editorial), *SMH*, 10 May 1996.

107 Anon. 'Beyond gun laws', (editorial), *The Age*, 7 May 1996: A14.

108 Humphries D. 'Carr to support people's gun vote', *SMH*, 16 July 1996: 9.

109 Darby A. 'Father who lost all speaks out', *SMH*, 20 July 1996: 2.

110 Anon. 'Out of the shadow of the gun' (editorial), *Daily Telegraph*, 11 May

Brokering bipartisanship

As discussed, reportage of the Police Ministers' agreement and Howard's role in it invariably referred to Australia's former political shirking of gun control. Since 1980 Australia's police ministers had met 20 times to discuss uniform national gun laws, but as one editorial commented, 'yet no [comprehensive national] laws are in place'.[111]

With the exception of Barrie Unsworth's 1988 efforts to seriously reform gun laws, successive NSW governments, along with those in Tasmania and Queensland, had long stood in the way of a national gun control policy. Queensland and Tasmania still allowed open access to military-style semi-automatic weapons and all three states had refused to introduce registration for rifles and shotguns. (All other jurisdictions had registration of all firearms, but these three renegade states required it only for handguns, which constitute only about 5% of guns). Three days before the 1995 Queensland election, then Premier Wayne Goss did a deal with the gun lobby, promising not to introduce gun registration in return for the lobby's electoral support.[112]

The Port Arthur massacre provoked immediate and passionate calls for gun law reform, many of them citing the appalling political record of inaction. The letters editor of the *Sydney Morning Herald* wrote, 'Not since the run-up to the Gulf War, when people feared an apocalyptic conflict, has our mail bag been so large.' In her weekly summary of letters received, she wrote:

> People had to find someone to blame that such a thing could happen – they homed in on politicians' inaction over gun control. The same words were used time and again: gutless, vacillating, weak-kneed, self-serving, cowardly, etc. Rarely have politicians been so out of touch with the public mood. Rarely has the public been more cynical about its politicians. John Howard's statements have been well received, but our

---

1996.

111 Anon. 'Success, or lethal shame' (editorial), *Daily Telegraph*, 10 May 1996.

112 *7.30 Report*, ABC TV, 29 April 1996.

readers have made it clear he'll be judged on his practical gun control achievements, not his rhetoric.[113]

Other typical comments included:

The time for excuses has passed. Now it is time for action.[114]

. . . such expressions of pain ring hollow [without political action].[115]

. . . the public was appalled by both the number and type of guns in circulation and the inability of state governments to keep tabs on their whereabouts.[116]

It is indicative of the sad state of politics in this country that it has taken the deaths of 35 people to bring our political leaders into a positive, non-partisan position of agreement.[117]

As the 10 May meeting of the Police Ministers approached, many editorials were scathing in their predictions that, yet again, no national consensus would be reached. Most described the approaching meeting as an opportunity to test political courage: 'Rarely in a federation of sovereign States such as our nation is there an opportunity to take decisive, united action to bring about instant change for the national good.'[118] Significantly, the pastor conducting the Mikac funeral on the day before the Police Ministers' meeting stated in his eulogy, 'To our national leaders we say, do not trade your votes for lives.'[119]

Four days after the massacre the front page of the *Daily Telegraph* showed 35 bullets, each with the name of a victim. Underneath was the statement:

113 Walsh G. Postscript, *SMH*, 6 May 1996: 14.

114 Anon. 'A cool look at gun laws', *SMH*, 30 April 1996.

115 Ibid.

116 Millett M. 'Howard's gun gamble', *SMH*, 11 May 1996.

117 Akerman P. 'Blasting the myths of the gun lobby', *Sunday Telegraph*, 5 May 1996.

118 Anon. 'Success, or lethal shame' (editorial), *Daily Telegraph*, 10 May 1996.

119 Freeman J. '1,000 mourn as tragic family is laid to rest', *SMH*, 10 May 1996.

Gentlemen, the people of Australia are weary of the gun
debate. In Tasmania, 35 people are dead because a killer was
able to arm himself with a semi-automatic rifle. Your responsibility is to make it illegal to own these guns, illegal to be in
possession of them, illegal to obtain the bullets they fire. All
this is within your power and the public demands nothing
less.[120]

The NSW Labor Party

After the 1988 defeat of the Unsworth Labor Government in NSW, gun
control had become a political sore for the NSW Labor Party – the party
in government in NSW – requiring regular band-aid applications such
as highly publicised voluntary gun amnesties. Before Port Arthur the
party had plainly ruled out any serious tightening of gun laws, particularly long-arm registration, due to its fear of electoral reprisal from
the gun lobby. In 1995 the CGC sought a meeting with Premier Carr
and his Police Minister, Paul Whelan. We met Whelan and Carr's senior
adviser and their message was unequivocal: the Labor Government
would not move alone to introduce gun registration. The only possible
avenue of hope lay in the remote possibility of brokering a bipartisan
policy between the Liberal-National Coalition and the Government.
But almost everyone we spoke to was highly sceptical that we would
have any hope of convincing the National Party arm of the Coalition to
support registration.

Premier Carr had gone on public record several times, both in
Parliament and in the media, saying he would not consider introducing registration unless there was bipartisan support between
the Government and the Opposition parties. The Liberal-National
Opposition agreed: 'The only way to provide for serious and lasting
reforms on firearm ownership, if there is bipartisan consensus, is to
have broad-based community support . . . Opposition members . . .
encourage a bipartisan and consensus approach in the future.' Despite
both major parties thus agreeing that bipartisanship was necessary and

---

120 Anon. '35 reasons why our leaders must act', *Daily Telegraph*, 2 May 1996: 1

even a good thing, both stood like shy brides, each refusing to take the initiative to consummate the arrangement. John Tingle noted after Port Arthur that he had 'an assurance in writing [dated November 1994] from Bob Carr when he was Opposition Leader that . . . his government if it came into power would not be moving toward any kind of registration *or anything else*'(emphasis added).[121] But Port Arthur changed this almost overnight.

On 2 May, four days after the Port Arthur massacre, Carr announced that he would introduce legislation to turn over the state's powers to regulate guns to the Commonwealth. Carr based his reasoning on the prospect that other states would refuse to act on gun control, arguing that the issue of national laws was too important to be left to flounder while it required identical legislation to be passed by six state and two territory governments.[122]

We suspected that many in the Carr Government – including Carr himself – privately sympathised with gun control, but their political pragmatism forced them to appease the gun lobby. Nonetheless we were highly suspicious of Carr's move, judging it as cynical posturing designed to make him appear tough on gun control while avoiding giving offence to John Tingle of the Shooters Party. He must have known the move would come to nothing, as it was highly unlikely that other states would want to hand powers back to the Federal Government. This would have then allowed Carr to blame other states for not having the 'courage' to hand over power to the Commonwealth, thereby derailing national gun law reform and allowing him to retreat behind the defence that he could not be expected to act alone. The CGC issued a press release deploring the move as buck-passing and hand-washing. Professor Charles Watson, a member of the CGC, said:

> The reason the State Government wants to hand it all over
> to the Federal Government is because it is too scared to do

---

121 Tingle J. 'What the Shooters Party is saying', *Guns Australia*, July/August 1996: 5–6.

122 Carr B. 'States have failed dismally with guns', *Sunday Telegraph*, 5 May 1996: 8.

anything. The Federal Government can only make gun laws if all the states cede their power, and Queensland will never do that, so it was a safe move for NSW.[123]

A *Sydney Morning Herald* journalist, Bernard Lagan, who had long reported gun control matters from the NSW Parliament, wrote an article under a particularly critical headline 'Hairy chested and hare brained'. He contrasted Carr's previous position on gun control with his new-found enthusiasm. Lagan wrote that Carr's

> new hairy-chested approach to tougher gun laws . . . smacks of a Premier anxious to position himself at the forefront of the gun control debate that has arisen out of the blood of Port Arthur . . . Carr won't be thanked by voters for using the current gun debate to advance his own political credentials.[124]

The same criticism was never made of Howard's motivations, probably because of his consistent position on gun control from the pre–Port Arthur period.

By the time of the 10 May Police Ministers' conference, NSW Premier Bob Carr and Police Minister Paul Whelan had apparently converted to gun control advocacy. The CGC believes it played an important role in brokering this radical transformation. But on the Tuesday after the massacre, the NSW Labor Party was in a dither about what to do. A motion by the Left faction to toughen the party's position was rejected in an emotional Caucus meeting. The proposer, Sandra Nori, had urged the Premier to develop a bipartisan approach with the State Opposition. Carr was reported to have rejected this in favour of his much-publicised move to hand over gun control powers to the Commonwealth Government.[125]

---

123 Carty L. 'Professor demands "bloody" Tingle's head', *Illawarra Mercury*, 10 May 1996.

124 Lagan B. 'Hairy chested and hare brained', *SMH*, 3 May 1996.

125 Humphries D. 'Emotions run high as Left loses bid to toughen laws', *SMH*, 1 May 1996: 8.

On 4 May, six days after the Port Arthur massacre, the CGC organised a mass rally for gun control in Sydney's Hyde Park. One of our intentions at the rally was to read out a four-point minimal position for gun law reform and to tell the crowd where the two main state political parties – the Labor Government and the Liberal-National Coalition – stood on these points:

> Uniform gun laws across Australia.
>
> Proof of reason required for all gun licences.
>
> Registration of the sale, transfer and ownership of all guns.
>
> No lifetime licences.

State Parliament was sitting that week, and four CGC members – Rebecca Peters, Geoff Derrick, Charles Watson and I – first sought an appointment with the leader of the Opposition, Peter Collins. What made us seek the views of the Opposition before those of the Government? The first reason was that the Liberal Opposition seemed more likely than the Labor Government to want to appear consistent with the position being advocated by the Liberal Prime Minister. If the Opposition signed, this would put pressure on Carr and his Labor Government who had long opposed gun registration. Second, we had sent the four-point list to all State MPs and asked for their faxed responses by the Friday morning. We received responses from all the minor parties and several Labor MPs, but nothing from the Opposition. We felt we held a card that, if publicised, would be embarrassing to the Opposition and so wanted to give them an 11-hour opportunity to state their views.

We telephoned on the morning of Friday 3 May to request a meeting with Collins, which was arranged for that afternoon. Collins arrived at the meeting with National Party leader Ian Armstrong, Shadow Police Minister Andrew Tink and National Party MP Peter Cochrane. It was the first time most of us had met any of these men in our capacities as gun control advocates. After briefly explaining the aims and structure of the CGC, we pointed out that we had received no response from the

Opposition to our four-point statement. We explained that we intended to read out a list of politicians who both supported and opposed our points at the rally the following day.

Peter Collins expressed surprise that we had not received his response – he was sure he had signed the statement. He then looked for and produced the statement, containing – sure enough – his signature. He passed it to Ian Armstrong, who (to our amazement) signed as well, without hesitation. Swiftly Collins then produced a typed list of Coalition MPs which he attached to the document, remarking airily that he and Armstrong were signing for every parliamentary member of the Coalition. To say we were speechless would be putting it mildly. Here, with little argument and no acrimony, the entire Opposition had been signed over to support gun registration and the other points in the document.

We left the building so jubilant that we momentarily overlooked trying to get the Government's agreement. Geoff Derrick then said, 'We've only got the job half done – we need Carr's signature.' We re-entered the Parliament building and called Bob Carr's office, explaining to a staff member what had happened. He replied that he thought 'the boss' would want to know about this urgently, so would we please come up to his rooms. We gave the staffer a photocopy of the statement signed by the Opposition – having first extracted a promise not to break the news publicly – and then we were left to wait. We waited for over an hour, during which (thanks to mobile phones) we ploughed ahead with the barrage of media interviews, which were still coming thick and fast, this being just five days after the massacre. After an hour we began to get nervous: Geoff Derrick suggested, only half in jest, that the Government was holding us hostage. Eventually we were taken to meet the Premier and the Police Minister, and they both promptly signed our document.

We had brokered the long sought-after bipartisan support. For the first time in recent NSW political history, all parties had agreed to introduce the gun lobby's bogeyman: gun registration. The next day at the Hyde Park rally, Rebecca Peters held aloft the signed agreements and declared: 'These documents mean the end of the power of the gun lobby in NSW. If Bob Carr or Peter Collins or Ian Armstrong renege on this commitment . . . they need never ask for the trust of the people of NSW again.'[126]

From that day on, the NSW Government became an open supporter of gun control, taking every opportunity to present itself as a leader of national reform. On the day of the 10 May Police Ministers' meeting – when several states were equivocating about details of the Howard plan – Carr convened a press conference where he had the temerity to refer to this obstruction to national agreement as coming from 'the usual suspects'.[127] NSW had for years, under both Labor and Coalition governments, been one of the principal states obstructing national agreements on gun law reform. But now things promised to be different.

On the eve of the 10 May Police Ministers' meeting, former NSW Premier Barrie Unsworth chronicled in the *Sydney Morning Herald* Australia's recent history of failure to achieve national gun laws. Unsworth had unsuccessfully attempted to introduce gun registration in 1988, thereby becoming a 'scalp' of the gun lobby. In the months after the defeat of Unsworth's Government in 1988, the SSAA and the Firearms Advisory Council distributed a publication to all politicians titled 'Rednecks, Reactionaries & Rambos: the true story of how a supposedly unsophisticated group of firearm owners helped bring down a government'.[128] The title came from a statement made by Unsworth. The booklet gloated over the gun lobby's alleged power in unseating the government. The gun lobby claimed its advertising expenditure during the election had been topped only by that of the two main political parties.

In the article, Unsworth attributed his failure to 'a lack of bipartisan

126 Larkin J. 'Gun crazy fools', *Sunday Telegraph*, 5 May 1996: 1; Warnock S. 'A city cries for the dead', *Sun Herald*, 5 May 1996: 2.

127 Lagan B. 'Howard's threat to expose the waverers pays off', *SMH*, 11 May 1996.

128 Sporting Shooters Association of Australia and Firearms Advisory Council, 'Rednecks, Reactionaries & Rambos. 'the true story of how a supposedly unsophisticated group of firearm owners helped bring down a government', undated (probably 1988).

political support' on the issue – Nick Greiner's Liberal Opposition had opposed Unsworth's reforms. Unsworth's article failed to mention any of the other factors to which analysts also attributed his defeat in 1988.[129] He concluded that after Port Arthur politicians were 'now all older and wiser'[130] – doubtless code for 'not foolish enough to try and ride out this one by doing nothing' or more optimistically, 'at last we have a pretext to show political courage'. It was as if the outrage of the event could not sustain another moment of procrastination. One analyst suggested: 'The devastation wreaked . . . had rendered gun control reform inevitable.'[131]

Reflecting the widespread community cynicism about politicians being soft on gun law reform, NSW Police Minister Paul Whelan (who had himself worn this accusation) said soon after the meeting, 'But those changes had to happen on Friday – it was a litmus test for politicians.'[132] Presumably the colour to be avoided was yellow. Similarly, Tasmania saw a dramatic turnaround in the Liberal Government, which still contained many of the parliamentarians who had endorsed former Police Minister Frank Madill's decision to do nothing about military and other high powered semi-automatic weapons. Tasmania was now to have the toughest gun laws in Australia, said Premier Rundle. The Tasmanian Liberal's U-turn mirrored that of the Labor Party's. For years both parties had courted the redneck shooters' vote by ignoring gun law reform. Following Port Arthur, they sang in unison with the Tasmanian Greens who were long-time gun control advocates.

The force of this discourse created a formidable definition of government as spineless and utterly out of touch with community concerns. At the beginning of his term in office, Prime Minister John Howard had the chance to reinvent himself as a model of political leadership rarely seen in Australia in recent years.

---

129 Cockburn M. 'Political cowardice stems from myth of Unsworth defeat', *SMH*, 30 April 1996.

130 Unsworth B. 'Failure on guns an affront', *SMH*, 10 May 1996.

131 Millett M. 'Howard's gun gamble', *SMH*, 11 May 1996.

132 Vass N. 'Owners won't give up weapons: Tingle', *SMH*, 13 May 1996.

The National Party

The National Party presented the greatest threat to political bipartisanship across the country. Conservative socially and politically,
perennially suspicious of having their interests ignored by city-domi-
nated parliaments, the Nationals had a long and ugly record of opposing
gun law reform. The Victorian Deputy Premier, the National Party's
Pat McNamara, had stood beside Ted Drane on the platform at a pro-
gun rally in Melbourne after the Cain Labor Government reacted to
the Queen St massacre in 1987.[133] Drane himself had formerly stood as
a National Party candidate in Victoria. In 1995 Queensland's National
Party Police Minister, Russell Cooper, announced his party would give
householders what the *Bulletin* magazine called 'the unfettered right to
shoot intruders',[134] following a series of populist articles in Brisbane's
tabloid press on the alleged rise in crime.

On the night after Port Arthur, Cooper told the *7.30 Report*: 'What
I don't want to do is one of these massive knee-jerk reactions . . .' going
on to explain that he didn't support gun registration and that he wanted
to see a prohibited person register 'with the cooperation of the AMA
[Australian Medical Association]'.[135]

The National Party's Federal leader, Deputy Prime Minister Tim
Fischer, fell in behind his Prime Minister and, despite being threatened with revolt in his party, consistently supported Howard's position
throughout the months of debate. Several commentators noted that
Fischer was emerging as a hero in his own right, because he had far more
to lose by supporting gun control than Howard did. His party's rural
seats were the main electoral targets of the Shooters Party, which cam-
paigned vigorously against the gun laws, distributing leaflets, organising
meetings and recruiting members. It was said the entire executive of at
least one National Party branch resigned *en masse* to join the Shooters
Party. Tim Fischer travelled tirelessly to country towns, explaining the

---

133 Archival footage shown on *7.30 Report*, ABC TV, 9 May 1996.
134 Roberts G. 'Break, enter and die', *The Bulletin*, 9 May 1995: 15, 17–19.
135 *7.30 Report*, ABC TV, 29 April 1996.

new gun laws and dampening down the hysteria fomented by the gun lobby.

In early June, the bipartisan unity in NSW appeared to be under threat when National Party leader Ian Armstrong suddenly announced that his party did not support gun registration, something to which he had signed his explicit agreement on the CGC's document on 4 May. Armstrong announced that he 'support[ed] the call by the Prime Minister for a national register of *gun ownership*' – that is, a record of the general fact that a person owns guns – but not a specific record of how many or what type of guns. He denied he had changed his stance, insisting this was the form of 'registration' he had always intended to support.[136] (Unfortunately the wording used in the CGC statement was 'registration of the ownership of all guns'. The words 'registration of every gun' would have expressed our intention more clearly. But since the principle of firearms registration is firmly established in other Australian jurisdictions, and even in NSW for handguns, there could never really have been any doubt about what was meant by the phrase.) The CGC attacked Armstrong's announcement as a pathetic attempt to weasel out of his signed agreement, suggesting that, 'Mr Armstrong may be being held captive to a hillbilly minority in the Coalition'.[137] To his credit, Liberal leader Peter Collins stood firm and said the Opposition's position was unchanged on registration and support for the full Howard package: 'Regardless of anything that may have been said today by Mr Armstrong, I guarantee that the Howard legislation will pass through the NSW Parliament'.[138]

And pass it did. Chapter 7 reviews several areas where state and territory governments watered down some of the principles of the 10 May APMC agreement when it came to incorporating these into legislation. Some of these were serious departures from the agreement and reflected obvious lobbying by conservative groups. Nonetheless, most

---

136 Morris R. 'Guns push Coalition to the brink', *Daily Telegraph*, 8 June 1996.

137 Simon Chapman on *ABC TV News*, 7 June 1996.

138 Peter Collins on *ABC TV News*, 7 June 1996.

of the APMC package passed into laws around Australia. Port Arthur had been the catalyst for transforming political cowardice. Federal Attorney-General Daryl Williams told the *7.30 Report*: 'I think the gun lobby is now being matched by an anti-gun lobby . . . The people of Australia expressed their own view of this issue quite emphatically and I think that gave the political will which was previously missing.'[139]

There will always be speculation about whether John Howard's resolve over gun law reform was opportunistic, or whether he would have been as resolute had the massacre occurred at a less politically 'safe' time. Howard's March election victory had been sweeping, giving him the confidence of huge electoral support. But would Howard have been so bold if the massacre had occurred toward the end of his first term as Prime Minister? Or if he had not enjoyed such a large parliamentary majority? Liberal-National parties were also in power in seven out of eight Australian states and territories. This allowed Howard, as Liberal leader, a huge advantage in dealing with state premiers who shared much of his political philosophy. Would the Federal Opposition have taken the same action if it had still been in power, with the same political situation prevailing in the states? Some have speculated that the coincidence of Bryant's rampage with the first weeks of Howard's sweeping political victory created a 'now or never' situation for gun law reform: even a massive backlash from shooters would not be sustained throughout a three-year political term. By this analysis, Howard had little to lose but everything to gain by stamping his mark of strong leadership on the community as his first major political act as Prime Minister.

On the first anniversary of Howard's prime ministership, a national poll asked respondents to rate 19 different issues in terms of how well the Howard Government had handled them. Only the handling of two issues – interest rates (55%) and gun control (63%) – was rated by more than half the respondents as 'good/very good'. The mean 'good/very good' rating across the 19 issues was only 27.5%.[140] Almost a year after

139 Williams D. *7.30 Report*, ABC TV, 10 May 1996.
140 Millett M. 'It's thumbs up', *SMH*, 1 March 1997: 34.

Over our dead bodies

Port Arthur, it seemed that no other issue could come close to gun control in community approval ratings.

2

The case for fewer guns

No blueprint of gun control promises to eliminate gun violence from communities. But the wide range of murder rates – between the extremes of Colombia (167.6 male homicides per 100,000), where guns are readily available and Japan (0.7 per 100,000),[1] which has the strictest gun control in the world – raises obvious questions about whether there might be some connection between gun availability and total and gun homicide rates. Similar questions can be asked about gun suicide rates.

The main reforms introduced after the Port Arthur massacre were designed to reduce the number of guns in the Australian community by making it much harder to qualify for gun ownership; tightening requirements on registration and storage; and removing certain weapons deemed unacceptable for civilian use. These policies were expected to reduce gun ownership, gun availability and therefore gun violence (murders, suicides, accidental deaths and injuries).

This chapter summarises the main arguments for reducing the number of guns in communities and the number of people permitted to own guns. The concern here is with the central question of whether reducing access to guns can be expected to reduce the number of people killed and injured from guns through murder, suicide and unintentional injury. I will summarise several key pieces of research on the relationship between the prevalence of guns in communities and their death/injury rates, and comment on the gun lobby's counter-arguments.

---

1 WHO: *World health statistics annual 1994.* Geneva, 1995.

Reduction not elimination

The tightest gun control laws imaginable would not eliminate all gun violence from a community. No nation has a zero death rate from guns. As with all preventive public health policies, gun control policies seek to reduce rather than eliminate the problems they address. Road safety policies are acclaimed when they reduce deaths and injuries. If someone condemned random breath testing or highway patrols because they only halved rather than eliminated drunk driving or speeding, they would hardly be taken seriously. Yet this was what the gun lobby sought to argue in regard to the new gun laws.

Mike Ascher, from the NSW Amateur Pistol Association, bellowed to the crowd at the 15 June 1996 pro-gun rally in Sydney, 'Get rid of the guns and you stop homicides. Get rid of the guns and you stop robberies. Get rid of the guns and you stop home invasions. What a load of unadulterated bloody rubbish!'[2] Similarly John Tingle argued: 'Handguns have been registered in NSW since 1927. It has not and will never stop their use in crime.'[3] Here Tingle, like Ascher, adroitly sets up the straw man argument that the only worthwhile test of gun registration is whether it eliminates *all* criminal use of guns. Anything less is presumably considered worthless.

International comparisons

The task of comparing countries head-to-head on two variables – for example, number of guns per population and number of incidents of violence (usually death from gun homicides, suicides and accidents) – is fraught with methodological problems. There are many cultural, historical and economic factors that can influence the scale of a nation's gun violence. The Colombian gun death rate, for example, plainly has much to do with the presence of cocaine cartels and their private armies – something few other nations share. Civil wars and persistent sectarian

---

2 *ABC TV News*, 15 June 1996.

3 Tingle J. *Channel 7 News*, 22 March 1996.

violence in places like Bosnia, Sri Lanka and Northern Ireland also confuse the gun availability/violence picture.

The extent of a nation's 'gun culture' depends on many factors including whether guns have been historically revered and glamorised, patterns of urbanisation, the extent of all violent crime, and whether guns are kept in homes as part of strictly regulated civil defence programs (as in Switzerland). These potentially complex and confounding variables are difficult to define and quantify, and make direct international comparisons problematic. All but the most intractable in both gun control and pro-gun factions admit there is clearly room for debate whenever *precise* claims are made about the relationship between availability and gun violence.

However, these groups differ radically over the question of whether there is an acceptable degree of research support for the general proposition that more guns means more deaths. The gun lobby argues this is nonsense and champions the case of nations with high rates of gun ownership and low rates of gun homicide (for example, Norway). Gun control advocates are less concerned about exceptional cases and more with the pattern across countries. There have been several recent studies comparing rates of gun ownership and gun violence between countries that are broadly similar culturally and economically.

A comparison of homicide rates between the US and Britain found that the non-gun US homicide rate (per 100,000 population) was 3.7 times higher than the British rate, while the rate of handgun homicides was 175 times higher.[4] This suggests that, even if Americans were inherently somewhat more murderous than the British, the easy availability of handguns has produced a massively disproportionate number of homicides.

A study comparing the cities of Seattle (US) and nearby Vancouver (Canada) found the cities had almost identical rates of burglary, assault and robbery without a gun; but that the Seattle rate of assault with a firearm and homicide with a handgun were seven and 4.8 times higher

---

4 Clarke RVG, Mayhew P. 'The British gas suicide story and its criminological implications', *British Journal of Criminology*, 1991, 31: 186–88.

respectively than the corresponding rates in Vancouver.[5] Again, handguns are much more accessible in the US than in Canada.

A later study by Centerwall[6] compared homicide rates from 1976–89 in Canadian provinces and US states on the US/Canada border. He concluded that there were no consistent differences between the homicide rates of the two countries, despite handgun ownership being much higher in the US. But other researchers have pointed out that Centerwall's comparison gives the same weight to sparsely populated states and provinces as it does to densely populated urban areas. If the comparison is made between states and provinces of similar population densities, the homicide rate is between two and four times higher on the US side of the border.[7]

The prolific suicide and homicide researcher David Lester examined the relationship between gun availability and both the total and gun homicide rates in 16 European countries. He used the proportion of all murders and suicides where guns were used, as well as the annual accidental gun death rate, as proxy measures for gun availability, commenting that 'no country of the world provides accurate measures of firearm ownership'. He found a strong correlation between these measures of availability and gun homicides, demonstrating that nations with more firearms have higher gun homicide rates. He also found that the rate of homicide by other means did not present any compensatory corollary; that is, in countries where guns were less available, there was

---

5 Sloan JH, Kellermann AL, Reay DT et al. 'Handgun regulations, crime, assaults, and homicide: a tale of two cities', *New England Journal of Medicine*, 1988, 319: 1256–62.

6 Centerwall BS. 'Homicide and the prevalence of handguns: Canada and the United States, 1976 to 1980', *American Journal of Epidemiology*, 1991: 1245–60.

7 Gabor T. 'The impact of the availability of firearms on violent crime, suicide, and accidental death', Department of Justice Canada, 1994; Mayhew P. 'A reply to comments on the research note in the government evidence', Lord Cullen's Inquiry into the Circumstances Leading Up To and Surrounding the Events at Dunblane Primary School on Wednesday 13 March. Home Office, July 1996: 12.

no significant increase in alternative methods of killing.[8]

Swiss criminologist Martin Killias published in 1993 a review of international correlations between gun ownership and rates of homicide and suicide in 14 countries,[9] later updating this to 18 nations.[10] The data on percentages of households with guns was obtained from the 1989 and 1992 International Crime Victimisation Surveys (ICVS) conducted by telephone interviews with householders. This is the largest international attempt to use a standard method to measure gun ownership. Table 2.1 shows Killias' results, listed by ascending levels of gun ownership.

Table 2.1. Homicide, suicide and household gun ownership in 18 countries (rates per million population)

Country	Overall homicide	Homicide with a gun	Overall suicide	Suicide with gun	% of households with guns
Holland	11.8	2.7	117.2	2.8	1.9
England & Wales	6.7	0.8	86.1	3.8	4.7
Scotland	16.3	1.1	105.1	6.9	4.7
CSSR	13.5	2.6	117.8	9.5	5.2
Nthrn Ireland	46.6	35.5	82.7	11.8	8.4
Germany	12.1	2.0	203.7	13.8	8.9
Spain	13.7	3.8	64.5	4.5	13.1
Sweden	13.3	2.0	182.4	21.2	15.1

8 Lester D. 'Crime as opportunity. A test of the hypothesis with European homicide rates', *British Journal of Criminology*, 1991, 31: 186–88.

9 Killias M. 'International correlations between gun ownership and rates of homicide and suicide', *Canadian Medical Association Journal*, 1993, 148: 1721–5.

10 Killias M. 'Gun ownership, suicide and homicide: an international perspective', in *Understanding crime: experiences of crime and crime control*. United Nations Interregional Crime and Justice Research Institute, Publication No 49, Rome, August 1993: 289–302.

Country	Overall homicide	Homicide with a gun	Overall suicide	Suicide with gun	% of households with guns
Italy	17.4	13.1	78.1	10.9	16.0
Belgium	18.5	8.7	231.5	24.5	16.6
Australia	19.5	6.6	115.8	34.2	19.6
New Zealand	20.2	4.7	137.7	24.1	22.3
France	12.5	5.5	223.0	49.3	22.6
Finland	29.6	7.4	253.5	54.3	23.2
Switzerland	11.7	4.6	244.5	57.4	27.2*
Canada	26.0	8.4	139.4	44.4	29.1
Norway	12.1	3.6	142.7	38.7	32.0
US	75.9	44.6	124.0	72.8	48.0

* The Swiss gun ownership rate excluding military guns is 12.2%.

Killias found that across the nations, the rate of household gun ownership correlated with the *rates* of homicide and suicide committed with guns, the *proportion* of all homicides and suicides committed with guns, and the *overall rates* of homicide and suicide. In other words, countries with high gun ownership rates tended to have higher rates of fatal gun violence than those with lower gun ownership. Nor did the study find a 'substitution' effect; that is, in countries with low rates of gun ownership, the rates of homicide and suicide by other means did not compensate for the lack of access to guns.

Killias noted:

> The correlation between gun ownership and suicide with a gun was stronger when the categories of firearms were combined instead of considered separately . . . One might conclude that, in the case of suicide at least, the mere presence of a lethal weapon [i.e., any type of gun] shapes the outcome of an acute crisis, whatever the legal status or the technical characteristics of the weapon may be.[11]

---

11 Ibid.

The gun lobby has criticised Killias' study because of the high non-response rates (47% averaged across all 18 nations).[12] It is also generally sceptical about surveys of gun ownership, arguing that many people will under-report ownership, due to fear of government persecution. But these critics cannot explain why the non-respondents would produce any systematic bias. In other words, they provide no compelling reasons why the correlations obtained would be any different had more people responded – if gun owners had consistently high rates of non-response to the surveys across the 18 countries, and the data were adjusted to account for this, this would not have altered the correlational results. Nor have they responded to the fact that the ICVS reported that rates of gun ownership generally corresponded well with estimates obtained by other surveys undertaken in some of the countries.[13]

The gun lobby also claims that the argument works the other way round: high homicide rates in a community may prompt people to purchase more guns for self-defence; that is, high gun murder rates lead to higher rates of gun ownership. This argument fails to explain why Killias and others have also found a link between high gun ownership levels and high suicide rates. It would be ludicrous to suggest that high gun suicide rates prompt communities to arm themselves more.

Gun violence in Australia

Table 2.2 shows the data on gun deaths in Australia for the five years 1990–95.

In summary:

- Between 1990 and 1995, an average of 560 people died from guns each year.
- Of all gun deaths, 81% were suicides; 14% resulted from violence; 4% were unintentional (accidents); 1% were of unknown intent.

---

12 Mayhew P. 'A reply to comments on the research note in the government evidence', *op. cit.*

13 Ibid.

In addition in 1994:

- 95.2% of gun suicides were males; 63.2% of gun homicides were males.
- Firearms were used in one in four homicides and one in five suicides.[14]
- One in four male suicides involved a firearm.
- One in 18 female suicides involved a firearm.
- 55% of female firearm deaths resulted from an assault.

Table 2.2. Firearm deaths, Australia 1990–95 (rate per 100,000 population in brackets)[15]

	1990	1991	1992	1993	1994	1995
Suicide	486 (2.9)	505 (2.9)	488 (2.8)	431 (2.4)	420 (2.4)	388 (2.2)
Assault (homicides)	79 (0.5)	84 (0.5)	96 (0.5)	64 (0.4)	76 (0.4)	67 (0.4)
Unintentional (accidents)	30 (0.2)	29 (0.2)	24 (0.1)	18 (0.1)	20 (0.1)	15 (0.1)
Total*	610 (3.6)*	623 (3.6)*	615 (3.4)*	519 (2.9)*	522 (2.9)*	470 (2.7)

* Column totals include gun deaths where intent was unknown. ** 1995 excludes legal interventions and deaths where intent was unknown.

In New South Wales, between 1984 and 1988, guns were the third leading cause of injury and death (8% of total), behind motor vehicle accidents (35%) and falls (12%).[16]

---

14 Mukherjee S, Carcach C. *Violent deaths and firearms in Australia: data and trends.* Australian Institute of Criminology. Research and Public Policy Series No. 4, 1996.

15 *Australian Injury Prevention Bulletin* 1994, Issue No 8; 1995 data from Moller J, Bordeaux S. 'Update of gun-related death data to 1995', National Injury Surveillance Unit, February 1997.

16 Lyle D et al. 'Firearm injuries in New South Wales', New South Wales Department of Health: NSW Public Health Bulletin, 1991, 2: 111.

Measuring the effect of gun laws in Australia has been difficult in the past because the eight states and territories all had different laws and the absence of interstate border checks meant guns were easily transported between jurisdictions, rendering the laws largely inoperable. This meant that guns bought freely in a state with a liberal law (for example, Queensland) could be carried into a stricter state where they would be illegal and not easily detected. The absence of gun registration in NSW, Tasmania and Queensland also meant there were no national records of number sand types of guns in circulation. Before the new laws, Australia's strictest gun law was in Western Australia, where many of the 1996 APMC agreement terms were law already.

The most striking feature of the distribution of firearm mortality in Australia is that the two states with the most permissive laws, Tasmania and Queensland, have gun death rates significantly above the average.[17] (The Northern Territory also has a relatively high rate, but it has such a small population (170,000) that a single gun death can dramatically increase the rate per population.) Gun death rates per 100,000 population in 1990–1994 were: Tasmania 7.97, Northern Territory 7.52, Queensland 5.04, South Australia 3.55, NSW 2.83, Victoria 2.66, Western Australia 2.55, Australian Capital Territory 1.56.[18] The Tasmanian gun death rate in 1994 was 7.2 per 100,000, based on 34 gun deaths for that year. Port Arthur doubled this rate in one afternoon.

One of the few Australian studies on the relationship between firearm availability and violence was conducted by Chris Cantor and Penelope Slater. They examined the effect of the *Queensland Weapons Act 1990*, which introduced firearm licensing and a 28-day waiting period for all applications.[19] The researchers said their study provided preliminary evidence that tightening gun control may reduce suicides

17 Harrison J, Moller J, Bordeaux S. 'Injury by Firearms Australia 1994', *Australian Injury Prevention Bulletin*, Issue No. 13, Supplement, October 1996.

18 Mukherjee S, Carcach C. *op. cit.*

19 Cantor CH, Slater PJ. 'The impact of firearm control legislation on suicide in Queensland: preliminary findings', *Medical Journal of Australia*, 1995, 162: 583–85.

rates, especially among young men. (They found reductions in both gun suicides and overall male suicides in provincial areas, and in gun suicides in the cities.)

Gun violence in the United States

As described in Chapter 1, the American gun problem has long imprinted itself in the Australian consciousness as the embodiment of all that should be avoided. For US gun control campaigners, the introduction of the most basic restrictions are seen as major victories; for example, the radical requirement that handgun buyers endure a six-day cooling-off period to allow background checks. The State of Virginia has introduced what the gun lobby bemoans as a tough handgun law, allowing residents to purchase a maximum of only one handgun per month.

The gun lobby likes to make the point that there is no shortage of gun laws in the US; rather, there are 20,000 separate gun laws which have not curbed the epidemic of violence.[20] The large number of gun laws illustrates the same fundamental deficiency which undermined gun control in Australia until 1996: the lack of national uniformity. A ban on military-style semi-automatics in her home state of Western Australia did not prevent 21-year-old Kate Scott from being killed when she visited Port Arthur, because Tasmania's law still allowed these weapons to be freely sold. The safety of an entire nation is undermined when gun laws are more feeble in some states than in others. But at least Australian gun laws are state and territory laws, so our legal patchwork was made up of only eight parts. US gun laws are often municipal ordinances – local bans which in reality have only symbolic value: the equivalent of banning handgun sales in downtown Perth while a brisk trade continues in neighbouring Fremantle.

In 1996, 31 of the 50 states in the US had laws permitting citizens to carry concealed loaded handguns[21] – a situation the National Rifle

---

20 SSAA. *Gun control: the facts. Is Australian going down the American path?* Pamphlet, December 1996.

21 Violence Policy Center. 'Concealing the risk: real-world effects of lax

Association (NRA) claims actually *reduces* the gun homicide rate. In 1996 a great deal of publicity was given to a paper by two American researchers, Lott and Mustard, focusing on 'shall issue' laws which require officials to issue permits for citizens to carry concealed guns.[22] The researchers examined whether these laws deterred violent crime. They concluded that states with such laws had lower rates of violent crime than those without. The gun lobby rapidly championed the study on the internet and in countless editorials. But reviews by other researchers found the study was methodologically weak enough to render its conclusions suspect.[23] The 'guns make us safe' perspective could probably only be advanced with a straight face in a country where gun violence is as rampant as it is in the US. For outside observers, the first and most obvious question to ask is: 'If carrying guns and arming homes prevents gun violence, why does the most heavily citizen-armed nation in the Western world have about 38,000 annual gun deaths, including 18,000 gun homicides a year, giving it the highest per capita rate of gun violence?' The debate on gun control in the US is profoundly parochial, with the horizons of many internal commentators seldom reaching beyond US shores to consider the perspective of other nations' gun violence records.[24] To argue from the US situation that guns make

concealed weapons laws', Washington DC: Violence Policy Center, 1996.

22 Lott JR, Mustard DB. 'Crime, deterrence, and right to carry concealed handguns', *Journal of Legal Studies*, January 1997, available at: http://www2.lib. uchicago.edu/~llou/guns.html.

23 Webster DW. 'The claims that right to carry laws reduce violent crime are unsubstantiated', Johns Hopkins Center for Gun Policy and Research, Johns Hopkins University, School of Public Health, Baltimore, MD, October 1996. See also: McDowell D, Loftin C, Wiersema B. 'Easing concealed firearms laws: effects on homicide in three states', *Journal of Criminal Law & Criminology*, 1995, 84: 193–206; McDowell D, Loftin C, Wiersema B. 'Additional discussion about easing concealed firearms laws: effects on homicide in three states', *Journal of Criminal Law & Criminology*, 1995, 86: 221–26; Nagin D. 'General deterrence: a review of the empirical evidence', in A Blumstein, J Cohen, D Nagin (eds), *Deterrence and incapacitation: estimating the effects of criminal sanctions on crime rates*. Washington, DC: National Academy Press, 1978.

24 The NCGC often receives email from American shooters upbraiding

communities 'safer' is rather akin to arguing that war-torn Bosnia is safer than Rwanda during the genocide. Ever since Port Arthur, the NCGC's web site has attracted virulent email from US shooters gasping in near apoplexy over our statements, apparently seldom realising that other nations' gun laws differ from those of the US and seemingly unaware that the benchmarks of 'safer' communities in the US are frequently outrageously high compared with other nations with tougher gun laws.

Here are some recent statistics on gun violence in the US (population about 254 million):

- From 1968 to 1991, annual deaths due to motor vehicles declined by 21% (from 54,842 to 43,536), while during the same period deaths due to firearms increased by 60% (from 23,875 to 38,317).[25] If this trend continues, by the year 2003 the number of US citizens killed annually by firearms will exceed the number killed in motor vehicle crashes.[26] In some states this crossover has already occurred.

- In 1993 there were 39,595 firearm-related deaths, a rate of 15.36/100,000. Of these, 18,940 (47.8%) were suicides, 18,571 (46.9%) were homicides, 1,521 (3.8%) were unintentional, and the remainder were of undetermined intent.[27] Firearm-related deaths were the fourth leading cause of 'years of potential life lost' before age 65.[28]

---

us for stating that there is no constitutional right to bear arms. Quite apart from the dubious existence of such a right in the US, these correspondents seem unaware that the United States ends at its shores: our website has many references marking it as an Australian site.

25 Centers for Disease Control. 'Deaths resulting from firearm and motor vehicle-related injuries United States, 1968–1991, *Morbidity and Mortality Weekly Report*, 1994, 43: 37–42.

26 Hinkle J, Betz S. 'Gunshot injuries', *AACN Clinical Issues*, 1995, 6: 175–86.

27 Mercy J. US Centers for Disease Control and Prevention. Email dated 9 September 1996.

28 US Centers for Disease Control. 'Firearm-related years of potential life lost before age 65 years – United States, 1980–1991', *Morbidity and Mortality*

- A total of 26,009 homicides were reported nationally in 1993, of which 71% (18,466) were firearm related. Overall rates of homicide increased from 1985 to 1991 and decreased from 1992 to 1994. During these two periods, rates for total firearm-related homicides and homicide among people aged 15–24 years increased and then stabilised, but remained at record high levels.[29]

- For every person killed by a gun, another 2.5 are injured seriously enough to be admitted to hospital. An estimated 99,025 people were treated for non-fatal firearm-related injuries in US hospital emergency departments in 1992.[30]

- In 1992 the US had more gun dealers (about 245,000) than petrol stations (about 210,000).[31] Since recent law reform outlawing 'kitchen table' dealerships, the number of dealerships has fallen to a mere 142,094.[32]

In summary, the US has nearly 14 times Australia's population. It has 69 times our total gun deaths, and 172 times Australia's gun homicides (Table 2.3). By contrast, Japan has nearly seven times Australia's population, yet has nearly six times fewer gun deaths and nearly three times fewer gun homicides.

Weekly Report, 1994, 43: 609–11.

29 US Centers for Disease Control. 'Trends in rates of homicide – United States, 1985–1994', *Morbidity and Mortality Weekly Report*, 1996, 45: 460–64.

30 Annest JL, Mercy JA, Gibson DR, Ryan GW. 'National estimates of non-fatal firearm-related injuries: beyond the tip of the iceberg', *JAMA*, 1995, 273: 1749–54.

31 Violence Policy Center. 'More gun dealers than gas stations: a study of federally licensed firearms dealers in America', Washington: 1992.

32 Violence Policy Center. 'Number of gun dealers plummets by 100,000 in two years', press release, 15 May 1996. Washington.

Table 2.3 Gun deaths and rates per 100,000 compared: US, Canada, Australia, Japan[33]

	US	Canada	Australia	Japan
Total annual gun deaths	36,985 (14.05)	189 (4.08)	536 (3.05)	93 (0.07)
Total gun homicides	16,524 (7.23)	176 (3.35)	96 (2.38)	34 (0.04)

Gun violence in England, Wales and Scotland

The gun control and gun violence situation in mainland Great Britain (excluding Northern Ireland, because of the continuing sectarian violence there) is particularly instructive. In a population of 57 million, Great Britain has very low rates of gun violence compared to those of Australia and the United States. Table 2.4 shows that the gun homicide rate in England and Wales is eight times less than in Australia, and nearly 56 times lower than the US rate. The gun suicide rate is nine times lower than Australia's and 19 times lower than it is in the US.

After the 1987 Hungerford massacre, Britain banned virtually all semi-automatic rifles in 1988 from private ownership. In response to the Cullen report on the March 1996 Dunblane massacre, the British Government passed The Firearms (Amendment) Act 1997 which banned all private possession of handguns over .22 calibre and all multi-shot .22s. Tony Blair's new Labour Government, elected in June 1997, lost no time in outlawing all private ownership of handguns, attributing the decision to the Dunblane shootings. Intriguingly, Lord Cullen's report did not apply the reasoning behind his recommendations about *ex*-residential handgun storage, to *all* guns. He wrote:

> the range of uses for [guns other than handguns] is very different. Thus the considerations relating to the possession and

---

33 Crime Prevention and Criminal Justice Division, United Nations Office at Vienna. United Nations Study on Firearm Regulation. Commission on Crime Prevention and Criminal Justice, Vienna 28 April–9 May 1997: 79.

use of shotguns are concerned with very different areas of activity from those relating to handguns. I am not persuaded that it is justifiable to approach all these types in essentially the same manner.

One cannot hunt or target-shoot with rifles and shotguns inside homes. But long arms are often stolen from homes, entering the criminal subculture. Being more common than handguns, shotguns and rifles are also more commonly used in domestic homicides and suicides. Having to take the time and trouble to check out a shotgun from a community armoury can put a critical cooling-off period between a raging impulse to shoot oneself or one's family and actually doing it. It is regrettable that Lord Cullen apparently chose to apply his terms of reference only to 'public' safety from guns, when gun murder and suicide behind the closed doors of gun owners' houses claim more lives each year.[34]

The NCGC frequently exemplified Britain's strict gun control post Hungerford and low death rates as the direction Australia should take. The gun lobby had no answers to this, except to claim that as Britain's gun laws had become tougher, its gun crime rate had risen. In fact, between 1993 and 1994 both gun homicide and armed robbery fell in Britain (Table 2.4). But this did not stop the gun lobby claiming that 'firearm deaths are increasing at a higher rate than [in] the so-called "gun crazy" United States'.[35]

34 Chapman S. 'Getting guns out of homes' (editorial), *British Medical Journal*, 1996, 313: 1030.

35 Howden J. 'Shooting from the hip on gun debate', *Newcastle Herald*, 3 April 1996.

Table 2.4. England, Wales and Scotland: offences in which a firearm was reported to have been used[36]

Year	All offences*	Homicide	Attempted murder	Robbery & assault
1993	15,727	82	1,388	6,014
1994	14,755	75	1,445	4,475
Change	-6.1%	-8.5%	+4.1%	-25.6%

* Includes offences such as criminal damage using a gun, reckless conduct.

The gun lobby has argued that high gun homicide rates in some nations result not from high gun ownership, but from high levels of 'violent culture', which manifests itself in gun homicides.[37] On this basis, nations which do not have 'violent cultures' can safely have access to guns without this translating into high rates of gun homicide. The gun lobby put this argument in submissions to the Dunblane inquiry. Unfortunately for the gun lobby, the argument that Britain is a 'less violent' and less crime-ridden nation than the US does not stand up to scrutiny. Table 2.5 lists rates of various crimes in the US and in England and Wales. It shows that property crime and non-gun assault rates are actually higher in England and Wales than in the US. This contradicts the suggestion that the British 'culture' is inherently less 'criminal' than the American, as the gun lobby seeks to imply. Gun-related crime rates, though, are dramatically different – suggesting that the availability of guns increases both fatal and non-fatal gun crime considerably more than might be expected from differences in recorded levels for other offences.

---

36 Evidence submitted on behalf of the Secretary of State for Scotland and the Home Secretary to Lord Cullen's Inquiry Into the Circumstances Leading Up To and Surrounding the Events at Dunblane Primary School on Wednesday 13 March 1996. 30 April 1996: 46.

37 Mayhew P. *op. cit.*, 7.

Table 2.5. Rates of various crimes in the US and England and Wales (per 1 million population, 1990–1994 averages)[38]

Crime	England & Wales	US	E&W/US ratio
Burglary	24,340	11,590	1: 0.48
Vehicle theft	10,960	6,290	1: 0.57
Non-gun assaults	3,860	3,290	1: 0.9
Non-gun robberies	890	1,540	1: 1.7
Non-gun homicides	12.4	30.4	1: 2.4
Gun assaults	53	1,045	1: 20
Gun robberies	98	1,033	1: 11
Gun homicides	1.2	63.6	1: 52

Gun violence in Japan

The extremely low gun death rate in Japan is an object lesson for other nations. Japan has the world's toughest gun laws. Citizens are not permitted to own handguns or swords. In 1971 the Japanese Government stopped the private transfer of all rifles then held by citizens, and required family heirs to surrender guns when the owners died. As a result, by 1986 only 27,000 people were licensed to keep a rifle or shotgun[39] and the number of licensed guns fell from 652,000 in 1981 to 493,373 in 1989.[40] In 1992 Japan had 133 million people (seven times Australia's population of 17.5 million), yet in 1995 just 34 people were murdered with guns – about one-third of Australia's gun homicide total. More people were shot dead at Port Arthur in one afternoon than in Japan in all of 1995.

---

38 Ibid, 10.

39 National Police Agency, Japanese Government. *White paper on police 1986* (excerpt), Trans. Tokyo: Police Association, 1986: 79.

40 National Police Agency, Japanese Government. *White paper on police 1990* (excerpt), Trans. Tokyo: Police Association, 1990: 80.

Despite this, the editor of *Australian Gun Sports* told his readers: 'Japan has a high murder rate and its people are prohibited from owning firearms.'[41] The NCGC repeatedly raised the example of Japan in media interviews and radio compere John Laws emphasised it many times. Yet a SSAA pamphlet distributed in December 1996 stated: 'Even though guns are virtually prohibited in Japan their murder rate is the same as Australia's – a fact gun prohibitionists never mention.' The pamphlet cited the World Health Organisation as its source.[42] The reason why 'gun prohibitionists' such as the NCGC never mention this 'fact' about Japan is because it is utter nonsense. At 0.7/100,000, Japan has the world's lowest homicide rate.

Gun violence in Switzerland

For many years the gun lobby has played what it believes is a rhetorical trump card in promoting the case of Switzerland, a nation whose civilian militia is said to hold some 400,000 military guns at home. By European standards, Switzerland has a low rate of homicide overall and a middle-range rate of homicide by guns (Table 2.1). The gun lobby believes this proves that heavily armed populations can live in safety. Immediately after Port Arthur it seemed that every second opponent of gun law reforms felt he had had the final word if he cited the case of Switzerland.[43]

Martin Killias, a Swiss resident, has pointed out that the image of Switzerland as a society with unrestricted access to guns is a 'criminological myth'.[44] The firearms kept in many Swiss homes are military guns that many citizens are obliged to keep as a part of their nation's civil militia. This kind of gun ownership differs fundamentally from that in countries like Australia and the US. The social meaning of gun

---

41 Galea R. 'Howard's hidden agendas?', Australian Gun Sports, 2 June 1996: 6.

42 SSAA. Gun control: the facts, op. cit.

43 Roudenko A. 'One in 10,000' (letter), *SMH*, 8 May 1996: 16.

44 Killias M. 'Gun ownership and violent crime: the Swiss experience in international perspective', *Security Journal*, 1990, 1(3): 169–74.

ownership has much more to do with Swiss civic responsibility than any personal interest in guns.[45] Further, as one writer to the *Sydney Morning Herald* pointed out, the gun lobby seldom acknowledges that in Switzerland both arms and ammunition must be kept under strict locked storage conditions that are checked every year.[46] The military weapons are heavy and difficult to carry inconspicuously, and military ammunition is not sold. There are extremely harsh penalties for failure to comply with these storage requirements and for any misuse of the military weapons. In terms of non-military firearm ownership, the Swiss gun law is 'definitely not among the most liberal in Europe'.[47]

As for gun violence, Killias noted that Switzerland has a high rate of gun homicide and one of the highest rates of gun suicide in Europe (see Table 2.1). This evidence, he says, contradicts the contention that the high gun ownership rate in Switzerland is not accompanied by frequent illegal use.[48] In fact the Swiss Government and people themselves believe guns are too easily available: in 1996 the population voted overwhelmingly to replace their patchwork of cantonal gun laws with one national law. At the time of writing, the new national law, which is stricter than the old cantonal laws, was expected to pass through Parliament.

Killias' work confirms what would seem to be intuitively the case: that societies with high rates of gun ownership pay the price with high rates of gun death, and those with strict gun controls tend to have low death rates. Easy access to guns places lethal and efficient killing instruments in the hands of people who might otherwise use less efficient means.

---

45 Harding R. 'Gun use in crime, rational choice, and social learning theory,' in Clarke RV, Felson M (eds). *Routine activity and rational choice.* Advances in criminological theory vol. 5. New Brunswick: Transaction Publishers, 1993: 95.

46 Looser E. 'Careless with the truth' (letter), *SMH*, 18 May 1996.

47 Killias M. 'Gun ownership and violent crime: the Swiss experience in international perspective', *Security Journal*, 1990, 1(3): 170.

48 Ibid, 174.

The gun lobby constantly disputes the relationship between gun availability and gun violence. A SSAA official agreed that the US as a whole had a high gun death rate, but insisted, 'there are many American States with murder rates as low as anywhere in the world that are safer to live in than parts of Australia. North Dakota and Nebraska are two examples'.[49] The reminder that there are some peaceful places in America was little comfort to Australians when our own quiet little backwater, Tasmania, was so savagely rocked by gun violence. (Although Tasmania's 'quiet' reputation was hardly deserved. Along with the most liberal gun laws in the country, it has the highest rate of firearm deaths.)

One senior journalist reviewing the gun control debate concluded: 'The crux of the guns lobby's argument – that there is no relationship between the murder rate and the level of gun ownership – simply is not tenable. It makes about as much sense as saying that there is no connection between the road toll and the number of cars, and moreover that Formula One cars should be allowed on the open road.'[50]

Suicide prevention

Since 81% of all Australian gun deaths are suicides, suicide prevention is clearly a major goal of gun control policy. Public gun massacres and other homicides capture more media attention, but are statistically overshadowed by gun suicides as the main type of gun death. Opponents of gun control believe restricting access to firearms will not prevent suicides because people who are unhappy will kill themselves anyway, by another method. But expert opinion suggests that only a proportion of people intent on suicide will substitute other methods. Of those who do, many will substitute less lethal methods and therefore have a greater chance of survival. Suicide prevention is the primary reason why the campaign for tighter gun laws has been strongly supported by the Royal Australian and New Zealand College of Psychiatrists, the Australian

49 Ziccone S. 'In defence of arms', *The Age*, 10 May 1996: A15.

50 Steketee M. 'Culture of violence demands tight controls', *The Australian*, 11 May 1996.

Medical Association, Suicide Prevention Australia, the Public Health Association, the Australian College for Emergency Medicine, and the Centre for Adolescent Health – among others.

Many suicide attempts are not planned well in advance. Many are relatively impulsive acts, precipitated by bouts of depression or incidents such as sexual conflict or financial crises.[51] A Scottish study of 522 self-poisonings, for example, found that two-thirds were impulsive.[52] Many suicide attempts occur when the person's judgment is impaired by intoxication.

Choice of suicide method by individuals and across different populations may be influenced by many factors: availability, cultural acceptability, technical skills (for example, being able to tie a fail-safe noose), whether planning is necessary, certainty of death, time taken to die, scope for second thoughts, chances of intervention, courage needed, perceived consequences of failure such as pain, disfigurement or humiliation, consequences for others (for example, danger, contaminating the family 'nest'), scope for concealing or publicising the suicide, symbolism, cultural ritual (for example, Japanese *hara-kiri*, *seppuku*, *shinju* and *oyako-shinju*) and dramatic impact.[53]

Whatever the relevance of the above to the choice of using a gun, three factors stand out as highly important:

Many more suicide attempts arise from temporary despair, rather than from a genuine decision to die. A Sydney hospital conducted an eight-year retrospective study of 33 survivors of self-inflicted firearm injury, finding that most were young men who did not suffer from major depression or psychosis. Most shootings occurred in the context

---

51 Easteal P. 'Homicide-suicides between adult sexual intimates: an Australian study', *Suicide Life Threatening Behaviour*, 1994, 24: 140–51.

52 Kessel N. 'Self-poisoning', in Shneidman ES (ed.). *Essays in self destruction.* New York: Science House, 1976.

53 Dudley M, Cantor C, de Moore G. 'Jumping the gun: firearms and the mental health of Australians', *Australian and New Zealand Journal of Psychiatry*, 1996, 30: 370–81.

of personal disputes with sexual partners or family members. They shot themselves impulsively in a crisis, were not psychotic, and had ready access to firearms.[54] Significantly, after medical and counselling intervention, almost none of the survivors attempted suicide again. This contradicts the popular misconception that 'they'll do it again anyway'; that is, that suicidal people will kill themselves no matter what efforts are made to prevent them from doing so. For every suicide in Australia, it has been estimated that there are 30–40 attempts (parasuicides).[55]

Guns are a particularly efficient means of killing. Different methods of attempting suicide have different 'completion' or fatality rates. In NSW, for example, attempts using guns are second only to hanging (see Table 2.6). The contrast in completion rates is particularly stark between firearms (75%) and the most common methods of attempting suicide – slashing oneself (6%) and drug overdoses (4%). The data suggest that if more people attempting suicide used guns, the number of suicide deaths would almost certainly rise. Alternatively, if more 'attempters' used knives, razors or drugs instead of guns, the number of suicides would fall. If access to guns was more difficult, some attempting suicide – particularly in impulsive contexts – might chose these less fatal methods.

Suicidal intent can dissipate in the time taken to locate or construct a method of attempting suicide. If a gun is not immediately available, by the time it is obtained or a substitute method found, the suicidal crisis may be over. US research suggests the availability of a highly lethal method like a gun in a house can precipitate an impulsive suicide attempt.[56] In other words, the availability of firearms influences not only

---

54 DeMoore GM, Plew JD, Bray KM, Snars JN. 'Survivors of self-inflicted firearm injury – a liaison psychiatry perspective', *Medical Journal of Australia*, 1994, 160: 421–25.

55 Davis AT, Schruder C. 'The prediction of suicide', *Medical Journal of Australia*, 1990, 53: 552–54.

56 US Centers for Disease Control. *Youth Suicide prevention programs: a*

the outcome of an attempt, but also the likelihood of a person attempting suicide at all.

Hanging has a suicide fatality rate comparable to that of firearms. So if a gun was not available, might not those seriously attempting suicide choose a rope, which of course is readily accessible? 'Why don't you try to ban ropes!' the gun lobby may sneer. Obviously some attempters may indeed choose hanging if a gun is not available. But hanging requires skill with knots, a suitable location and a degree of organisation. Some may reject this method as too difficult and too likely to fail.

Table 2.6. Suicide attempts resulting in death or hospitalisation in NSW, 1992[57]

Method	Attempts	Died without hospitalisation	Hospitalised	Died in hospital	Survived	Fatality rate (%)
Hanging	230	186	44	2	42	82
Firearms	211	145	66	13	53	75
Motor vehicle exhaust gas	203	127	76	4	72	65
Jumping from a high place	102	56	46	3	43	58
Cutting & piercing instruments	382	19	363	4	359	6
Poisoning with drugs	2975	99	2876	13	2863	4
Others	360	56	304	14	290	19
Total	4463	688	3775	53	3722	17

resource guide September 1992.

57 Sayer G, Stewart G, Cripps J. 'Suicide attempts in NSW: associated mortality and morbidity', *NSW Public Health Bulletin*, 1996, 7(6): 55–59, 63.

There is an extensive body of research on whether people intent on suicide switch to alternative methods if the first choice of suicide is unavailable.[58] There is compelling evidence from the UK on the importance of limiting access to easily accessible, culturally accepted means of suicide. In England and Wales between 1963 and 1975, the number of suicides suddenly and unexpectedly declined from 5,714 to 3,693 when suicide rates were rising in most European nations.[59] The fall was almost wholly attributed to the detoxification of domestic gas when carbon monoxide was removed from the gas supply. Many people attempting suicide did not switch to other means when they were no longer able to kill themselves in their homes using a gas oven or heater.

But what about gun control? Does restricting access to firearms prevent suicides? Canadian criminologist Thomas Gabor identified 16 local, national or international studies conducted since 1980 on firearm availability and suicide rates.[60] He observed that 15 of the 16 studies found a strong link between gun availability and gun suicides. (The only study not confirming this relationship was conducted by Gary Kleck, the researcher whose work is most heavily relied on by the gun lobby.) Gabor found eight of these 15 studies also concluded that high gun availability led to higher suicide rates overall. Six found no relationship, and one study did not consider overall suicide trends. But Gabor noted that if the two factors were not connected at all, one would expect to see a balance of positive and negative correlations in the research results; for example, some studies suggesting that high gun ownership *reduces* suicide rates. The absence of any such studies led Gabor to conclude that the research is 'strongly suggestive of a link between suicide and firearm availability'. Even more important for clinicians, counsellors

---

58 Clarke RV, Lester D. *Suicide: closing the exits*. New York: Springer-Verlag, 1989; Marzuk PM et al. 'The effect of access to lethal methods of injury on suicide rates', *Archives of General Psychiatry*, 1992, 49: 451–58.

59 Clarke RV, Mayhew P. 'The British gas suicide story and its criminological implications', *Crime and Justice*, 1988, 10: 79–116.

60 Gabor T. 'The impact of the availability of firearms on violent crime, suicide, and accidental death', Department of Justice Canada, 1994.

and families to keep in mind is the evidence from case-control studies of the relationship between domestic gun availability and suicide. Three important US studies have found that the presence of a gun in the home increases the risk of suicide.[61]

Domestic violence

Gun control has long been a concern of those working to reduce domestic violence in Australia. The largest category of homicides (around 40%) is domestic, and guns are more commonly used in family killings than among homicides in general. A NSW Bureau of Crime Statistics and Research study noted: 'The difference between a fatal and a non-fatal episode of domestic violence may be entirely due to the presence of a dangerous weapon such as a gun.'[62] US Research shows that domestic assaults involving guns are three times more likely to result in death than those with knives; 23 times more likely than unarmed assaults; and 12 times more likely than non-firearm assaults overall.[63]

Victim surveys confirm abundant anecdotal evidence from domestic violence groups that guns are frequently used to intimidate women and children in their homes. For example, 14% of victims who contacted the 1988 Queensland domestic violence phone-in said they had

---

61 Brent DA, Perper JA, Allman CJ, Moritz GM, Wartella ME, Zelenak JP. 'The presence and accessibility of firearms in the homes of adolescent suicides: a case-control study', *Journal of the American Medical Association*, 1991, 266: 2989–95; Brent DA, Perper JA, Goldstein CE, Kolko DJ, Allman MJ, Allman CJ, Zelenak JP. 'Risk factors for adolescent suicide', *Archives of General Psychiatry*, 1988, 45: 581–88; Kellermann AL, Rivara FP, Somes G, Reay DT, Francisco J, Banton JG, Prodzinski J, Fligner C, Hackman BB. 'Suicide in the home in relation to gun ownership', *New England Journal of Medicine*, 1992, 327: 467–72.

62 Devery C. 'Domestic violence in NSW: a regional analysis', NSW Bureau of Crime Statistics and Research, 1992: 9.

63 Saltzman LE, Mercy JA, O'Carroll PW, Rosenberg ML, Rhodes PH. 'Weapon involvement and injury outcomes in family and intimate assaults', *Journal of the American Medical Association*, 1992, 267: 3043–47.

been threatened or injured with a gun.[64] In 1991 Sydney's Domestic Violence Advocacy Service (DVAS) reported that 15% of clients said their partners had a gun.[65] The DVAS and other agencies have described some of the ways guns are used to terrorise family members, including direct threats, shooting pets as a warning, mock executions, sleeping with the gun nearby, and cleaning the gun during or after arguments, especially during custody disputes.

Danielle Mazza's recent study of 1,500 women attending their doctor found that of those women who were in couple relationships, one in 50 had been threatened with a knife or a gun in the previous year, and one in 100 had had a knife or gun used against them.[66] The 1996 Women's Safety Survey revealed that 0.5% of all Australian women – that is, about 34,500 – had been either threatened or harmed with a knife or gun in the previous 12 months.[67] However vicious and traumatic a knife threat or attack may be, the availability of a gun greatly increases the likelihood of conflict or depression leading to death.

---

64 Queensland Domestic Violence Task Force. 'Beyond these walls', Brisbane 1988.

65 Domestic Violence Advocacy Service (NSW). *Domestic Violence Advocacy Service 1986–1991: the first five years*. Sydney 1991.

66 Mazza D. 'Guns and domestic violence', Paper presented to Guns, Violence and Victims, Australian Medical Association conference, Canberra, 28 June 1996.

67 Australian Bureau of Statistics. *Women's Safety Australia 1996*. ABS Canberra, 1996: 16.

3

The campaign for gun control

The Port Arthur massacre was at least the fifth tragedy in recent years to expedite reform of a country's gun laws. In August 1987, after Michael Ryan shot 16 people at Hungerford, Berkshire, UK, the British Government introduced the Firearms (Amendment) Act 1988 which effectively prohibited the private ownership of most self-loading rifles and shotguns in Britain. In 1989 Patrick Purdy, 24, returned to his elementary school in Stockton California and fired at least 105 rounds from an AK–47 military-style semi-automatic rifle with a 75-round drum magazine. He killed five children and injured another 30 before killing himself. The outrage over these killings is widely held to have precipitated the eventual banning of newly manufactured or imported assault rifles in the US on 13 September 1994. (This law did not prevent the possession or sale of any such weapons already in the country, nor of the vast numbers of them stockpiled by gun dealers before enactment of the bill).[1]

The 6 December 1989 shooting murder of 14 women at Montreal's Ecole Polytechnique also set in train what eventually became gun control Bill C–68, passed in the Canadian Parliament on 6 December 1995. Among its most important provisions, this law required the registration of all firearms – something always implacably opposed by gun lobbies throughout the world.

---

1 McCarron SM. Summary of Firearms Provisions of Federal Crime Control Law, enacted 13 September 1994. Undated Fact Sheet, US Bureau of Alcohol, Tobacco and Firearms, Washington DC.

The Dunblane Primary School massacre on 13 March 1996, when Thomas Hamilton killed 16 children and their teacher, prompted the British Government to ban all handguns of a higher calibre than .22, and ban people from keeping any handguns in the home.[2] This was subsequently extended to a ban on all private ownership of handguns.

Like the Hungerford, Californian, Canadian and Dunblane shootings, the Port Arthur massacre became the catalyst for a quantum leap in gun law reform. Australian gun control groups had long advocated the measures agreed by the Australasian Police Ministers Council (APMC), both in the media and in representations to politicians. But before Port Arthur, national uniform gun laws based on the registration of all guns and banning all semi-automatic rifles seemed only a remote possibility.

Advocacy for gun control before Port Arthur

The gun control movement in Australia had its first manifestations in the Committee to Register all Guns, set up by families and friends of two teenage girls, Margaret Bacsa and Ella Rosvoll, shot dead in the late 1960s in Victoria. In 1981 Professor Richard Harding of the University of Western Australia published his pioneering book, *Firearms and violence in Australian life*,[3] and convened the first Australian conference on the subject.[4] Around this time the Council to Control Gun Misuse was established in Victoria and began lobbying the state government there.[5] Advocacy for gun control accelerated after the shooting murder of four

2 Lord Cullen. 'The Public Inquiry into the Shootings at Dunblane Primary School on 13 March 1996', Report presented by the Secretary of State for Scotland by Command of Her Majesty Oct 1996 London: The Stationary Office; The Public Inquiry into the Shootings at Dunblane Primary School on 13 March 1996. The Government Response.

3 Harding R. *Firearms and violence in Australian life*. Perth: University of Western Australia Press, 1981.

4 *Firearms: laws and use*. Proceedings of First Australian National Conference, Perth, Western Australia, 25–27 June 1981.

5 Crook J. *Issues in gun control*. 2nd edn. Chelsea: Gun Control Australia, 1994.

teenage girls in the Sydney suburb of Pymble in 1987, followed by a spate of mass killings in the late 1980s in Sydney, Melbourne and South Australia. Coalitions for Gun Control were established in Tasmania (1987), Victoria (around 1988), and NSW (around 1990). Another group, Gun Control Australia, formed under the leadership of John Crook, a retiree who had written a masters thesis on the subject.

By the time of Port Arthur, these years of advocacy, supplemented by efforts from a diverse range of health, legal, academic, church, trade union, women's and community groups, had established widespread public support for the main platforms of gun control. Table 3.1 sets out some recent opinion poll data on gun control in Australia, showing the consistently huge community support for stronger controls. But progress had been slow and *ad hoc*, with isolated legal reforms made by individual states and territories. A rational, comprehensive and national uniform gun control scheme was urgently needed.

Table 3.1: Recent surveys of community opinion about gun control

Poll	Question asked	Results (percentages)
Saulwick Poll, August 1991[6]	'Should semi-automatics be banned?'	Yes: Sydney 90, Melbourne 89
AGB-McNair, July 1995[7]	'Would you support or oppose gun laws that make it more difficult to buy guns in NSW? Is that strongly support/oppose or support/oppose?'	64 strongly support; 18 support
North Sydney Local Govt Elections, September 1995	'Should there be tougher gun control legislation in NSW including gun registration?'	93.1 in favour
AGB McNair national phone poll 2,058, 3–5 May 1996	'Do you support or oppose [a ban on all automatic and semi-automatic guns]?'	Support: National 90, NSW 91, Vic 90, Qld 86, SA/NT 89, WA 91, Tas 95, ACT 92. City: 91, Rural: 88

6 Hicks I. 'Most support bans on guns', *SMH*, 20 August 1991· 4

7 Herald AGB McNair Poll. 'Should gun purchase be more difficult?', *SMH*, 8 August 1995.

Poll	Question asked	Results (percentages)
	'Do you support or oppose a register of all guns?'	National: 95, NSW 95, Vic 97, Qld 93, SA/NT 96, WA 96, Tas 92, ACT 97. City: 96, Rural: 93
Morgan national poll 526 voters, 1–2 June 1996[8]	'Do you agree or disagree with John Howard's new gun control laws?'	Agree: 80; Disagree: 18
Morgan national poll 526 voters, 1–2 June 1996[9]	'Would you vote against a political candidate if advised by a gun group?'	Yes: 4; No/don't support: 96

A National Gun Summit convened by then Prime Minister Bob Hawke on 22 December 1987 – after the Queen Street massacre in Melbourne – failed to achieve consensus on national gun laws or even a national ban on military-style semi-automatics.[9] The most entrenched opposition came from Tasmania and Queensland. Ironically, as it transpires, NSW Premier Barrie Unsworth walked out of that meeting declaring with disgust: 'It will take a massacre in Tasmania before we get gun law reform in Australia.'[10] Victorian Premier John Cain echoed this: 'I hope it's not true that some other disaster has to occur, maybe to our south [that is, Tasmania], to try and make those people understand the gravity of the problem we have.'[11] (After Port Arthur, Unsworth commented on the huge advances that had occurred: 'It has been remarkable how [Tasmania's Premier] Rundle has changed [his mind] so quickly, because back then Tasmania did not care what happened . . . these things did not happen in its backyard.')[12]

From 1987 most jurisdictions did make some improvements in their gun laws. For example:

---

8 Murphy D. 'Popgun politics', *The Bulletin*, 11 June 1996: 14–8.

9 Unsworth B. 'Failure on guns an affront', *SMH*, 10 May 1996.

10 Byrne A. 'Unsworth gloomy on summit', *SMH*, 3 May 1996.

11 Archival footage from 23 December 1987, *7.30 Report*, ABC TV, 10 May 1996.

12 Byrne A. *op. cit.*

- Victoria tightened restrictions on semi-automatic long-arms after the 1987 Hoddle Street and Queen Street massacres.
- The ACT introduced a new *Weapons Act* in 1991, requiring firearm registration and (in some cases) proof of reason for ownership.
- In NSW, the Labor Government completely overhauled the gun law between 1985 and 1988. (Ironically, Labor's legislation at that time was very similar to the scheme established after Port Arthur by the APMC.) Labor's law was overturned when the government changed in 1988; and the new Liberal-National Government waited until 1992 to introduce a few improvements such as compulsory cancellation of gun licences for domestic violence offenders.
- In 1990 the Queensland Parliament enacted that state's first law regulating rifles and shotguns – henceforth a licence was required to own or buy guns.
- In 1991 Tasmania passed a similar law. The Bill was still before the Tasmanian Parliament in September 1991 when Wade Frankum killed eight people with a military-style semi-automatic in Sydney's Strathfield shopping mall. The Tasmanian Parliament responded by giving the Police Minister the power to ban rapid-fire centre-fire weapons. He did not use that power until one week after the Port Arthur massacre.

Gun control had been on the agenda of 20 out of 29 meetings of the nation's police ministers' conferences, and two previous special meetings had been held on the subject.[13] Despite the efforts of some states and individual police ministers to broker a workable agreement on uniform laws, in early 1996 Australia seemed no closer to achieving it. The most fundamental element of any uniform scheme had to be universal firearm registration, and the refusal by NSW, Queensland and Tasmania to cooperate over this left Australia with a legal patchwork of astonishing inconsistency.

13 Millett M. 'Howard's gun gamble', *SMH*, 11 May 1996.

For example, the differences between the states meant that guns declared illegal in one state could be purchased in another and then taken back over the border. With no requirement for gun registration in the first state, there would be no record of the guns bought, or taken out of that state. In Australia as in the US, this inconsistency allowed people to exploit state laws by freely moving banned weapons interstate.[14] In 1995, a journalist from Channel 9's *A Current Affair*, who did not have a shooter's licence, travelled to Tasmania, looked in the 'for sale' section of the *Hobart Mercury* for a military-style semi-automatic, bought two (plus ammunition) with consummate ease and then handed the guns to the Tasmanian police – all on national television.[15] The embarrassed Tasmanian Government threatened to charge the journalist with obtaining a gun without a licence. The Police Minister ordered an investigation into the matter, and police interviewed the journalist and gun control activist Roland Browne (who had been interviewed on *A Current Affair*). This was the same Police Minister who had refused to ban military weapons, while Tasmania had banned free access to fireworks in 1992 because of the annual injury toll to children.

After the Strathfield massacre in 1991, the military-style semi-automatic rifles Bryant used at Port Arthur were banned from sale in all jurisdictions except Tasmania and Queensland, where they remained freely available. Tasmania even had its own gun manufacturing industry: Hobart boasted Australia's only private factory, Australian Automatic Arms, producing military-style semi-automatic rifles until 1993 for export and local sales. Anyone travelling to Queensland or Tasmania could readily purchase such a weapon from a local gun owner and take it to their home state where, though technically illegal, it would be unregistered and therefore highly unlikely to come to the attention of police.

Just a month before the Port Arthur massacre, the *Sydney Morning Herald* reported the findings of a state-wide public opinion poll

---

14 Anon. 'Historic pact on gun reforms', *SMH*, 11 May 1996.

15 Darby A. 'Nightmare shatters the island of dreams', *SMH*, 30 April 1996.

conducted for the NSW Health Department.[16] Three questions on attitudes to gun control were asked among some 90 covering a wide range of health issues. In the developmental stages of the survey, I had been invited to submit questions on gun control that would be important to future policy debate. The number of people questioned (2,251) made this the largest Australian sample ever invited to answer questions on gun control. As with the previous opinion polls shown in Table 3.1, a large majority of those interviewed (90%) supported gun registration. Support was also very high among rural respondents (83%) and among gun owners, or at least those who reported having a gun on their property (69.3%).

Despite these figures, Health Minister Dr Andrew Refshauge publicly dismissed the study and its findings, claiming it to be 'no better than an opinion poll' – referring to the very same tool political parties routinely use to guide policy-making in most fields of government. He told a news conference: 'It is not found that there is any link between gun control and reduction of gun violence.' I learned that Refshauge's office had angrily demanded an explanation from Health Department officials: Why had the gun questions been included in the questionnaire? Why had their release not been cleared through his office? This strongly implied an intention to suppress release of the results, given an opportunity. NSW Labor still feared upsetting the gun lobby or having to take positive steps about gun control.

In NSW the gun control campaign focused on universal firearm registration, without which other gun control measures are doomed to fail. The Carr Labor Government, like its immediate predecessors (the Fahey and Greiner Liberal governments) had been constantly pressured to introduce registration. Almost every reported shooting brought a reiteration of public and media criticism of these governments being 'soft on guns'. The standard policy response from governments was an amnesty allowing shooters to surrender their guns. Voluntary, uncompensated amnesties prompt a relatively small number of gun owners

---

16 Lagan B, Lamont L. 'Major push to register all weapons', *SMH*, 22 March 1996: 1.

to hand in their weapons', but there are usually enough to create public relations opportunities for governments to boast that they are 'doing something'.[17] NSW Police Minister Paul Whelan admitted as much on ABC TV's *Lateline*:

> *Whelan*: It [the latest amnesty] actually went up to nine-and-a-half thousand . . . it worked quite successfully . . . that's nine-and-a-half thousand guns that had been removed from New South Wales.
>
> *Maxine McKew*: But it's a drop in the bucket, isn't it?
>
> *Whelan*: Well it is in the totality . . . it's a step in the right direction.[18]

In NSW the latest amnesty began seven months before Port Arthur, in response to the shooting of two police at Crescent Head. On 21 September 1995, an ebullient Premier Bob Carr sat in the parliamentary press room next to Police Minister Paul Whelan and the Shooters' Party's solitary MP, John Tingle, to announce an all-new amnesty for unlicensed shooters. Under the plan, unlicensed gun owners could shuffle their feet over the next 12 months and ponder surrendering their weapons to police or selling them to gun shops. Backed with a K-Tel-style offer of a $15 smoke detector voucher from a hardware chainstore – a set of free steak knives was seen as inappropriate – this, in the words of Carr's press release, was 'action' to reduce guns in the community.

But wait! There was more! Without presenting a shred of evidence, and notwithstanding that licences were already free for farmers, Tingle had convinced the Government that the $75 licence fee should be dropped during the amnesty. Designed as an incentive to encourage

---

17 Bearup G. 'Amnesty reaping an ugly harvest', *SMH*, 3 January 1996; Larkin J. '4000 weapons handed in', *Sunday Telegraph*, 28 January 1996. Larkin J. 'Minister to extend gun amnesty', *Sunday Telegraph*, 18 February 1996; English B. 'Illegal weapons given to police', *Daily Telegraph*, 20 February 1996; Anon. 'Prolific weapons amnesty may be extended', *Newcastle Herald*, 20 February 1996; Anon. 'Premier praises weapons amnesty', *SMH*, 20 February 1996.
18 *Lateline*, ABC TV, 9 May 1996.

unlicensed shooters to go legal, the free licence would also have been a huge incentive for thousands of low-income youths to consider buying a gun for the first time. No wonder Tingle looked chipper.

At 2.15pm Carr told the House that the plan followed 'extensive consultations' with Tingle and the Coalition for Gun Control. In fact, CGC representatives had been told of the forthcoming announcement by Paul Whelan only an hour previously. The group had not been consulted at all, and told Whelan the plan was pitiful, refusing to endorse it.

The day before, on 20 September, the parents of 15-year-old Dali Handmer-Pleshet, shot dead near Mudgee in June 1993, had called for stronger gun laws based on gun registration.[19] A week earlier, Australia's first referendum on gun control, held during the North Sydney local government elections, resulted in 93.1% support for registration of long-arms – the same sort of system that had operated smoothly since the 1920s for handguns.[20]

In Parliament, Carr said further progress would depend on bipartisan support from the Opposition. Opposition leader Peter Collins immediately got to his feet, supported the campaign and soberly endorsed the need for bipartisanship. If ever there was an opportunity for a leader to seize the day and accept the offer, here it was. Yet minutes later, Carr resumed the circus that passes for parliamentary process, launching into an extended ridicule of Collins' performance as Treasurer in the previous Government. Carr basked in vainglory and Collins sat glumly. Carr's minutes-old condolences to the families of Dali Handmer-Pleshet and the Crescent Head police were dutifully recorded in Hansard, but were already out of political sight.

This sort of tokenism led some in the NSW Labor Party to become critical of the party's performance on gun control. Just weeks before Port Arthur, one of Carr and Refshauge's parliamentary colleagues, backbencher Ann Symonds – who had a long record of gun control advocacy – led factional criticism in the Labor Party about its poor

19 Brown M. 'Gun jokes led to girl's death, court told', *SMH*, 22 October 1993: 1.
20 Llewellyn M. 'Shooters scoff at local gun vote', *SMH*, 21 September 1995: 3.

record on the issue and its willingness to appease the interests of the Shooters' Party MP, John Tingle.

Tingle was a strident opponent of gun registration; instead he championed the rights of crime victims and advocated stiffer penalties for crimes involving guns.[21] In promoting these two issues, his position was consistent with that of gun lobbies around the world, relying on the basic premise that there are two sorts of shooters: the responsible ones and the irresponsible criminals, with little or no overlap. Like most gun lobbyists, Tingle framed the gun control issue entirely in law and order terms, rather than seeing guns as in any way relevant to public health and safety. For Tingle, it followed that any measures designed to make guns less accessible to the general population should be opposed, while measures designed to punish those who had already misused guns should be supported. As discussed in Chapters 5 and 6, this convenient division of gun owners into safe versus dangerous, good versus bad, bears little resemblance to the facts about gun violence.

Early in 1996, another NSW parliamentarian, Alan Corbett of the Better Future for Our Children Party, announced his intention to introduce a comprehensive private member's Bill on gun control.[22] Corbett had extensively consulted the CGC on the content of his Bill. Without the support of the Government or the Opposition – none was expected from either – there was no chance that his Bill would be passed. Nonetheless, two hopes were held for it: it would represent a model Bill lying ready for action in the right political climate; and it would temporarily resurrect the debate in the media, thereby accelerating growing public cynicism about the mainstream political parties' cowardice before the gun lobby (see Chapter 5).

In early April 1996 Professor Fred Stephens, an eminent Sydney surgeon, spoke for many in the community when he wrote to the *Sydney Morning Herald*:

---

21 Macey R. 'Shooters want tough penalties', *SMH*, 9 June 1992: 7.

22 Sharp M. 'Gun register push fails to win Carr over', *SMH*, 27 February 1996; Anon. 'Sensible gun laws now' (editorial), *SMH*, 23 March 1996: 36.

successive leaders of both sides of politics show the spinal fortitude of a jellyfish when it comes to doing something really meaningful [about guns] . . . It is humbling for me to reflect that a political leader with integrity and a modicum of insight and courage could, in one act, surpass as a service to humanity all I have achieved in almost 40 years as a practising surgeon and professor of surgery. That one act would be effective limitation of gun ownership and gun availability . . .[23]

Just three days before the Port Arthur massacre, the *Sydney Morning Herald* published an article from the CGC arguing for universal gun registration. The article anticipated the imminent findings of a coronial inquiry into the fatal shooting of two police at Crescent Head, NSW, in 1995.[24] The coroner had received submissions from hundreds of health, legal, and community organisations advocating firearm registration, and we believed his report would include this recommendation. We also expected the Carr Government would try to dismiss or shelve the recommendation, and we wished to shame such a move before it happened. In fact another month passed before the coroner's report was released, but it vindicated the CGC. The report recommended the two most important propositions in the CGC's submission to the coroner: not only registration but also that proof of reason for gun ownership should be required for all gun licences. By that time the coroner's inquiry had been overtaken by the APMC agreement.

Even before taking office in March 1995, Bob Carr's public position had been consistently opposed to registration, because the gun lobby had threatened political retaliation against any government considering such a measure. These threats dated from a resounding defeat suffered in 1988 by a previous NSW Labor Government after then Premier Barrie Unsworth had introduced tougher gun controls. His massive defeat was seen within Labor circles as a prime example of the gun lobby's power to direct votes away from anti-gun candidates. After the 1988 defeat,

---

23 Stephens F. 'A spinal transplant called for' (letter), *SMH*, 9 April 1996.
24 Chapman S. 'A timely trigger for gun control', *SMH*, 25 April 25 1996: 11.

the NSW Labor Party hierarchy proclaimed that any talk of serious gun control a political no-go zone.

In 1994, when Carr was Leader of the Opposition, a coroner recommended tightening the gun laws in his report on the murder-suicide of twin three-year-old girls by their father. Carr responded: 'After our experience in gun laws in 1988, we will take no initiative that doesn't reflect the consensus in Parliament.'[25]

The view that Unsworth's stance on guns led to his Government's defeat has been criticised as superficial and expedient, insofar as it avoided a more searching examination of the public hostility to many initiatives of his Government linked to politicians still highly placed in the Labor Party in the post-Unsworth years. At worst, one analyst argued, only five of 20 seats lost by Labor at the 1988 election could have been affected by an anti-gun control vote.[26] Any power the gun lobby had was due to the lack of bipartisanship on gun control in NSW state politics, which allowed the gun lobby to play one party off against the other. The gun lobby would typically threaten any politician or party supporting gun control, urging shooters to direct their preference votes away from that candidate.

These developments illustrate the climate of gun control in Australia's most populous state just before the Port Arthur massacre. In summary, apart from the publicity potential of Alan Corbett's Bill, and the possibility that the State Coroner might table a set of strong recommendations on gun control, there was no tangible prospect of substantial law reform on the political horizon.

Meanwhile in Tasmania, the Parliament had struggled with gun laws for almost a decade. Green Independent Dr Bob Brown's Dangerous Weapons Control Bill, which provided for gun licensing, registration, safe storage and a ban on military firearms, was defeated in 1987. In 1988 the Liberals introduced a Guns Bill modelled on a 'prohibited

25 Morris L. '60,000 decline in licensed shooters', *SMH*, 30 April 1994: 5.

26 Cockburn M. 'The gun lobby's electoral support is much weaker than many people think', *SMH*, 4 August 1995: 10; Cockburn M. 'Political cowardice stems from myth of Unsworth defeat', *SMH*, 30 April 1996.

persons register' (see Chapter 6). It was passed but never proclaimed. In 1990 Dr Brown tried again with his Firearms Bill. It was again defeated, though in 1991 Tasmania finally enacted the *Guns Act 1991*, the weakest gun law in Australia. All this would change radically after Martin Bryant's rampage on 28 April.

Just 12 days later, in what was universally described as an historic moment, the APMC released its agreement at 6.20pm, after meeting for more than seven hours. Previous parliamentary opponents of gun registration, notably NSW Labor leader Bob Carr and Tasmanian Premier Tony Rundle, rushed to proclaim their passionate support for the Prime Minister's initiative. There had seldom been greater chameleon acts in Australian political history.

Media interest in gun control

Port Arthur and the many facets of its aftermath will probably rank, after the two world wars, as one of the largest news events in Australian media history. In terms of volume alone it is likely to rival the 1991 Gulf War, the 1975 sacking of the Whitlam Government, and the 1974 destruction of Darwin in Cyclone Tracy. It will quite easily surpass reportage of several Olympic games.

Multiple murders, particularly of people unknown to the gunman, unleash huge news media interest. Debate on gun control receives most prominence in the days after mass shootings or poignant individual homicides, particularly if these occur in public settings. Table 3.2 lists some mass killings by civilians in peacetime that attracted heavy media coverage.[27]

---

27 For details of many of these murders see Crook J, Harding A. *Gun massacres in Australia*. Chelsea: Gun Control Australia, 1994.

Table 3.2: Mass shootings that received extensive reportage

Good Friday 1996: Vernon, British Columbia	Mark Chahal shoots nine people at a pre-wedding celebration.
25 January 1996: Hillcrest, Queensland	Peter May shoots six then himself.
5 December 1994: Fawkner, Victoria	Fotios Diakonidis fatally shoots two then himself with M1 30/30 carbine after shooting indiscriminately.
20 June 1994: Dunedin, New Zealand	David Bain shoots five family members.
26 August 1993: Burwood, Sydney	Josip Jankovec shoots landlord and two boarders.
21 August 1993: Melbourne	John Lascano shoots three people in a suburban gunshop.
31 March 1993: Cangai, NSW	Len Leabeater and two others shoot five.
27 October 1992: Terrigal, NSW	Malcolm Baker shoots six.
29 July 1992: Burwood, Victoria	Ashley Coulston murders three.
20 May 1992: Paerata, New Zealand	Brian Schlaepfer shoots four, then himself.
18 October 1991: Luby's Cafe Killeen, Texas	George Hennard Jr shoots 22 dead in a cafe.
17 August 1991: Strathfield, NSW	Wade Frankum kills six, then himself in shopping plaza.
5 January 1991: Camp Hill, Brisbane	Peter Forrest murders his former de facto, her father and baby daughter then suicides.
13 November 1990: Aramoana, New Zealand	David Gray shoots 13 in village, before being shot by police.
30 August: Surry Hills NSW	Paul Evers shoots five neighbours.
8 April 1990: Burleigh Heads, Queensland	Rodney Dale, armed with a .22 rifle and a pump-action shotgun, kills one and wounds 13.
12 March 1990: Girrawheen, Western Australia	Gun enthusiast Don Clemensha kills his ex-wife and her two teenage daughters, then suicides.
26 March 1990: Wynnum, Brisbane	Michael Woods murders his two children then suicides.

3 November 1989: Evandale, Tasmania	15-year-old Wayne Johnson murders his parents and young brother.
5 February 1988: Patterson Lakes, Melbourne	Mayer Kaldas kills wife, his two children then himself with shotgun.
25 September 1988: Oenpelli, Northern Territory	Dennis Rostron shoots six.
27 December 1987: Winkie, South Australia	Frank Pangallo kills wife and two relatives with pump-action shotgun.
8 December 8, 1987: Queen Street, Melbourne	Frank Vitkovic shoots eight in office block, then himself.
10 October 1987: Canley Vale, NSW	John Tran shoots five, then himself.
19 August 1987: Hungerford, England	Michael Ryan kills 16 people then suicides.
9 August 1987: Hoddle Street, Melbourne	Julian Knight shoots seven strangers.
19 June 1987: Northern Territory	Joseph Schwab shoots five over nine days, then himself.
23 January 1987: West Pymble, Sydney	Richard Maddrell armed with a pump-action shotgun kills four teenage girls.
2 September 1984: Milperra Viking Tavern	Rival motorcycle gangs fought one another in carpark: eight dead, 20 wounded.
July 1984: San Ysidro California	James Huberty kills 21 and wounds 19 others in a McDonald's restaurant.

When the Port Arthur massacre occurred on 28 April 1996, the Australian public and the media were already concerned about gun violence. In the Dunblane massacre in Scotland on 13 March, 16 small children and their teacher were killed in a school gymnasium, a tragedy that flooded the Australian newspapers with articles and letters to the editor. One week later, extensive coverage was given to the shooting of Jean Majdalawi (Lennon) by her former husband outside the Family Court at Parramatta, Sydney, where they were due for a child custody hearing.[28] The letters editor of the *Sydney Morning Herald* wrote that the

---

28 Horin A. 'At least mum doesn't have to run from him any more', *SMH*, 22 March 1996; Cornford P, Lamont L. 'Bloody ending to a bitter custody battle',

volume of letters about the Majdalawi murder

> threatened to destroy Letters' fax machine . . . [it] overlaid
> the despair in the community already felt after the massacre
> at Dunblane, Scotland. The Parramatta killing turned weepy
> grief to anger at the lack of political resolve over our gun
> laws. If our fax machine is any guide, politicians on both
> sides would be foolish to ignore such intense public feeling.[29]

A *Sun Herald* editorial yet again called on the Carr Government to 'stop fudging the issue of gun control' after the Majdalawi shooting.[30] The week ending 28 April was National Stop Domestic Violence Week, and the issue of domestic gun homicide weighed heavily on the minds of everyone, including journalists, who took part in rallies, vigils and meetings around the country. Proposals for gun control had also received prominence after the discovery of large caches of armaments, publication of reports on the rising rate of youth suicide involving guns, and after reports about controlling violence in the community.

In the ten years before the Port Arthur massacre, Australia and New Zealand had 13 mass shootings in which five or more people died, sometimes including the perpetrator.[31] Consistent with the overall homicide pattern in the community, nine of these incidents involved men shooting people known to them (usually family members or neighbours). In the other incidents, gunmen ran amok in public places or stalked and killed total strangers over a number of hours or, in two cases, days.

These latter incidents (particularly Queen Street, Hoddle Street, and Strathfield) received huge media coverage compared to that given

---

SMH, 22 March 1996: 1; Powell S. 'Domestic violence victims fear Jean's fate', *The Australian*, 23 March 1996; Morris R, Gelastopoulos E. 'Instant AVOs to protect women from their violent partners', Daily Telegraph, 23 March 1996.

29 Walsh G. 'Postscript', *SMH*, 25 March 1996: 12.

30 Anon. 'Need for firm action', *Sun Herald*, 24 March 1996: 30.

31 Alpers P. The people most likely to kill with a gun, NZ Mental Health Commission Fact Sheet, http://www.gunpolicy.org/documents/doc_download/5347-the-people-most-likely-to-kill-with-a-gun-nz-mental-health-commission-fact-sheet.

to family and neighbour killings. The number of people shot in family massacres has often equalled or exceeded the numbers in public incidents, but they tend to attract less media interest and seldom provoke political comment or action. The same can be said about media and political interest in the most common forms of gun death – suicides and family murders of individuals. If reported at all, they tend to be reported briefly without major display. Yet cumulatively, each year these deaths far exceed the annual death tolls from mass shootings. For every victim of a mass shooting in Australia and New Zealand, nine more died in a less newsworthy gun murders. Every one of these deaths leaves a trail of grief. The NCGC refers to these other gun deaths, which receive little media coverage, as 'the slow massacre' in which hundreds of people die each year.

The disparity between the coverage of stranger killings and reports of domestic homicides is often remarked on by domestic violence agencies. It may be that journalists are susceptible to society's general discomfort about confronting the reality of domestic violence; or that they believe domestic homicide is a 'private' matter; or that the victims have somehow provoked their own deaths; or because of the 'there by the grace of God go I' factor – the possibility that they could have been victims themselves.

The sheer magnitude of the Port Arthur massacre – described as the 'biggest', 'worst ever', 'monstrous' and so on – was reflected in its media coverage. The event and the discussion of gun control became the leading news item in both print and electronic media recorded by monitoring agencies. Even in late June, gun control remained the 'most discussed' news issue on NSW radio and TV stations,[32] and letters to the *Sydney Morning Herald* were still flowing in steadily, 'most of them in favour of Prime Minister Howard's plans.'[33]

Almost universally, the Australian media's editorial line on the issue supported the NCGC's gun control platform. Much of this support was

32 'The public eye', Rehame Australia Monitoring Services. cited in *SMH*, 24 June 1996: 24.

33 Walsh G. 'Postscript', *SMH*, 17 and 24 June 1996: 16.

confined to the commentary and opinion sections of newspapers, but it was occasionally revealed in news headlines, for example: 'Amnesty reaping an ugly harvest',[34] 'Modest heroes defy the bullies'.[35]

34 Bearup G. 'Amnesty reaping an ugly harvest', *SMH*, 3 January 1996.
35 Warnock S. 'Modest heroes defy the bullies', *Sun Herald*, 25 July 1996.

4

The main reforms

This chapter outlines the main reforms introduced after Port Arthur. It examines the rationale and supportive evidence for each reform, the gun lobby's efforts to attack each proposal and how gun control advocates sought to respond to these attacks. In summary, the key provisions of the new laws were:

- A ban on the importation, ownership, sale, resale, transfer, possession, manufacture or use of semi-automatic rifles and pump-action shotguns.
- A compensatory 'buyback' scheme funded by an increase in the Medicare levy, whereby gun owners would be paid the market value of prohibited guns they handed in.
- The registration of all firearms as part of an integrated shooter licensing scheme.
- Shooter licensing based on a requirement to prove a 'genuine reason' for owning a firearm.
- Requirements that all guns be stored securely.
- Uniform national gun laws (See Introduction for more details.)

Ban on semi-automatics

Martin Bryant carried three weapons at Port Arthur. Inside the café he pulled an AR–15 semi-automatic .223 calibre rifle from a tennis bag and began shooting the patrons. In the next 90 seconds he fired 29 shots, killing 20 people in the café. A bus driver and passengers parked outside were killed, along with passers-by, hotel patrons and motorists of all ages. The killer used his second military-style semi-automatic rifle, a .308 FN, or 'SLR', as he drove through the community, took a hostage whom he later killed, then drove to the Seascape Cottage. There he had access to an SKS–46 semi-automatic rifle which he fired at police and helicopters ferrying the wounded. Early the next morning Bryant set fire to the house and finally rushed outside in flames, dropping his rifles and surrendering to police. In the ashes police found weapons described as 'highly unusual and very distinctive' including a military-style Belgian-made shotgun. The third gun in Bryant's bag had been a 12-gauge semi-automatic shotgun, but this was not used in the killings. Before the killings, Bryant answered a private newspaper advertisement to purchase one of his weapons, an AR–10 military-style semi-automatic rifle. When he took the AR–10 to a gun shop for repairs two days before the shootings, the dealer refused to hand it back until he'd sighted a firearms licence. Bryant had purchased the AR–15 and the shotgun from a Hobart dealer who probably also sold him the SLR. Bryant did not have a firearms licence, and had not applied for a drivers' licence as he felt he was too unintelligent to pass the test. The son of the owners of the Seascape was a gun collector, and this may be where Bryant obtained the SKS.

Self-loading or semi-automatic firearms are guns which reload automatically after each shot, so the user does not have to insert a fresh round of ammunition by hand after each bullet is fired. Each time the trigger is squeezed, a shot fires. (By contrast, a fully automatic weapon, or machinegun, fires continuously while the trigger remains depressed.) Different magazine sizes can be fitted to many semi-automatic guns, with some capable of firing dozens of rounds in rapid succession. This capability can make a gunman particularly difficult to approach and disarm. Under the new gun control scheme, pump-action shotguns, which reload with a sliding movement by the shooter, are also classed as semi-automatic.

Before the APMC agreement, the laws governing self-loading weapons varied widely across Australia. All states and territories had banned fully automatic rifles completely from private ownership, except for those held by a few collectors. With the exceptions of Queensland and Tasmania, all had also banned new sales of military-style semi-automatic rifles. (The definition of 'military style' is based on appearance and accessories rather than on its functional capacity.) Otherwise all states and territories allowed private ownership of non-military, self-loading weapons, mostly with additional restrictions on centre-fire semi-automatic rifles with large-capacity or detachable magazines. Rim-fire semi-automatics and pump-action shotguns were treated no differently from ordinary single-shot weapons in most Australian jurisdictions.

Along with the buyback scheme, the ban on self-loading rifles and shotguns attracted more controversy than any other aspect of the APMC agreement (see Chapter 6). No longer were 'military-style' weapons singled out as the only really dangerous firearms. They were joined by *all* self-loading long-arms that were labelled as prohibited weapons (Categories C and D in the new licensing scheme). Category C firearms were semi-automatic rim-fire (low-power) rifles with a magazine capacity up to 10 rounds, as well as semi-automatic and pump-action shotguns up to five rounds. These were prohibited except for occupational use by police, farmers, and professional shooters. A further exemption was added for certain clay target shooters. Category D included all semi-automatic centre-fire (high-power) rifles, whether military style or not; and semi-automatic and pump-action shotguns with a magazine capacity over five rounds. These were prohibited except for police, military and professional shooters.

The APMC's decision to prohibit ownership of all self-loading rifles and shotguns from all but a tightly defined group of shooters was based on community concern about the ability of these guns to fire a rapid stream of bullets, and the potential danger this posed to public safety. Guns that were capable of killing large numbers of people quickly were no longer considered 'sporting' weapons.

119

In any case, the ability of shooters armed with semi-automatics to spray a target with bullets always sat awkwardly with notions that these guns were 'sporting' in the usual sense of the term. Semi-automatic weapons allow lazy or mediocre shooters to miss their targets but simply blast away until they achieve their purpose – quite the opposite of the high-level technical ability associated with skilled sporting shooters and hunters. Greg Carlsson, spokesperson for the Association of Professional Shooters (APS), told the media that semi-automatics were favoured by incompetent amateurs: 'The basic people who own semi-automatic firearms come from the city and are more interested in blowing away anything that moves . . . The common terminology out here for them are weekend shooters – that's when we are being nice about them . . .'[1] A professional kangaroo shooter from western Queensland with 22 years experience, Carlsson said semi-automatics were 'too inaccurate to be humane'.

The use of semi-automatics on the battlefield lends them an additional negative connotation. Dr Brian Walpole, the doctor in charge of the Royal Hobart Hospital's Department of Emergency Medicine which received the Port Arthur victims, described the bloodshed he witnessed: 'We went to war for a day in Tasmania and we saw on the bodies of all those people the havoc the weapons of war can wreak.'[2] Many commentators picked up the military analogy, for example:

- 'They are killing machines – those guns were designed to kill people.'[3]
- 'Weapons designed for rapid mass killing.'[4]
- 'These hideously dangerous ego-boosting toys.'[5]

---

1 Collins C. 'Single-shot Greg takes aim at the semi-automatics lobby', *The Australian*, 11 May 1996.

2 Wright T. 'A doctor can look forward with hope', *SMH*, 11 May 1996.

3 Anon. 'Success, or lethal shame' (editorial), *Daily Telegraph*, 10 May 1996.

4 McGuinness PP. 'Fanatics cause discomfort for the Nationals', *The Age*, 8 June 1996: A23.

5 Kinson K. 'The overkill factor' (letter), *The Age*, 9 May 1996: 14.

The ban on semi-automatics thus arose from a concern to remove weapons from the community which might be used in public massacres like Port Arthur, Strathfield, Terrigal, Queen Street and Hoddle Street – as opposed to single homicides and suicides, which constitute the great majority of gun deaths in Australia. Massacres are rare events; the average gun homicide incident involves only 1.09 victims per offender.[6] But when a semi-automatic is involved, the number of victims can climb dramatically. As the Federal Government pointed out, the past decade had seen 116 people killed in 14 massacres in Australia and New Zealand where four or more people were shot; only six of the 14 perpetrators used military-style semi-automatics, but these accounted for 74% of the victims.[7] In early June, publicity was given to a report published in the *Journal of the American Medical Association* that showed that the increasing popularity of semi-automatic handguns in the US was a major factor in the escalation of handgun deaths there.[8]

The gun lobby's reaction

In the first week after Port Arthur, the gun lobby probably hoped that the mooted ban on semi-automatics would simply bring the two most recalcitrant states, Tasmania and Queensland, into line with the other jurisdictions by banning military-style semi-automatic weapons. John Tingle repeatedly asserted that he had always argued the ban on such weapons should be national, later appearing to carefully change his words to say that he supported a 'reduction in semi-automatics'.[9] After the NSW Government had acted to ban military-style semi-automatics

6 Gallagher P, Huong MTND, Bonney R. 'Trends in homicide 1968–1992', *Crime and Justice Bulletin*, 1994, 21: 1.

7 'Australian Firearm Statistics', The Australian Firearms Buyback (fact sheet) November 1996.

8 Wintemute GJ. 'The relationship between firearm design and firearm violence: handguns in the 1990s', *JAMA*, 1996, 275: 1749–53.

9 Lawnham P, McGarry A. 'Shooters will defy news laws, MP warns', *The Australian*, 11 May 1996.

after the Strathfield massacre in 1991, Tingle nonetheless joined other groups in mapping out a strategy to fight the new laws.[10]

A profile of Tingle published in *Guns Australia* in 1993 quoted him as saying: 'My wife Gail and I are members of the RAE Military Rifle and Holsworthy Pistol Clubs . . .' and that his wife had once said to former NSW Police Minister Ted Pickering that 'no one will take her M1 Carbine away if she can help it'.[11]

The SSAA's Ted Drane had publicly lobbied to increase access to military-style weapons as recently as April 1995 ('Mr Drane . . . supported some of the recommendations [of the Victorian Firearms' Consultative Committee, such as the proposal to increase access to some military weapons.'[12]), but most gun lobby leaders and many shooters immediately threw in the towel on the argument for citizen access to military assault rifles, and agreed with the Police Ministers that these guns should be banned. As one gun owner wrote: 'While I approve of stringent gun laws and the banning of semi-automatic high-powered rifles, I must protest at the proposed mass confiscation of the legally held property of hundreds of thousands of law-abiding Australians.'[13])

Ted Drane predictably described the ban on all semi-automatics as 'an invasion of law-abiding citizens' rights'.[14] Others described the ban as 'undemocratic and un-Australian',[15] despite the huge community support for the move (see Chapter 1). Ian McNiven, of the Firearms Owners' Association (see Chapter 6), obligingly dampened the gun lobby's new-found efforts to distance themselves from military-style guns by saying on national television: 'There is no reason to compromise on

10 Fitzpatrick E. 'Shooters Party to fight new gun laws', *SMH*, 18 May 1992: 2.

11 Palladino T. 'Men of calibre. John Tingle', *Guns Australia*, January/February 1993: 60–61.

12 Brady N. 'Gun report criticised', *The Age*, 6 April 1995: 4.

13 Lawson JB. 'Punished just for being a gun owner' (letter), *The Age*, 15 May 1996: A16.

14 Lawnham P, McGarry A. 'Shooters will defy news laws, MP warns', *The Australian*, 11 May 1996.

15 Rees P. 'Shooters call crisis talks', *Sunday Telegraph*, 12 May 1996.

military-style semi-automatic rifles. They are an essential part of our nation's defence system.'[16]

.22 'rabbit rifles'

Along with gun registration, the element of the APMC agreement that most angered the gun lobby was the ban (apart from limited exemptions) on *all* self-loading long-arms, including pump-action shotguns and the 'innocent' .22 semi-automatic. Gun lovers attempted to draw a distinction between the frighteningly labelled 'military-style' weapons and other semi-automatics that were positioned by comparison as benign.[17] One wrote, 'Rim-fire self-loading rifles have not proved to be a public danger, although many thousands of them are in use. Centre-fire self-loading guns, not necessarily military weapons, do have a very useful and legitimate place . . .'[18]

The gun lobby often referred to these rim-fire semi-automatics as 'rabbit guns' or 'pea rifles', seeking to portray them as inconsequential 'toys'. The Northern Territory's Chief Minister, Shane Stone, described them in this way on *Lateline* the night before the Police Ministers' first meeting. Later in the program, I replied, 'I was concerned to hear Mr Stone refer to them as "pea shooters". They don't shoot peas. They shoot bullets.'[19] The SSAA's Sebastian Ziccone wrote: 'Self-loading rabbit rifles . . . have been safely owned in this country since 1903. This is too stupid for words.'[20]

Gun control advocates both in and outside government were adamant that all semi-automatics, regardless of calibre, should be included in the ban. Low-calibre bullets like .22s can easily kill humans, so the ability to fire many such bullets in rapid succession increases their lethal

---

16 McNiven I. *7.30 Report* ABC TV, 9 May 1996.

17 Aubert E. 'Blackmore digs in over weapons decision', *Newcastle Herald*, 11 May 1996.

18 Heinze J. 'The gun curbs just won't work' (letter), *The Age*, 10 May 1996.

19 Chapman S. *Lateline*, ABC TV, 9 May 1996.

20 Ziccone S. 'In defence of arms', *The Age*, 10 May 1996: A15.

potential enormously. As the Western Australian Police Commissioner stated: 'Whether or not they are small calibre and high velocity or heavy calibre – in other words military-style weapons – is not really of great interest. It's the rapidity of fire [which is critical].'[21]

When it became apparent that most people in the gun lobby were prepared to roll over on military semi-automatics, but would concentrate their opposition on rim-fire weapons, the NCGC set about emphasising that .22 rifles could and *did* kill more Australians than any other category of weapon and should therefore not be trivialised as harmless 'pea shooters.' Several journalists noted this point.[22] The advocacy task became one of supporting this contention and attacking gun lobby arguments that sought to trivialise the .22 as being 'innocent.' Ted Drane had said: 'The main argument against [banning them] is that they have never been involved in any of these [mass murder] incidents. They are innocent, if you like.'[23])

This was demonstrably not the case and so it was a straightforward task to refute Drane's claim. One journalist wrote a profile of the use of the .22 semi-automatic in mass killings. She recalled the multiple murders in Hope Forest, South Australia in 1971 (Clifford Bartholomew killed 10 people including his seven children with such a gun) and Campsie, NSW in 1981 (Fred Daoud shot his wife and four children, then himself). The journalist cited Australian Institute of Criminology data showing that the generic class of .22s (single shot and semi-automatics combined) had been used in 40% of gun homicides in Australia in 1992–93, making it the most common type of gun used. Shotguns accounted for 30% and high-powered semi-automatics like the type used at Port Arthur only accounted for 7% of the homicides.[24]

In the *Sydney Morning Herald* I pointed out: '

> Although two-thirds of the victims of local mass shootings were shot with military-style semi-automatic rifles using

21 Chapman S. 'For the Howard plan' (vox pops), *SMH*, 10 May 1996.
22 Anon. 'Deaths can't be in vain' (editorial), *SMH*, 10 May 1996.
23 Lamont L. 'The calibre favoured by killers', *SMH*, 10 May 1996.
24 Ibid.

'high power' centre-fire ammunition designed for the battlefield, a large proportion also died at the hands of men
wielding the most common semi-automatic rifle of them all:
the ubiquitous .22 calibre 'bunny gun'. Although these fire
'low power' rim-fire rounds, .22 semi-automatic rifles have
been used as the principal weapon in four recent mass shootings in Australia and New Zealand. In these events alone,
27 people were shot dead. The .22 rabbit rifle also features
in many family violence shootings and hold-ups. The police
killed at Crescent Head were shot by such a gun.[25]

On *Lateline* on the night before the first Police Ministers' meeting,
when debating Ted Drane, I listed several mass killings in recent years
where .22 semi-automatics had been used. Drane avoided acknowledging the particulars of the deaths listed. Instead he replied lamely:
'Simon Chapman's point is based on somebody's research called Alpers,
a radio announcer from New Zealand, and there's no official research
in Australia.'[26]

For the record, Philip Alpers was a radio announcer for two months
in 1974. He is now a researcher and journalist who has compiled information for the New Zealand Police Association. Alpers' meticulous
records on mass killings in Australia and New Zealand over the past
decade became an invaluable source of information supporting several key debating points regarding the new laws. The gun lobby was
never once able to deny the facts that Alpers had documented[27] and so
resorted to gratuitous personal attacks on his bona fides as a researcher.
Ironically, John Tingle of the Shooters Party had been a radio announcer
most of his working life.

On the eve of the Police Ministers' conference, the Victorian Police
Minister reportedly advocated exempting pump-action shotguns and
.22s from the ban because they were 'ineffective after 40 metres'. Asked
to comment, I described this 'watering down' as 'an obscenity. His

---

25 Chapman S. 'Now, about those guns . . .', *SMH*, 9 May 1996: 15.

26 Drane T. *Lateline*, ABC TV, 9 May 1996.

27 http://www.health.su.oz.au/cgc/fp_2_3.htm [no longer active, 2013].

amazing comments on how pump-action shotguns and .22 rifles are ineffective after 40m are . . . cold comfort to the Broad Arrow Café victims.'[28] These people, and indeed most victims of shootings, were shot at very close range. At the gun control rally in Sydney on 4 May 1996, Virginia Handmer spoke of her 15-year-old daughter Dali's death by a semi-automatic .22. Dali was killed instantly at a distance of 106 metres.

> One of the most delightful retorts to the gun lobby's demands for open access to semi-automatics came from a sarcastic Sydney resident: For some time I've been petitioning the authorities to legalise the private use of armoured personnel carriers and the smaller tanks on our roads. The modern tank and the APC are very efficient, spacious and, need I say, safe means of transport, ideal for the family and the proposed 40 km/h speed limit . . . Moreover, their banning makes it more likely the authorities will try to ban other types of vehicles. There will be those . . . who will go on about the safety issue. They never seem to understand that it isn't the shells or tracks which kill, but the driver the doctors didn't weed out . . . If a disturbed person does grab the neighbour's Leopard, all it should take is one or two people responsible people with anti-tank rockets or just plain armour-piercing ammunition to ensure the situation is defused.[29]

On *Four Corners* on 4 November, Rebecca Peters used a similar analogy:

> Military weapons are made for killing large numbers of people and they should have never have been allowed in the first place. You can't be a collector of plutonium for fun, and you shouldn't be allowed to use military rifles for fun. Times have changed, and this is not acceptable any more.

---

28 Chapman S. 'For the Howard plan', (vox pops) *SMH*, 10 May 1996.

29 Lowe A. 'The hills are alive with them' (letter), *SMH*, 20 May 1996: 14.

Crimping

A major debate that emerged soon after the Police Ministers' meeting concerned the issue of 'crimping' – the structural alteration of a five or seven-shot semi-automatic or pump-action weapon to allow it to fire a maximum of only two shots before reloading was required. Such an altered weapon would be a much-limited killing machine in a massacre or siege scenario. The main argument for crimping – strongly advocated by the Queensland, West Australian and Northern Territory governments in the weeks preceding a 17 July Police Ministers' meeting – was that if guns could be mechanically altered in an irreversible way, many semi-automatic gun owners might take this option instead of surrendering their guns in the gun buyback. Since crimping would have been less expensive than the buyback cost of the entire gun, it promised to reduce the buyback cost by an estimated $100 million – although the basis of this figure was never explained.[30] Many rural politicians also perceived crimping as an option that would placate many gun owners and reduce their electoral anger. 'Crimping would have placated 60 to 80% of gun owners,' said a National Party backbencher.[31] 'It is better to achieve 90 per cent compliance to a modification regime than 50 per cent compliance to a confiscation regime,' said another.[32] National Party Leader and Deputy Prime Minister Tim Fischer had 'gone into bat' to support crimping in Federal Cabinet.[33]

On 4 July the SSAA put out a press release saying: 'After conducting private polls around Australia, the SSAA is convinced that the public overwhelmingly supports the concept of crimping and believe that if

30 Millett M, Riley M. 'Rural MPs pressure Cabinet on guns', *SMH*, 29 June 1996: 2.

31 Millett M. 'Howard stands firm against gun crimping', *SMH*, 11 July 1996: 1; Millett M, Riley M. 'Rural MPs pressure Cabinet on guns', *SMH*, 29 June 1996: 2.

32 Middleton K. 'WA to defy gun-crimping decision', *The Age*, 12 July 1996: 4.

33 Kitney G. 'Why Fischer will fight on', *SMH*, 12 July 1996: 11; Hughes J, Emerson S. 'Court alone as Borbidge reins in gun opposition', *The Australian*, 20–21 July 1996: 5.

law abiding gun owners are given the opportunity to retain their firearms using this method they won't reverse the procedure.'

The details and results of these 'polls' were never revealed.

The main debate on crimping began around mid June[34] and continued until just after the second Police Ministers' meeting on 17 July when, one by one, those States supporting crimping agreed to drop their demands. The Prime Minister was forthright in his opposition to the option from the outset.[35] His uncompromising stance on crimping prompted still more praise of his political courage ('Doing so has required considerable political spine.')[36] The Federal Government had finally referred the issue to the Department of Defence for advice after an initial report from a ballistics expert had concluded that most gun owners would find it difficult to reverse modifications carried out by a gunsmith. The Defence Department's report advised that the crimping process was reversible 'within an hour'[37] and Howard declared it an unacceptable option.

Given the gun lobby's support for crimping, it was not hard to discern that the shooters saw it as an ineffective control. The old principle in advocacy – that if your opposition supports a particular proposal, it is wise to be immediately suspicious of it – impressed itself on NCGC members. Ted Drane made the tactical mistake of admitting that it was reversible[38] and so the NCGC began to argue for the crimping option to be abandoned, framing it as an attempt to 'walk away' from the tough, uncompromising agreements reached by the Police Ministers on 10 May. The Prime Minister used this expression in speaking of his reservations.[39]

---

34 Savva N, Farouque F. 'Deal could permit owners to keep guns', *The Age*, 19 June 1996: 3; Middleton K. 'WA to defy gun-crimping decision', *The Age*, 12 July 1996: 4.

35 Millet M. 'Howard stands firm against gun crimping', *SMH*, 11 July 1996: 1.

36 Anon. 'Press on, Prime Minister' (editorial), *The Age*, 12 July 1996: A14.

37 Roberts G, Middleton K. 'Be rational on guns, PM urges states', *The Age*, 15 July 1996: A3.

38 Grattan M. 'Integrity survives the 'crimp' snag', *The Age*, 11 July 1996: A8.

39 Millett M, Vass N. 'Don't walk away on guns: PM', *SMH*, 13 July 1996: 13.

The *Sydney Morning Herald* published a lengthy article by Rebecca Peters on the morning of the Police Ministers' second meeting.[40] She argued that the states' concern to save money through crimping was disingenuous because the Commonwealth was paying for the buyback. She also argued that the compensation scheme – the major item of business at the meeting – should be extended to provide funds for gun owners who wished or would be obliged to surrender single-shot rifles.

The new laws would require gun owners to demonstrate that they had a legitimate need for a gun. Not having such needs, many current owners would not qualify, and if they owned single-shot weapons, there was no provision to buy back these guns. This would be a huge disincentive for such people to surrender their guns. Arguing that the buyback system should be extended not only introduced a salient point that was hard to refute, but made any move to reject the buyback for semi-automatics and pump-action shotguns that much harder. The call to extend the buyback, while entirely serious, could have also functioned as an ambit claim, allowing opposing politicians to appear before the gun lobby as having at least opposed moves to encourage even more guns to come out of the community.

One NCGC supporter pointedly asked: 'Has anyone from the pro-gun group given a coherent reason for wanting a 'crimped' semi-automatic? How long will it be before a gun publication (or Internet) generously gives advice on DIY 'uncrimping'?'[41] A *Sydney Morning Herald* editorial stated that 'the real objective of the defenders of crimping is not to save the community money but to be able to hold onto semi-automatic guns . . . when the heat [of Port Arthur] dies down, they can be uncrimped.'[42] The issue of crimping faded away very rapidly under the threat of Howard's referendum.

---

40 Peters R. 'Ministers in the line of fire', *SMH*, 17 July: 17.

41 Hudson L. 'Crimping' (letter), *SMH*, 6 July 1996: 34.

42 Anon. 'PM right on gun caution' (editorial), *SMH*, 12 July 1996: 10.

Buyback

Australia's gun buyback scheme appears to have been the first attempt anywhere in the world to combine a mandatory requirement to surrender particular categories of gun with an offer of full market value for them. Tony Blair's Labour Government in Britain became the second government to use such a scheme when it acted swiftly in 1997 to ban all handguns from civilian use. In recent years, several cities and counties in the United States have organised voluntary buyback schemes where small, sometimes token payments have been given for surrendered guns.[43] For example, Seattle organised a buyback program in 1992, but only $US50 was paid for each handgun. A total of 1,772 firearms were collected – less than 1% of handguns owned in Seattle – and 66% of those who handed in their gun continued to own at least one other firearm after the exchange. There was no evidence of any effect of the program on homicides, suicides, unintentional deaths due to firearms, firearm-related trauma admissions, or firearm related crimes.[44]

Before the details of the Australian buyback scheme were even announced, the gun lobby sought to anger shooters by spreading rumours that the amount of compensation to be offered would be minimal: 'As we heard at the meeting, they're offering probably $200 for my pump-action shotgun which is worth over $600,' claimed one gun owner.[45] Ted Drane said on television: 'A $2,000 firearm – if somebody says they're going to give you $100 for it, you're unlikely to get it.')[46] He also sought to argue that the estimated budget for the buyback was hugely underestimated. Independent MP Graeme Campbell told Federal Parliament: 'Ted Drane . . . says that he estimates compensation

---

43 Plotkin MR (ed.) *Under fire: gun buy-backs, exchanges and amnesty programs*. Washington: Police Executive Research Forum, 1996.

44 Callahan CM, Rivara FP, Koepsell TD. *Money for guns evaluation of the Seattle gun buyback program*. Public Health Reports 1994, 109: 472–77.

45 Roberts G, Zinn C. ' "Pineapple" extremism takes root', *The Age*, 11 June 1996: A11.

46 Drane T. *7.30 Report*, ABC TV, 9 May 1996.

to be $500 million. I suspect Mr Drane is talking about Victoria alone, because the cost will be substantially higher.'[47] Ted Drane regularly used the figure of $1 billion,[48] having apparently decided to double his initial figure of 'up to $500 million',[49] which presumably did not have the same sort of impact. John Tingle claimed that 'some semi-automatics were worth as much as $70,000'.[50] This tactic seemed designed to show that the bureaucrats were out of touch with gun marketplace realities and to introduce a spectre of aggregated payments that were so massive, that people could start comparing other community priorities on which such vast sums might have been spent.

On 30 July, newspapers published lengthy lists of what the Government would be paying for prohibited weapons. The figures were based on the average sale prices listed in gun dealers' catalogues in March 1996. Prices ranged between $60 and $10,000, well short of Tingle's alarmist $70,000 figure. Owners of expensive (more than $2,500) non-military semi-automatics were given the option of submitting the weapons to approved dealers who would try to sell them overseas for higher prices. Gun dealers would be compensated for any unsold prohibited firearms, ammunition, spare parts, maintenance equipment and manuals.[51] Gun owners would not have to pay tax on the money gained in compensation.[52]

The media began showing film and pictures of the destruction of surrendered guns from mid-August. Victoria was the first state to implement the buyback, and TV news programs and newspaper reports showed queues of men lining up to receive cash for their guns, metal

---

47 Australian House of Representatives *Hansard* for 9 May 1996.

48 Grattan M, Brady N. 'Tax to buy up banned guns', *The Age*, 13 May 1996: 1.

49 Farouque F, McKay S. 'Angry shooters plan a $1 million protest', *The Age*, 11 May 1996: A6.

50 Vass N. 'Owners won't give up weapons: Tingle', *SMH*, 13 May 1996.

51 Farouque F, Darby A. 'Owners able to sell guns overseas', *The Age*, 24 July 1996: A3; Millett M. 'Lock, stock and barrel compo for gun owners', *SMH*, 30 July 1996: 9.

52 Middleton K. 'Tax-free vow on gun cash', *The Age*, 25 July 1996: A8.

crushers pulverising the weapons and heavy machinery scooping up mountains of crushed guns to dump them in smelters.[53] The states and territories began their respective buybacks at different dates and with a variety of different administrative arrangements. Victoria, for example, paid shooters cash on the spot, while NSW had a system where cheques were posted about two weeks after surrender. Table 4.1 shows the state of the buyback at 5pm, 31 October 1997. In South Australia the buyback ended on 28 February 1997. In all other states and territories, the buyback and amnesty continued until 30 September 1997 although some states such as Tasmania have since continued with it.

Table 4.1 Gun buyback: numbers and dollars outlaid, 1 October 1997

State and population (millions)**	Buyback commenced	Number of guns surrendered	Adult population per gun surrendered***	$ paid	Mean $ per gun
Vic* (4.5022)	1 September	207,220	16.0	101,324,241	489
SA* (1.474)	9 September	52,348	20.7	26,080,422	498
ACT (.3041)	1 September	5,380	41.7	2,803,918	521
Tas (.473022)	1 September	32,132	10.9	14,277,331	444
NT* (.177720)	1 October	9,472	13.8	5,000,433	530
WA* (1.7317)	1 September	50,804	22.0	18,135,426	357
NSW (6.1151)	14 October	154,262	29.2	70,500,000	457
Qld (3.272)	13 January '97	128,783	18.7	66,230,973	514
Total (18.0498)		640,401	20.8	304,374,176	475

* States that previously had gun registration ** population estimated as at 30 June 1995 *** 73.7% of Australia's population is aged 15–74 years. I assume a negligible proportion of people aged under 15 and over 75 would have owned semi-automatic weapons.

53 Adams D. 'On-the-spot payment for gun owners', *The Age*, 14 August 1996: A8; Costa G. 'Thousands of guns go into crusher', *The Age*, 26 August 1996: A2; Boreham G. 'Long delays at gun centres', *The Age*, 20 August 1996: 2.

An ABC Radio report in October 1996 on the buyback in South Australia described it as reaping a bonanza for gun dealers who reportedly said many people used their compensation payments to immediately purchase legal single-shot weapons. Most of those interviewed commented that this was further evidence of the folly of the new laws: how stupid the Government was to have thought the ban on semi-automatics would reduce the net number of guns in the community. Shooters were simply replacing one sort of gun with others 'just as capable of killing', they argued. Here again, the gun lobby wanted it both ways: law abiding shooters would never commit homicide, yet the new guns they were purchasing were argued to be potentially dangerous.

When the NSW buyback began in November 1996, gun dealers similarly predicted a boom in new rifle sales.[54] This argument, of course, neatly avoided all the previous protests that few shooters would surrender their semi-automatics and that these guns were considered indispensable to their owners. Reports of a windfall for gun dealers also invited questions about whether the dealers were not seeking to use the publicity opportunity to suggest to shooters that they might use their compensation money to buy another gun, rather than use it for another purpose. Until gun registration update data became available, there was no way of knowing how much of this was marketing hype. But a press comment in December from the Victorian secretary of the Firearm Traders Association, Robert Brewer, suggested that this was exactly what was happening. Brewer said there had been a big increase in the number of firearms sold, but the surge would drop off. 'Out of every 100 firearms handed in, only eight are being replaced. That means a massive drop in the number of firearms. Not everyone is buying a replacement.'[55]

In late September 1996 the NSW and Queensland governments began publicly criticising the Federal Government, claiming there was a large shortfall in the funding allocated to their states to pay for the

---

54 Sandham S. 'Shooters will thwart buyback, say dealers', *SMH*, 5 November 1996: 5.

55 *Herald Sun*, 13 December 1996: 1–2.

buyback. The NCGC was asked for comment on NSW, which while having long passed the legislation, had not started a buyback several months later. Part of the costs the NSW Government complained were not being adequately met by the Commonwealth were infrastructural costs for regional police centres to record the buyback transactions. Gun control advocates argued that Victoria, Western Australia and South Australia had funded their own gun registration schemes when they had implemented these before Port Arthur. If these states had borne the costs of gun control without Commonwealth help, we believed NSW might be unreasonably trying to milk money it would otherwise have paid had it acted on guns previously. Additionally, if Victoria and South Australia could start their buybacks promptly, we felt little sympathy for NSW's claim that they were being short-changed. This deadlock was eventually resolved with the Federal Government agreeing to fund all of the buyback.

Gun registration

Martin Bryant – who did not have a shooter's licence – lived in a state which had no long arm registration. He obtained his guns from a Hobart gun dealer. Below are excerpts from the record of interview between two Tasmanian police officers and Bryant.[56] They illustrate the frightening simplicity with which a licensed gun dealer knew he could sell a high-powered military weapon to someone like Bryant in a state where lack of registration meant that the purchaser of the gun would not be recorded.

> Q: Do you remember where you bought that one [the Colt AR-15 semi-automatic]?
>
> *Bryant*: Yeah Terry Hill, Terry Hill.
>
> Q: At Guns and Ammo?
>
> *Bryant*: Mmm.

---

56 http://www.theage.com.au:80/special/bryant/t1.htm [no longer active, 2013].

Q: And you can remember how much you paid for that one?

Bryant: Ahh, five grand with the scope.

Q: Five.

Bryant: Five thousand dollars with the scope on it. It was gonna be four and a half thousand without the scope but it was five thousand with the scope and strap and also got, got some ammunition thrown in.

Q: All right. How many rounds of ammunition did you get with that, can you remember?

Bryant: Ohh, about eighty rounds. Eighty to a hundred rounds.

Q: Have you purchased any more rounds, umm, since you know you've bought the firearm itself?

Bryant: Umm, yeah I've probably purchased eight packets of, be twenty rounds in each . . . Terry, yeah. Terry's, have you met Terry before?

Q: Yes, [I] know Terry.

Bryant: Still in business is he?

Q: Yes, he's still in business . . . why do you ask that ahh, Martin, if Terry's still in business?

Bryant: Ahh, 'cos I didn't have a licence. I had no gun licence.

Q: So, just let me get this straight. You didn't have a gun licence?

Bryant: No.

Q: Did you make out you had a gun licence when you purchased them?

Bryant: No, I never discussed it, I never, I just said I had the cash on me and he said that's all right.

Q: Did he ever, did he ask to see if you had a gun licence?

Bryant: No, never.

135

Gun registration – the recording of a gun's ownership against a licence-holder's name – has been the most vehemently and consistently opposed measure in the Australian gun control debate. Gun registration and shooter licensing are two terms that can be confusing. Perhaps the easiest way to understand the two is by analogy with the car. Each person who drives is legally required to have a driver's licence, and each motor vehicle being driven is required to be individually registered. Driver licensing enables motor traffic authorities to test the competency of a driver to use a motor vehicle and for persons deemed unsuitable (for example, those with poor driving records, the poorly sighted and people with uncontrolled epilepsy) to have their driving licence cancelled or their application refused. The public benefits of vehicle registration include the ability to certify road-worthiness for each registered vehicle and to trace cars involved in crime, dangerous traffic incidents and those that are stolen.

There are key similarities in the arguments for shooter licensing and gun registration. No sensible person would argue that people with dangerous driving records or the poorly sighted should be allowed to drive. Nor should shooters – even the gun lobby would agree – be licensed if they are demonstrably unfit to own a gun; for example, if they have threatened or committed violence. Similarly, few would maintain that an unsafe car should be let onto public roads or that it is a bad idea to be able to trace a car via registration if it was involved in a hit-and-run incident. Gun registration allows authorities to track the movement of a gun from owner to owner, to note if people are building arsenals, and to link a gun found to be used in a crime to its owner. All of these benefits, of course, assume that shooters would register their guns. Obviously, people intending to use a gun criminally would not register it, but in many ways this consideration should have been irrelevant to the gun lobby, because of its continual insistence that it spoke only for law-abiding citizens (see Chapter 6).

The most important argument for firearm registration is simply that without it, the shooter licensing system is undermined. Licensing is cardinal to the gun control policies of all countries with gun laws.

Legislators use licensing to exclude people such as those with violent criminal records and domestic violence offenders from owning guns. Licensing places a major obstacle in the way of known criminals and domestic violence offenders wishing to obtain the authorisation they would need to buy guns from a shop. However, firearms are often (and until the new laws, quite legally) obtained from sources other than gun shops. In the past, nearly half of all gun owners obtain their guns through private sales, gifts, as heirlooms or other means.[57] Anyone disposing of a gun privately is still legally required to ensure the new owner holds a current gun licence – but without registration, many would think 'why bother?'. Without gun registration there is no trail for police to follow.

Guns originally bought legally by a licensed shooter can pass easily into the hands of those forbidden from holding a licence because of a history of violence. This can happen quite innocently: how could someone selling a gun be expected to know the criminal or domestic violence record of any potential purchaser? 'Straw man' purchases also occur (when someone with no criminal record buys guns on behalf of others whose criminal record would preclude them from having one).

Registration also provides licensed gun owners with the incentive to remain licensed after their licence expires: if you can only retain a (registered) gun while you have a current licence, then you may be concerned that cherished guns might be confiscated if you failed to renew your shooter's licence. The importance of this was tragically demonstrated by the double police killings at Crescent Head, NSW in July 1995. The gunman there, John McGowan, was a licensed shooter who had not renewed his licence when it had expired a few years before. The two police who responded to a domestic violence call-out involving McGowan therefore had no way of knowing he had ever owned a gun and were therefore perhaps unprepared for what was to happen. They were shot dead.

Those opposed to gun registration often argue that police should always assume there may be a gun at such incidents. This is analogous to

---

57 Harding R, *Firearms and violence in Australian life*, Perth: University of Western Australia Press, 1981: 84.

expecting police to assume every car they see on the road is stolen, but never to obtain positive confirmation. Australian police routinely check by radio the names, vehicle details, criminal record, unpaid parking fines, history of stolen property and firearm ownership (among other things) associated with premises they are called to. Gun registration can boost incalculably the precision of this information.

It is naive to expect that all shooters with expired licences would conscientiously renew their licences or dispose of their guns legally when there is not the remotest possibility that they will be found to be breaking the law. The NCGC believes the absence of registration has been the main reason why such a large proportion of NSW licence-holders have failed to renew on expiry (see below).

Domestic homicide prevention

Attempting to prevent guns being used in domestic violence, including homicide, has long been a major reason for restricting access to guns. But whatever improvements that might be made in laws on guns and domestic violence cannot hope to work without registration. When a gun licence is automatically suspended or cancelled after a protection order is issued, this does not guarantee that a guns are not still available to domestic violence perpetrators. If the licence is seized, this only prevents the former licensee from legally buying more guns. It does nothing to remove guns the violent person already has and may be hiding. Without knowing how many firearms a person owns, police can only guess whether the offender has any weapons they cannot locate.

The NSW Central Coast (Terrigal) massacre in 1992 illustrates this point. The gunman was Malcolm Baker, a licensed shooter with no criminal record. Three weeks before the shootings, his de facto wife, Kerry Anne Gannan, had left him and obtained an apprehended violence order (AVO) against him. When the AVO was issued, the local police cancelled Baker's licence and searched his house for guns. They seized five firearms, assuming these were all he owned. But there was one more that was not found: a pump-action shotgun which he used to kill Gannan and her sister, their father, his adult son, a former business associate and this man's de facto.

The Central Coast massacre was widely publicised because of the extent of the carnage. Yet in important respects it was a very 'usual' homicide. It occurred within a family, was preceded by domestic violence, motivated by sexual possessiveness, and accomplished with a common firearm owned by a 'law-abiding' licensed shooter.

'Registration has never helped to solve a crime'

The SSAA's Ted Drane at one time argued 'there has never been a crime solved in Australia through registration', citing the case of murdered Federal Police Assistant Commissioner Colin Winchester, who was killed with a Ruger .22. According to Drane, police contacted 'everyone who had Rugers. They still haven't found it.'[58] But Drane was never heard to use this argument again after the notorious backpacker murderer Ivan Milat was traced through a gun shop's sales records, a de facto form of gun registration.

The gun lobby are fond of quoting a former Victorian police officer who is opposed to registration. But research by another Victorian police officer, Errol Mason, and criminologist Dr Jo Herlihy, has shown that registration can greatly assist police 'even when it is administratively clumsy and reputedly operating at less than maximum efficiency'.[59] Mason and Herlihy's interviews with police found many examples of cases in which firearm registration was crucial in investigating crimes. They cite seven examples, including homicides, armed robberies and drug offences, which could not have been solved without the use of the firearms registration system. Most of these involved professional criminals – precisely the type of gun owners for whom the gun lobby repeatedly claims the new gun laws would be irrelevant. If a gun is lost or stolen, registration can aid in its recovery. If police know the gun (or

---

58 Aiton D. 'Out for a duck', *The Sunday Age*, 21 March 1993: 4.

59 Mason E, Herlihy J, 'Firearms registration: the controversy revisited (first draft)', unpublished manuscript, Australian Institute of Criminology 1993: 15.

even the type of gun) used in a crime, registration provides a starting point for tracing the owner and piecing together the chain of events surrounding the crime – as the Milat backpacker investigations showed. Knowing that a gun is registered provides a disincentive to experienced criminals contemplating stealing it, because registration could link them to a crime.[60] Few people bother to note down the manufacturer's number on every household item such as video and sound equipment they own. Consequently, when stolen these items can usually find ready purchasers. But stolen guns – like stolen cars – can only be re-sold to people prepared to risk owning a numbered and identifiable gun. Even when serial numbers have been ground off the gun, forensic science techniques can often identify at least part of the original number.

Many arguments against registration have become redundant because of technological developments. Early registration systems depended on bookkeeping or carded record systems. Today's computer based systems such as the national fingerprint database for Australia and New Zealand and the National Exchange of Police Information (NEPI) database that will link the gun licensing and registration systems of all eight Australian jurisdictions, allow information to be accessed almost instantly, updated and preserved.

'Shooters won't register their guns'

One of the gun lobby's principal arguments against gun registration was that it would be administrative folly and a waste of taxpayers' money to establish a registration system because many shooters simply would refuse or neglect to register their guns. Before Port Arthur, Western Australia, South Australia, Victoria, the Northern Territory and the ACT required long-arm registration. The gun lobby argued (almost certainly correctly) that even in those jurisdictions many shooters do not register their weapons. After the buyback concluded on the 30 September 1997, NSW's comparatively low ratio of guns handed in per adult population (see Table 4.1) was widely attributed to many gun owners thinking 'they don't know I've got the gun, so why should I bother handing it in?'

---

60 Ibid, 10.

Part of the reason for this has undoubtedly been because no state had taken gun registration particularly seriously. No state engaged in random checks of houses for guns. None publicised the seriousness of owning an unregistered gun through, for example, the conduct of community policing campaigns (similar to the annual Operation Noah campaign where the public can inform police about suspected illicit drug dealing). And all states with gun registration seldom prosecuted anyone for having an unregistered gun, unless these guns were detected in the course of charging people with other offences. All this combined to send a message to shooters that failure to register a gun would most likely go unnoticed. Again, many probably thought 'why bother?'

NSW has never had rifle registration, but some indication of the extent to which shooters might be ignoring gun laws could be gained by considering the situation of shooter licensing in the state between June 1991 and April 1993, when tougher, although still very inadequate, gun laws were introduced. In this period the number of licensed shooters fell from about 240,000 to about 180,000. The gun lobby and its political sympathisers attributed the fall to shooters refusing to take out licences, while the NCGC suggested that many of people no longer having licences may have decided that, not being active shooters, they no longer wanted a gun licence. Many may have given up shooting.[61] The answer probably lay in a combination of the two factors.

In summary, the gun lobby was certainly correct in maintaining that many shooters did not register their guns in states that already had gun registration, and that many would not register guns under the new trans-Australia laws. Much of this was doubtless due to a rational belief that with gun registration having so far been given low priority in police law enforcement efforts, they had little to lose by failing to register their guns. But to leap from this assessment to open public advocacy against registration was, as the NCGC regularly argued, equivalent to saying that all drivers should not drive within the speed limit because people often sped and were not caught by highway patrols. The gun lobby's argument reduced to saying, 'plenty of people break the law and get

---

61 Morris L. '60,000 decline in licensed shooters', *SMH*, 30 April 1994: 5.

away with it ... so the law is stupid and should be opposed'. A *Sydney Morning Herald* editorial argued that the failure of many to register was no argument against registration but rather 'speaks of a disturbing propensity among gun owners for flouting the law'.[62] This theme is examined further in Chapter 6.

'Criminals won't register their guns'

A related argument was that 'the basic flaw in the argument for firearm registration [is that] it would only apply to the law-abiding citizen ... and would have absolutely no effect on the criminal or the violent person ... The fact is that you cannot legislate against insanity or against massacres ...'[63] Yet again, the gun lobby sought refuge behind its convenient dichotomy of good and bad shooters (see Chapter 6). Their argument here presupposed that all who would commit violence with a gun would be planning to do this when they acquired their guns. Hence, those intent on wrongdoing wouldn't be silly enough to be licensed or register their guns. This argument attempted to frame the advocates of registration as utterly naive in their pursuit of bureaucratic solutions to problems that allegedly defied all regulation.

The problem for the gun lobby here is that the example shown by the facts on gun licensing simply do not support them. Philip Alpers presented a paper to the Third International Conference on Injury Prevention and Control in Melbourne in February 1996 and showed that in 11 multiple killings (five or more dead) in Australia and New Zealand between 1987 and 1993, 50 of the 70 victims were shot by licensed gun owners. Sixty of the dead (86%) were shot by someone with no previous history of mental illness or violent crime.[64] Again the gun lobby had no specific response to Alpers' analysis, with Ted Drane resorting to a vague and unsubstantiated slur: 'Claims by Philip Alpers from New Zealand about licensed gun owners being killers were debunked after

---

62 Anon. 'A cool look at gun laws' (editorial), *SMH*, 30 April 1996.

63 Tingle J. 'The crossfire on gun legislation', *SMH*, 11 July 1995: 15.

64 Allison C. 'Licensed gun owners are main killers', *SMH*, 19 February 1996.

scrutiny in NZ,' he claimed in a Sporting Shooters' Association press release, providing no information about what exactly was debunked.[65] Drane's informant on this point was the Sporting Shooters'Association of New Zealand. That country's Police Commissioner later wrote to the local pro-gun group suggesting an apology for claiming, wrongly, that the Alpers study had been judged inaccurate. There was no response.

'Gun registration is irrelevant to violence'

Shooters often claimed that the registration status of a gun was irrelevant to whether it would be used in a violent act ('Mrs Majdalawi was killed by an unregistered pistol, even though all pistols are supposed to be registered. The children of Dunblane were murdered by registered pistols. What does it prove? Registration is irrelevant.'[66]) Obviously no one was arguing that registration would somehow stop a gun owner from shooting someone – just as no one would argue that a registered car would never be involved in an illegal act. But the gun lobby was not in the business of rational argument. Its aim was to present a simplistic vision of gun laws that sought to make them look facile. Drane's clever rhetoric here framed registration as a solution around the wrong problem – guns – while his argument simultaneously framed the real issue as one of 'bad' men who presumably needed to be controlled, counselled or 'educated' not to be bad. As Drane's point indicated, registration would not prevent any given murder, and if the debate stopped and ended there, the gun lobby would have succeeded in framing registration as a pointless exercise.

The task for gun control advocacy was to move the debate away from any particular murder to consider the population-wide benefits of registration, much in the same way that the community appreciates the car analogy. One of the NCGC's most used debating points over the years when advocating gun registration had been: 'We register cars, we register boats . . . we even register dogs! Why on earth can't we register

65 SSAA website, 19 February 1996.
66 Downes DA. 'Guns and damned statistics' (letter), *SMH*, 27 March 1996.

guns?'[67] We often found that to use this phrase in radio or television interviews almost guaranteed that it would be the 'sound bite' used in news reports. The argument followed that any community bothered enough to set up dog registration systems but not act on guns had perverse priorities. Professor Duncan Chappell said: 'We have a better idea how many dogs we have in this country, rather than guns.'[68]

We also used the dog analogy to counter the gun lobby's point that criminals would not register guns: 'Some, often with criminal intent, don't register their cars, boats or vicious dogs either. So do we hear a call for the abandonment of car registration?' But guns are easier to hide than cars, ran the next stage of the argument. This can be countered by arguing that by this logic, handguns are the easiest to hide of the lot, yet they have been registered successfully since 1927.[69]

All Australian states have for many years required handguns to be registered, something the NCGC raised whenever appropriate. In public debate, this created an awkward precedent for the gun lobby when it tried to justify its opposition to long-arm registration. It obliged them to either criticise handgun registration or implicitly admit that the same sensible arguments applied, regardless of the type of gun. On no occasion did anyone from the gun lobby argue that handguns should not be tightly controlled. Their usual debating approach was to try to wave the issue away by vague references to irrelevant 'past history'. But the point was often noted by journalists and editorial writers: 'If it's good enough for handguns, it's good enough for all guns.'[70] We had sown this argument in media commentary during the years before Port Arthur.

---

67 Peters R, Chapman S. 'Cars, boats, dogs . . . why not guns? The case for national gun registration in Australia', *Aust J Public Health*, 1995, 19: 213–15.

68 Chappell D. *Lateline*, ABC TV 9 May 1996.

69 Chapman S. 'Now, about those guns . . ', *SMH*, 9 May 1996: 15.

70 Anon. 'A cool look at gun laws' (editorial), *SMH*, 30 April 1996.

The gun lobby's deepest fears

So why then did the gun lobby reserve its most vehement opposition for gun registration? On the morning of the Police Ministers' meeting, the *Sydney Morning Herald* published a lengthy, anonymous article by a woman who had lived with a man who had threatened her and her children with gun violence. Most of the article described how hitherto ordinary, 'good' men who have guns in the house can lose self-control and use guns threateningly after things begin to go wrong in their domestic or working lives. In one highly sarcastic passage, the writer explored the gun lobby's objections to gun registration by asking two most pertinent and obvious rhetorical questions:

> Why does the pro-gun lobby object to gun registration? Because someone might be able to trace an illegally possessed gun back to an irresponsible gun license holder who indiscriminately off-loaded one of his excess guns? Surely not. Because it might attract attention when your average citizen accumulates an arsenal to rival a small nation's defence force? Not likely.[71]

Here, so simply and eloquently expressed, were two of the main fears held by the gun lobby about registration; that is, a system of keeping records of gun ownership and transfers which:

- Governments could use to confiscate further categories of weapons that might be later declared illegal.

- Police could use to note if individuals were building up arsenals of weapons.

- Police could use to trace the sale of a weapon to someone not authorised to own it (that is, a person without a gun licence or without the correct class of licence).

- The Tax Office could access to assess whether tax has been paid on any income gained from selling guns.

---

71 Anon. 'Life in the firing line', *SMH*, 10 May 1996.

Of these, the fourth, concerning tax evasion, is never publicly voiced by the gun lobby for obvious reasons – there would be no political advantage in trying to argue for a scheme that facilitated easy tax evasion. But I have been told on several occasions that there is an extensive and (for some) lucrative black market in guns organised through gun fairs and various gun networks. Registration would severely restrict this trade and so is vehemently opposed. A press advertisement placed by 'The Shooters Task Force' listed as one of its gripes that the new laws would require that 'all sales must go through a licensed gun dealer, thus reducing their value'.[72] This was an understandable concern for shooters because dealers will always offer a lower price than could be obtained from a private sale. But it may also have been an allusion to the end of unrecorded cash transactions for guns, and hence tax avoidance by those who sold guns this way for a living.

One gun lobby advertisement expressed horror that the computerised gun register would mean that 'licensed gun owners' names will be placed on the National Exchange of Police Information database *alongside real criminals.* An insult to every decent gun owner.'[73] (our emphasis). This was a truly astonishing statement, revealing much about either the sheer innocence of some in the gun lobby about databases, or else about their resentment at even being remotely associated with criminals. A parallel claim of outrage might well have been drivers with flawless driving records feeling outraged that their names appeared on the Department of Motor Transport's computerised list of all drivers 'next to' people who had culpable, drunk, or negligent driving charges recorded against them. Horror!

The bottom line to the futility of the gun lobby's resistance to registration can be simply expressed. It seemed that many among the public were satisfied that there was an obvious reason behind opposition to gun registration: that anyone wanting to own a gun for peaceful, legal purposes would have nothing to fear in registration, while those who

---

72 The Shooters Task Force. 'Firearm owners don't be duped' (advertisement), *Daily Telegraph*, 17 June 1996.

73 Ibid.

implacably opposed registration must have something to hide ('There's nothing undemocratic about being asked to register your gun, and unless you have malevolent intent, what is there to hide?').[74] At the end of the day, we were left with an indelible sense that this sentiment was foremost in most people's minds whenever this debate arose.

Genuine reason to own a gun

The ban on semi-automatics and the introduction of national gun registration were the two changes that caused most apoplexy among the gun lobby. But arguably the most significant reform attracted far less attention, despite its immense potential to reduce the number of Australians who would be allowed to own guns. This was the requirement that anyone wishing to own a gun needed to prove a genuine reason for being granted a licence.

Most Australians probably assumed that gun owners were required by law to prove that they had a legitimate reason for wanting to own a gun; the idea that one could legally acquire a firearm on virtually any pretext might seem incredible to non-gun owners. Yet under the existing law in most states and territories, pistols were the only guns where ownership required justification. All pistol owners needed to do was to prove they were active members of a target shooting club, or needed a pistol for occupational reasons, such as working in the security industry. Some jurisdictions also required proof of reason for high-capacity semi-automatic rifles. Only Western Australia required proof for all types of firearms. Applicants elsewhere were asked to simply name their reason for wishing to own guns – no proof was required. Thus, outside Western Australia, any adult without a criminal record was eligible to own unlimited numbers of ordinary rifles or shotguns.

Resolution 3 in the APMC agreement requires applicants for all types of gun licences to establish a 'genuine reason' for owning or using a gun. The set of genuine reasons was short and seemingly unambiguous:

---

74 Gordon H. Letter, *SMH*, 30 March 1996: 36.

- Applicants claiming to be target shooters must demonstrate membership of an authorised club.
- Those claiming to be recreational hunters must produce permission from a rural landowner allowing shooting on their land.
- People claiming an occupational requirement must prove that their occupation actually does require a gun (for example, farmers with feral animal infestations).
- Gun collectors must prove to police that they are bona fide collectors.
- Other limited purposes (such as the use of guns in theatrical productions) could be authorised by special permit.

In addition, those wishing to own self-loading firearms (Categories C and D) needed to prove a 'genuine need' that could not be met by single-shot weapons. Only farmers, professional shooters and authorised clay target shooters (the latter may only apply for one type of Category C weapon, a self-loading shotgun) could apply to prove 'genuine need'. However most farmers would not qualify, as their needs (for example, routine feral animal control) could be met with an ordinary rifle or shotgun. Recreational hunters and the vast majority of target shooters were simply ruled out.

Being a farmer and member of a target shooting club were relatively unproblematic. Both of these 'genuine need' categories would easily allow applicants to produce evidence of rural residence or property ownership, or of gun club membership. Those stating hunting as their reason would have to obtain a letter from a landowner giving permission for the shooter to shoot on the landowner's property. This was always going to be a big problem for many shooters and for governments in having to rule out past stated reasons for gun ownership.

Many people owning guns before the new reforms had indicated when applying for a licence that they wanted them for hunting. They were not obliged to provide evidence for this, nor any landowner's authorisation. Many urban gun owners probably would not even know a farmer, and on the strength of many comments made during the post–Port Arthur debate by farmers who supported the new laws, would be very unlikely to get such permission. Farmers signing a letter of authorisation risked entangling themselves in legal problems if a shooter to whom they had given permission to use their property was involved in some incident. It seemed likely that most cautious landowners would be deeply uninterested in providing such permission, particularly to strangers.

The criteria for 'need to own' a gun threatened to prove a huge headache for governments. They would exclude many thousands of angry shooters, particularly those living in cities, who were not farmers, did not belong to a gun club, and could not find a landowner willing to provide authorisation for hunting. In short, it promised to 'disenfranchise' thousands of people who held shooters' licences under the old laws. Not only would thousands of shooters be required to surrender their semi-automatics, but thousands more would be told that, not satisfying the criteria for having genuine need to own a gun, they could not continue to legally own *any* gun. And if these guns were single-shot rifles and shotguns, there was no provision for any compensation to be paid for their surrender. The NCGC regularly called for the provisions of the buyback to be extended to cover compensation for *any* gun surrendered. No state took up our suggestion.

Throughout the debate that followed the Port Arthur massacre, the NCGC noticed that politicians paid little attention to this issue. We took this as a sign that governments had privately decided it was something they would simply not take on. Several times we heard reassurances on radio from politicians that people who already held shooters' licences had 'nothing to fear'. This was plainly very much against the intent of the Police Ministers' agreement on the nature of a 'genuine reason' to own a gun.

Safe storage

The new proposals reiterated and strengthened provisions in some states requiring licensed gun owners to securely store their weapons at home. A national standard for storage required that guns be stored in a locked hardwood or steel receptacle that could not be easily penetrated. To avoid easy removal, the receptacle must weigh more than 150 kg when empty, or be fixed to a building. All ammunition must be stored in a locked container of an approved type, separate from the firearms. Farmers and professional shooters with special permits to own a semi-automatic gun or pump-action shotgun must store these in a locked steel cabinet bolted to a building.

Safe, secure storage in locked gun cabinets is considered important for two reasons: preventing theft and minimising access to guns by people (often children) not trained to use them. Guns are often stolen when found by thieves in break-and-enter situations. In the USA, a study of 1,678 criminals found that 47% reported having stolen a gun. When asked where they would go to steal a gun, the most common response (58%) was a home or apartment.[75] In England, Scotland and Wales a 1994 study showed 1,339 offences were recorded when guns (excluding air rifles and starting pistols) were stolen. These included 690 occasions when shotguns, pistols or rifles were stolen from houses.[76] (In Australia, there is no database on how many guns are stolen during robberies, but these statistics are available from crime reports of break and enters.)

We did not notice any public objections from the gun lobby to safe storage: to have done so would have required them to advance reckless arguments about leaving guns lying about in houses, which would counter their frequent efforts to position shooters as responsible. But there was behind-the-scenes lobbying against any move that granting a licence would be conditional on installation of a safe. The Australian Police Ministers' Council resolutions required all governments to introduce laws that would only allow shooter's licences to 'be issued subject

---

75 Wright JD, Rossi PH. *Armed and considered dangerous: a survey of felons and their firearms*. New York: Aldine de Gruyter, 1986: 194–95.

76 Evidence submitted on behalf of the Secretary of State for Scotland and the Home Secretary to Lord Cullen's Inquiry Into the Circumstances Leading up to and Surrounding the Events at Dunblane Primary School on Wednesday 13 March 1996, 30 April 1996: 50.

to undertakings to comply with storage requirements, to provide details of proposed storage provisions at the time of licensing'. Most people would imagine this means shooters can't get licences until they undertake to store their guns in ways that make them difficult to access. And given the seriousness of guns getting into the hands of criminals, people might be forgiven for thinking governments would arrange for these hand-on-heart 'undertakings' to be backed up with inspection. This was not to be the case in NSW.

In November 1996, only days after Martin Bryant's sentencing, NSW independent politician Peter Macdonald sought to amend the NSW Act by requiring police to inspect safe storage arrangements before shooters were given a gun licence. Police Minister Paul Whelan replied that this was 'unfair . . . It would mean that all applicants for firearms would be required to install expensive safes and other storage equipment before they knew whether their licence application had been approved'. Instead Whelan was content with applicants simply stating that they would comply with the requirements. While the Act allowed for inspections, it did not require them and the government gave no undertakings that it would set any target levels. Almost unbelievably, Whelan went on to explain that 'police can inspect storage facilities at a time mutually agreed with the licence holder'.[77] Just picture it. 'Er, hello, Constable Plod here. Would it be convenient for me to drop around just to check that your guns are securely stored so that you won't be hit with a whopping fine and possible jail sentence? Not tomorrow? Week after next, you say? Right. See you then.'

In many aspects of daily life, issues of public safety are backed with requirements for inspection. Would we accept the unchecked assurances of owner-builders that they comply with electrical circuitry and building standards? From drivers that they promise not to drive with bald tyres and faulty brakes? Or from nightclub owners that their fire escapes will be adequate? Do Food Act inspectors bow to the privacy

---

77 NSW Legislative Assembly *Hansard*. Firearms Amendment Bill. Second Reading. 26 November 1996.

of café owners and arrange mutually convenient times to check for rat droppings?

The National Party's Peter Cochrane, who had earlier unsuccessfully tried to have the Act amended so that guns would not be distastefully referred to as 'weapons' but as benign 'devices'[78] ('Come out with your hands up and drop your device!'), told the NSW Parliament when supporting the Government's rejection of Macdonald's amendment that country police officers 'have far more pressing law and order issues to attend to than the inspection of storage facilities for firearms'. Or registering guns, he would have doubtless agreed.

Macdonald argued that a user-pays approach, so favoured by both government and opposition in practically every other facet of life, could be used to pay for the obvious costs that inspections would entail. Just like drivers pay for annual motor vehicle safety inspections, for example. If drivers can't afford compulsory insurance, we deem they can't afford the car. So if shooters aren't prepared to pay for storage inspections, should they be able to have a gun licence? Cochrane pointed out that country police would need to travel hundreds of thousands of kilometres each year to undertake the inspections. With inspections only being one-off at the time of licensing, there was doubtless some hyperbole in this. But at a very minimum, it invited the solution of quotas of random inspections.

Under such a scheme all shooters would be on notice that each police station would be required to randomly inspect, unannounced, say 200 licensees a year. Any station which reported rates of compliance much higher than the state average would have a further random sample inspected by external police. This was one very glaring example of the (thankfully rare) backsliding that many had predicted would begin when the Port Arthur case faded from the media's gaze.

---

78 Ibid.

5

The gun lobby in Australia

This chapter and the next examine three of the main groups that make up the gun lobby in Australia and the range of arguments they used against the reforms. First, I look at the gun lobby's reaction to the Port Arthur massacre and the announced gun law reforms, and particularly at how the lobby was described and discussed in the media. In the next chapter, I examine in detail their main arguments against gun control.

As described in Chapter 3, the public and media discourse on gun control in the three months after Port Arthur reached an unprecedented intensity. Australia's gun lobby probably received more exposure in these months than in its entire political history. The spotlight fell particularly on three prominent spokespeople: Ted Drane, of the Sporting Shooters Association of Australia (SSAA); John Tingle, of the Shooters' Party; and Ian McNiven, of the Queensland Firearm Owners' Association of Australia (FOAA). A few supportive politicians, particularly West Australian Independent Graeme Campbell and Queensland National Party backbencher Bob Katter Jr, also had significant exposure. The great majority of Australians, urging governments to fulfil the 10 May Police Ministers' agreement, found their views opposed by these wilful men. In an important way, the nation's media hosted a social drama that retold an age-old 'good versus evil' story about the struggle between two groups. Whatever image the gun lobby hoped to project, to the great majority of the population it simply represented a dark force trying to block Prime Minister John Howard's gun law reforms.

If Howard and Attorney-General Daryl Williams were secular priests offering the new laws as a way of absolving governments from past sins of omission, gun lobbyists were the infidels intent on disrupting this attempt at reparation. The nation watched this drama unfold over the months after Port Arthur, with each new gun lobby strategy looming as a threat to force a retreat on reform.

Immediate reaction to the massacre

Voices from the gun lobby joined in the general expression of abhorrence over what happened at Port Arthur. Especially in the early days after the massacre, and at most of the gun lobby's rallies, great care was taken to open their protest meetings with expressions of sympathy and outrage over Martin Bryant's acts. These rallies would then quickly resume their bellicose chanting about shooters' rights, ridiculing any politicians acting against gun violence. In what one editorial described as a 'nakedly opportunistic drive for new members',[1] the SSAA ran full-page 'fighting fund' advertisements in major newspapers on the morning of the 10 May Police Ministers' meeting, calling for donations.[2] These advertisements opened with the words, 'Responsible gun owners were shocked and horrified, as were all Australians, at recent tragic events in Tasmania.' While these expressions of sympathy may well have been genuine, they were plainly calculated by the gun lobby to present itself as a group of compassionate, decent people whose first concern was to share the nation's grief and outrage before getting down to the main agenda: opposing the new gun laws.

In the July/August 1996 edition of *Guns Australia* magazine, the editor appeared willing to dispense with all this grief talk and start putting Port Arthur in a different, no-nonsense perspective: 'Sure, innocent people lost their lives at the hands of a criminal, but innocents have

---

1 Anon. 'Historic pact on gun reforms', *SMH*, 11 May 1996.

2 Sporting Shooters Association of Australia. 'An urgent message to all gun owners' (advertisement), *Daily Telegraph*, 10 May 1996.

been losing their lives in a similar manner for thousands of years, and on a scale which makes the death toll of Port Arthur look insignificant,' he shrugged.[3] Apparently not realising that Port Arthur was the largest civilian gun massacre by a lone gunman recorded this century, the editor went on,

> Why have this country's governments, media and most of the general public reacted in such a way as to suggest that the massacre at Port Arthur is a tragedy on a global scale; that the loss of life is something this nation will never recover from, and that the world will never know the pain of Port Arthur. The world does know – it has known that kind of pain for many centuries and on a more frequent basis than us.

His blood brothers from the FOAA issued a statement on the Tuesday after the massacre saying: 'A few hundred murdered by nut cases is infinitesimal in comparison to what Mao, Stalin . . . have committed.'[4]

The SSAA's Ted Drane lost no time in turning to his principal task: to distract attention away from gun control and on to more ponderous solutions that would allow the passage of time to dissipate community demands for reform. On the Monday after the Sunday massacre, Drane told the *7.30 Report*: 'We don't believe that any so-called tougher firearm laws will actually do anything. What we need is to look at the reasons . . . what went wrong with the laws that were in Tasmania now and try to come up with a solution.'[5] The gun lobby made predictable calls to establish committees to examine the proposed reforms. Amid his criticism of the actions taken by the Police Ministers, John Tingle said an inquiry was needed to find out why Australia had suffered a spate of gun massacres in the past 10 years. Neither Drane nor Tingle appeared to remember that the National Committee on Violence (NCV) had already carried out a two-year inquiry involving hearings throughout

3 Bostock I. 'From the editor's desk', *Guns Australia*, July/August 1996: 4–5.

4 Roberts G, Cornford P. 'Buying spree as shooters try to beat the ban', *SMH*, 1 May 1996: 1.

5 *7.30 Report* ABC TV, 29 April 1996.

Australia, and had recommended a national gun control scheme very similar to the one agreed on by the APMC in 1996.[6]

Formidable reputation

The gun lobby's reputation as a politically powerful force derived not from the Shooters' Party's ventures into directly contesting elections (see Chapter 1), but by constantly talking up its ability to swing votes against any political party candidates supporting gun law reform. Gun magazines are full of gun lobby swagger about the role shooters claim to have played in the defeat of the Unsworth Labor Government in NSW in 1988, and threats about what they will do to any candidate stupid enough to run a gun law reform platform. The leaders of the lobby at times seemed drunk on the sense of their own power. Ted Drane said: 'The firearms lobby ... are very powerful, we don't resile from that, and there are a couple of governments in Australia that are just hanging on by the skin of their teeth at the moment.'[7]

The term 'gun lobby' referred to what one analyst described as:

> Something of a movement championing a reactionary, right-wing political agenda including advocacy of individual liberty in the face of perceptions of excessive government, opposition to immigration, opposition to multicultural-ism, rabid opposition to any group whose moral or sexual perspectives deviate from anything the far right considers normal, and claims that law and order is breaking down to the extent that citizens need weapons to defend themselves.[8]

Another writer, analysing the appeal of right-wing politicians like Campbell and Katter, suggested that the gun lobby was

---

6 National Committee on Violence. *Violence: directions for Australia.* Australian Institute of Criminology, Canberra 1990: 175–89.

7 Gibson R, Chamberlain P. 'Wheeling out the big guns', *The Age*, 11 May 1996: A20–21.

8 Economou N. 'The far right makes its move on power', *The Age*, 8 June 1996: A8.

reflecting and responding to a set of social and political fears that are widespread throughout rural Australia. To these rural people, the Federal Government's move on automatic and semi-automatic weapons is the latest manifestation of broader concerns. Essentially, the problem is one of rural alienation and economic hardship, with lashings of personal paranoia and religious fundamentalism, encouraging a feeling ... that politicians either won't respond to people's needs and desires or are engaged in a conspiracy against them.[9]

Many similar analyses were published during 1997 about the political appeal of federal MP Pauline Hanson – another independent politician who expressed open solidarity with many of the aims of the gun lobby.

But hundreds of writers emphasised that the gun lobby should be seen as a minority group of extremists. Here is a small selection from the print media:

- 'Powerful but misguided ... an outspoken but blinkered minority whose political influence has traditionally been grossly out of proportion to their numbers.'[10]

- 'But the debate is also being driven by extremists – the ugly face of the nation.'[11]

- 'A noisy, misguided minority.'[12]

- 'We should not be put off by the rantings of the militant few.'[13]

- 'Protect us from those rednecks of Australia's deep north as well as from any lone madman with murderous intent.'[14]

- 'Some, of course, are genuinely around the twist, others in the grip

9 Barker G. 'Rural rebels have Coalition on the run', *Australian Financial Review*, 11 June 1996.

10 Anon. 'Historic pact on gun reforms', *SMH*, 11 May 1996.

11 Anon. 'The people expect new gun laws' (editorial), *Weekend Australian* 22–23 June 1996: 20.

12 Anon. 'Deaths can't be in vain' (editorial), *SMH*, 10 May 1996.

13 Anon. 'Fair price for a peaceful society', *Sunday Telegraph*, 12 May 1996: 129.

14 Benson R. (Letter), *The Australian*, 18–19 May 1996: 20.

of a peculiarly paranoid obsession of the kind that has ugly manifestations in the United States.'[15]

- 'What baloney the shooters come up with. Are only the uneducated
  and crazed allowed to become members of the shooters' groups in
  Australia? Perhaps compulsory psychiatric tests are needed next?'[16]
- 'Vociferous cowboys . . . self-centred and besotted by gun-toting
  America . . .'[17]
- 'Extreme splinter groups whose frothing spokesmen have achieved
  notoriety in recent weeks.'[18]
- 'The arguments of the gun group have proved incontrovertibly
  that it is little more than a shelter for a sad collection of right-wing
  extremists.'[19]
- 'We are dealing with wilful children in grown-up bodies.'[20]
- 'The tiny minority who oppose tougher gun controls are able to
  exercise an influence out of all proportion to their numbers because
  some political parties have been prepared to pander to them in a
  sleazy quest for votes.'[21]
- 'Only a handful of gun lobbyists have attempted to defend the lunatic gun laws of Tasmania and Queensland . . . the puny gun lobby
  . . .'[22]

---

15 McGuinness PP. 'Fanatics cause discomfort for the Nationals', *The Age*, 8
June 1996: A23.

16 Gilchrist BR. 'Careless with the truth' (letter), *SMH*, 18 May 1996.

17 McMahon P. 'It's not Dodge City' (letter), *The Age*, 9 May: 14.

18 McGregor M. 'Blow to fading National force', *Australian Financial Review*,
17 June 1996.

19 Akerman P. 'Australia's despair has turned to hope', *Sunday Telegraph*, 12
May 1996: 129.

20 Finney J. (Letter), *SMH*, 5 June 1996.

21 Anon. 'Deaths can't be in vain' (editorial), *SMH*, 10 May 1996.

22 Akerman P. 'Blasting the myths of the gun lobby', *Sunday Telegraph*, 5 May
1996.

After a rally organised by the CGC on Saturday 4 May, the front-page headline of the *Sunday Telegraph* borrowed a phrase used by Professor Charles Watson at the rally: 'Gun crazy fools'.[23] All this was clearly too much for Brian Robson, director of the Victorian Field and Game Association, who defiantly told a Wodonga pro-gun meeting: 'We are not a minority group. We are a majority and we are very angry.'[24]

The gun lobby was astounded by the scope and unanimity of the Police Ministers' resolutions: 'We believed John Howard was flying a kite of draconian laws which would be watered down at the conference . . . Everybody assumed that responsible shooters and farmers were still going to have access to [semi-automatics].'[25] The SSAA claimed Howard had been 'grandstanding' as a tough leader to put himself in a good light for a double dissolution of both houses of parliament, so he could gain control of the Senate where his party lacked a majority. This prediction came to nothing. More than 12 months after the 10 May agreement, no double dissolution had been called. The SSAA claimed to have had 'politicians from all political parties expressing their disgust at what has happened here'.[26] Few were ever named.

In addition to the contempt directed at the gun lobby from the public, many people commented on the act of shooting, focusing on the thrill hunters get from killing: 'Sporting shooters kill for fun. Think of it: they actually *enjoy* killing, they *like* it!'[27] One shooter attempted to sanitise this aspect of shooting: 'A good hunter shouldn't get pleasure from the kill, just an element of satisfaction,'[28] an interesting distinction. The phallic shape of guns and the concept of guns as a means of expressing power, caused some to speculate unkindly that some gun owners

23 Larkin J. 'Gun crazy fools', *Sunday Telegraph*, 5 May 1996: 1.

24 Millett M, Wright T. 'Under fire', *SMH*, 22 June 1996: 35.

25 Wainwright R. 'We'll take to streets, say sporting shooters', *SMH*, 13 May 1996.

26 Rees P. 'Shooters call crisis talks', *Sunday Telegraph*, 12 May 1996: 8.

27 Mauntner T. 'A shooter's choice beyond cruelty' (letter), *The Age*, 6 June 1996: 16.

28 Nolan S. 'Against', *The Age*, 7 June 1996: A11.

cherished the gun as a means of sublimating sexual inadequacy. The *Sun Herald* – perhaps mischievously – included a large advertisement for an impotence clinic on the same page as its report on the Sydney shooters' rally.

Respectable, responsible shooters

The gun lobby was acutely aware of its redneck public image and constantly emphasised that its membership was diverse, intelligent and responsible. Tingle and Drane were articulate and highly plausible representatives, although Drane was easily provoked and frequently appeared to be only just suppressing his anger. When the SSAA brought Bob Corbin, president of the United States' National Rifle Association (NRA), to Australia in 1992, Drane had explained the visit as a public relations exercise to counter the gun lobby's image as 'a bunch of raving lunatics, subversives and right-wing fanatics'.[29] Defensively, he described Corbin as 'an extremely intelligent, articulate guy. He's not a redneck'.[30] In 1993 Drane told a journalist that through the SSAA's magazine, 'We belt the readers with ethics'.[31]

In defence of semi-automatics, a Tasmanian gun dealer told a reporter that people who bought these guns were 'respectable people . . . They are not untrustworthy people. They are professional people, high up in the business world. They're not Rambos or rough-heads'.[32] 'We [shooters] are such innocuous people. Really, no one could be more conservative than a shooter,' said one speaker at a gun rally.[33]

Some shooters were even prickly about having their guns described as 'weapons': '[They] keep referring to our sporting firearms as being "weapons" and the crowd reacted very strongly against that because

---

29 Bicknell J. 'Fears held over visit by US rifle club chief', *SMH*, 9 November 1992: 5.

30 O'Neill M. 'Other arms reach out . .', *The Bulletin*, 14 July 1992: 32–34.

31 Aiton D. 'Out for a duck', *The Sunday Age*, 21 March 1993: 4.

32 Hayes B. 'Rifles sold near Bryant's home', *SMH*, 10 May 1996.

33 Gora B. 'Protesters vow to keep fighting', *Sunday Telegraph*, 16 June 1996.

that's part of the stigmatisation that firearm owners is being forced upon them [sic]; said the Field and Game Association's Ian McLachlan.[34] In November 1996 National Party MP Peter Cochrane tried unsuccessfully in the NSW Parliament to have the *Firearms Act* amended so that guns would not be distastefully referred to as 'weapons' but as 'devices'.

At the NSW National Party Conference in June 1996, a delegate named Jim Looney told the assembled members, 'We all must remember that Australia was founded on guns, in the normal sense, and saved by the gun.'[35] ABC Radio commentator Mike Carlton had a wonderful time ridiculing Mr Looney's comment, speculating on how the Aboriginal community would react to his comments about the 'normal sense' of Australia being 'founded on guns.'

The NCGC took care to never besmirch gun owners as a general class. Philip Alpers, our New Zealand colleague, is a licensed shooter and I owned and regularly shot a .22 when growing up in the NSW country. We readily acknowledged that most gun owners were responsible and 'law-abiding'. This was not saying much, because the old gun laws demanded so little of them. Before Port Arthur, those who wanted guns but had no legitimate use for them could still buy and keep any number of weapons in most parts of Australia – and still be within the law. Anyone with an ordinary shooter's licence could legally own rapid-fire weaponry. In three states one could buy guns without giving notice of any kind to the police. This was 'law-abiding' behaviour.

Associated negative publicity

During the first few months of the debate several incidents unrelated to Port Arthur amplified the call for gun control. In early June it was reported that a blind man who had held a shooter's licence since 1987 took his pump-action shotgun to work and threatened to kill his

---

34 *7.30 Report* ABC TV 17 June 1996.

35 Aubert E. 'National MPs endorse federal move on gun laws', *Newcastle Herald*, 15 June 1996.

supervisor,[36] raising the obvious question: 'What was a blind man doing with a shooting licence?' Days later a licensed shooter with no history of mental illness, carrying a shotgun and a substantial amount of ammunition, held staff in a Melbourne suburban solicitor's office hostage before surrendering. Again, the media did not fail to make the connection: 'New laws will ban gun used in siege'.[37] And on the very day of the gun lobby's biggest rally against the new laws, yet another man ran amok with a pump-action shotgun in Darwin, shooting five people including four police. No one was killed, but the man was charged with seven counts of attempted murder.[38] The media nationwide ran the story of the Darwin shootings alongside the Melbourne gun rally story.

The gun lobby provided journalists with a constant supply of lurid copy that made a sinister contrast with the quiet, responsible, community-minded determination of people like John Howard and Daryl Williams. Members of the public, including ordinary reasonable shooters, often contacted the NCGC with tip-offs that we were happy to share with the media. For example, a suburban gun shop in Campsie, Sydney, featured in its window display a mannequin's head marked out with the concentric circles of a shooter's target, and we alerted a television crew to this valuable footage. A newspaper revealed that gun shops were selling videos explaining the best ways to kill with guns. One such video suggested which parts of the body to aim at, and the journalists noted, 'which is how Martin Bryant allegedly shot dead his 35 victims'. The same video reportedly counselled its viewers to act confused when questioned by police after a gun death.[39]

36 Donovan P. 'Blind man is placed on bond after shooting threat', *The Age*, 7 June 1996: 3.

37 Adams D, Costa G, Koutsoukis J. 'New laws will ban gun used in siege', *The Age*, 13 June 1996: A2.

38 Anon. 'Man charged in police shootings', *The Age*, 3 June 1996: A4; Anon. 'Gunman injures five in rampage', *Sunday Telegraph*, 2 June 1996: 5.

39 Anon. 'Guns summit just a start' (editorial), *Sun Herald*, 12 May 1996: 30;. Cumming F, Abbott G. 'Killer videos on sale', *Sun Herald*, 12 May 1996: 1, 3.

Three days after the Port Arthur massacre, the CGC alerted the media to the fact that in NSW – where military-style semi-automatic riles were already banned from sale – ammunition which could be used only in these weapons was freely available for as little as 20 cents a bullet. This received extensive coverage, and showed that the NSW Government had been half-hearted about the ban.[40]

An American mail order catalogue, *US Cavalry*, distributed from a Sydney suburban postal address, was sent to one of our colleagues presumably by a bulk mail house. The catalogue featured every conceivable accessory for gun lovers and those who like to dress up in military combat gear and play war games. It also invited mail orders for semi-automatic handguns that fired lead pellets. We also supplied this to the media.

The notorious backpacker serial killer, Ivan Milat, was tried for murder during the aftermath of the Port Arthur shootings. Extensive reportage was given to Milat's obsession with guns,[41] which added urgency to the argument that current laws allowed virtually anyone to own a gun. Sydney's largest gun shop, the Horsley Park Gun Shop, was found to have handled the sale of Ruger rifle parts found in Milat's home. By law, gun dealers are required to record full serial numbers of all guns they sell, plus the name and address of the purchaser and anyone selling them a gun second-hand. This requirement was intended to act as a de facto system of gun registration, at least for guns sold through licensed dealers. But it was found that the Horsley Park Gun Shop had not kept any such record and the shop was charged with more than 800 breaches of the law.[42]

---

40 Skelsey M. 'The tools of slaughter', *Daily Telegraph*, 2 May 1996: 4.

41 Curtin J. 'Milat liked guns, ex-wife tells court', *SMH*, 29 March 1996: 3.

42 Fife-Yeomans J. 'Milat's gun shop owner cited for 800 firearm register breaches', *The Australian*, 25–26 May 1996: 7.

The SSAA

The Sporting Shooters Association of Australia is the largest of the organisations that make up the gun lobby in Australia. In mid June 1996 it was said to have a national membership of 45,000 spread throughout 156 branches.[43] This meant that it was bigger than some trade unions, yet the membership figure represented less than 5% of the number of licensed shooters in Australia. Annual membership of the SSAA costs $45, yielding it an annual income from fees of $2,025,000. Annual returns for 1995 showed that the Victorian branch had $519,034 in assets, while Queensland had $1,031,249.[44]

Sections of the Australian gun lobby openly revere the powerful gun lobby in the United States. Before Port Arthur, the SSAA declared its ambition to become a clone of the National Rifle Association (NRA). Ted Drane told an NRA board meeting in the United States in April 1992: 'I believe we could not do any better than become the NRA of Australia.' He told *The Bulletin*, 'I love it,' when Australians linked him with the NRA. Drane said the NRA 'frightens the shit out of [US politicians]. We want to scare the shit out of them here too.'[45] In 1993, Drane returned to the US and boasted to an Australian journalist that he had been given a hotel room right next to the NRA's chief executive, Wayne LaPierre.[46]

NRA President Bob Corbin visited Australia and New Zealand in November 1992 at the invitation of the SSAA and the SSANZ. In his monthly column in *American Rifleman*, Corbin wrote:

> They're [the SSAA] now studying NRA and building an Australian Institute for Legislative Action. Modelled after our own NRA-ILA, the lobby will unite gun owners and shooters' groups throughout Australia and New Zealand to defend

---

43 'Thriving gun trade turns to dead stock', *The Age*, 17 June 1996: A4.

44 Ibid.

45 O'Neill M. 'Other arms reach out . . .', *The Bulletin*, July 14: 1992: 32–34.

46 Clark P. 'Mom, apple pie and guns', *SMH*, 28 April 1993: 19.

their rights as one united front. I'm ... proud to help with all the guidance and advice I can give them.'[47]

Corbin advised the SSAA to 'go after the anti-gun politicians. Get rid of them.'[48]

Inviting Bob Corbin to Australasia in 1992 was possibly the worst public relations mistake the local gun lobby ever made. Years later, many Australians still retain a vivid memory of this wild-eyed elderly American barking on current affairs programs: 'Guns made America free!' The very idea that the leader of the American NRA – the group dedicated to defeating even the most modest controls on gun ownership in a country besieged by gun violence – could visit Australia and avoid being lashed with 'Yankee go home!' anger showed how profoundly out of touch some local gun lobby leaders were.

In an effort to harness whenever possible, the powerful discourse about avoiding 'the American road' on guns, the NCGC reminded the public of the connection between the two gun lobbies. After Port Arthur, I debated Ted Drane on ABC Radio's *AM* program and introduced this dimension as early as possible. I also said that the NCGC had heard that the US NRA had offered to bankroll the formation of local branches of the SSAA in rural areas. Drane went apoplectic at this suggestion. I had struck a raw nerve.

One of the most important routine tasks in advocacy is to maintain a file of instances where your opposition has said or written something that could be strategically useful in particular debates. The NCGC keeps numerous examples from gun lobby literature such as magazines and pamphlets, and quotes obtained from the mainstream media. The worst examples of gun lobby venom are received almost daily via email.

One such example occurred on the ABC's *Lateline*, screened on 16 November 1992, when two senior members of the SSAA made frank admissions about their organisation's relationship with the NRA. We reviewed the tape of the program on 9 May 1996, the day before the

---

47 Corbin R. 'The President's Column', *American Rifleman* February 1993: 50
48 Lewis J. 'Aust. gun lobby told to toughen up', *SMH*, 27 November 1992: 15.

Police Ministers' meeting, and issued a press release resurrecting some of the most damaging quotes (see below). We knew that the next day's press would contain full-page advertisements calling for donations to the SSAA. Our press release alerted journalists to the ads and to the NRA's proposal to bankroll the SSAA.

> *Keith Tidswell (SSA):* 'We don't differ a lot from the NRA (US National Rifle Association) at all. In fact we're very close in terms of our overall philosophy. The only differences might be in the way in which we are structured.'

> *Kerry O'Brien (Lateline host):* 'On what basis did you accept money from the NRA's political action arm, the Institute for Legislative Action?'

> *Ted Drane (SSA):* 'On the basis that they offered it to us. They offer it to us, we'll take it. And I'll ask for more and if they give it, that'll be great.'

O'Brien asks then, how much?

> *Ted Drane:* 'They [people] can guess whatever they like. They can make it 250, 300, 4 [hundred thousand] . . . whatever they like.'

Drane maintained his coyness until at least June 1993 when he told *The Sunday Age*, 'We did ask and we did receive. It's specific. They don't care what we do with it but they know what we're going to do.'[49] Drane has since claimed that the NRA gave the SSAA only $20,000.[50] Never in the entire debate did anyone in the SSAA repudiate the relationship with the NRA.

The Shooters' Party

Urbane radio announcer John Tingle and six friends from his pistol club formed the Shooters' Party in June 1992. It contested its first

---

49 Debelle P. 'Brothers in arms', *The Sunday Age*, 26 June 1993: 20.

50 Gibson R, Chamberlain P. 'Wheeling out the big guns', *The Age*, 11 May 1996: A20–1.

election in 1993, gaining 1.8% of the vote and exchanging preferences with the Australians Against Further Immigration Party. Tingle told the *Sydney Morning Herald* that the party was 'a grievance party for people pushed around by governments and told what they can't do.'[51] It had no electoral success until Tingle himself stood as a candidate and scraped into the Upper House of the NSW Parliament, the Legislative Council, in March 1995. Apart from being a symbolic triumph, his election gave the gun lobby a significant practical advantage: henceforth the NSW taxpayers, who overwhelmingly supported tighter gun laws, were obliged to fund his campaign against gun control. In addition, the tight numbers in the Upper House gave Tingle a disproportionate amount of voting power. Soon after his election it became clear that the Labor Government was doing deals: in return for his support on other legislation, the Government had apparently agreed to take no positive action on gun control (See Chapter 3). As a Member of the Legislative Council, Tingle was elected for a term of eight years. If the Port Arthur massacre had not occurred, NSW might have continued to block the push for national uniform gun laws into the next century. Tingle's media skills and status as a politician made him one of the gun lobby's most prominent spokespeople. The letters editor of the *Sydney Morning Herald* noted in her summary of the first week's massive mail on the massacre, 'Not surprisingly, one politician was singled out for special mention – John Tingle of the Shooters' Party.'[52]

As discussed later in this chapter, the Australian gun lobby is bitterly divided, apparently due to personality clashes as much as to disagreements on policy and strategy. The Shooters' Party shared many policy directions with the SSAA, but made a much greater effort to appear reasonable and moderate in the debate after Port Arthur. By cultivating this moderate image, Tingle presented himself as a more mercurial and reasoned opponent than Ted Drane and the SSAA, whose routine

---

51 Loane S. 'They're Shooters' Party men, and they're going to war', *SMH*, 4 March 1995: 7.

52 Walsh G. 'Postscript', *SMH*, 6 May 1996: 14.

outbreaks of anger and incitement to shooters to hold onto their guns contrasted starkly with their claim to be peaceful, law-abiding citizens.

Angling for support from an outraged community, Tingle claimed to have criticised the Tasmanian gun laws as a national disgrace. In a letter to a newspaper he stated that he did 'not believe civilians need a fully automatic firearm; and I do not support military firearms in the civilian population.'[53] This statement seemed to contradict his admission in 1993 that he belonged to a military rifle club.[54] And fully automatic firearms had long been banned throughout Australia except for bona fide 'collectors', so Tingle was flying a kite for a position that was not even under debate. Tingle claimed to agree that some law reforms were needed, but he objected to every major element in the APMC agreement. He refused to admit there was any benefit in national uniformity, railed against firearm registration, and predicted mass flouting of the ban on semi-automatics. In fact, he declined to nominate which main gun law reforms he would support, insisting that the solution lay in harsher penalties for offenders.

Ian McNiven and the Firearm Owners' Association of Australia

On 15 May 1996 a significant development in the debate occurred in the Queensland town of Gympie. One of the lesser-known enclaves of the gun lobby, the Firearm Owners' Association of Australia (FOAA), held a meeting in the town's bowling club. Among those who addressed the meeting of about 200 were the vice-president and president of the FOAA in Queensland: Ian McNiven, a ruddy-faced electrician; and Ron Owen, a portly Gympie gun dealer and publisher of the extreme pro-gun magazine *Lock, Stock and Barrel*. In what became one of the most repeated news items of the debate, McNiven blustered in front of the TV cameras:

---

53 Tingle J. 'Don't blame me' (letter), *SMH*, 9 May 1996: 14.

54 Palladino T. 'Men of calibre. John Tingle', *Guns Australia*, January/February 1993: 60–61.

> You can send a message all the way down to Canberra to that
> sawn-off little dickhead Jackboot Johnny . . . The only cur-
> rency that you can purchase freedom back with is blood. I
> know that you're [the meeting] a bit angry about this shit.
> You're a bit pissed off. Well I can assure you I haven't calmed
> down yet. I'm still wild![55]

McNiven provided a hint of theatrical menace two days before
when he said on *Today Tonight*: 'I would point out to Mr Howard and
his Liberal ministers that we also know where they live.'[56]

In the March 1996 federal elections, McNiven had stood for the
Senate as number one on a ticket of three candidates for a party called
The Constitutionalists. Between them they attracted 152 votes, McNiven
himself getting all of 121 votes. This was the man who now threatened
to 'purge our Parliament' of left-wing traitors.[57] McNiven's appearance on television after the Gympie meeting unintentionally gave the
gun control lobby one of the most enduring and damaging images of
our opponents. If 'the gun lobby' had previously conveyed something
vaguely sinister and obsessive to many Australians, here now were two
men who embodied it.

McNiven was a glutton for media attention and made himself available for dozens of interviews. Several feature articles were written about
him and other extremists.[58] Politicians repeatedly commented that his
performance had destroyed much of the gun lobby's credibility. The
Sydney Morning Herald published eight scathing letters under the title
'Gun lobby proves PM's point'. One joked that Drane and Tingle must
have hired actors to play rabid shooters at Gympie to make the SSAA
and the Shooters' Party look moderate;[59] several made the point that the

---

55 *TV News* Channel 7, 15 May 1996.

56 *Today Tonight* Channel 7, 13 May 1996.

57 Chan G. 'Gun lobbyist stood for Senate', *The Australian*, 18–19 May 1996: 2.

58 For example: Roberts G. 'Pineapple extremists arm for freedom', *SMH*, 25
May 1996: 37.

59 Wong W. 'Gun lobby proves PM's point' (letter), *SMH*, 18 May 1996.

Gympie performance 'convinced the peaceful majority that these are exactly the type of people that should not be bearing arms'.[60]

- 'Having just read the manic ravings of Mr Owen and Mr McNiven . . . I'm convinced the only gun I'd feel safe with in their hands is a water pistol.'[61]

- 'It has flushed out some of the mega-nutters who make up the gun lobby.'[62]

- '. . . there are some real ratbags out there, like Mr Ian McNiven, vice-president of the Firearm Owners Association, which is headquartered, you will not be surprised to learn, in darkest Queensland.'[63]

- 'A couple of rounds short of a full magazine.' (description of Ian McNiven)[64]

- 'After watching highlights from the Firearm Owners Association's Gympie rally, I'm no longer sure [the film Deliverance] wasn't a documentary.'[65]

Journalist Richard Glover's analysis was particularly penetrating:

> That's what's alarming about Gympie: it revealed the way that those who care deeply about guns also have a world-view that's startlingly unhinged . . . the gun is central – these are people who define the removal of their guns as the removal of a central part of themselves. The gun is a prop to their personality and they see themselves dissolving without it. It's a crutch without which they cannot walk as men . . . It was all there – a textbook lesson in the features of the socially inadequate: the pathological fear of community, the anger at

---

60 Ellis G. 'Gun lobby proves PM's point' (letter), *SMH*, 18 May 1996.
61 Breeze BH. 'Killing animals for sport' (letter), *SMH*, 24 May 1996: 14.
62 Carlton M. 'Mike Carlton' (column), *SMH*, 11 May 1996.
63 Ibid.
64 Carpenter B. 'Gun lobby proves PM's point' (letter), *SMH*, 18 May 1996.
65 Fleming T. 'Alive and well' (letter), *SMH*, 5 June 1996.

authority, the tendency to talk about blood and violence as the proper response when you don't get your own way . . . And yet these are the people who ask us to believe than the gun lobby has different values [from mass killers] . . . They remind us that the more sick passion these people show, the less we should budge. Every cry that their very soul has been removed is proof of their weirdness.[66]

A few days after the Port Arthur massacre, McNiven debated Rebecca Peters on Channel 7's *Today Tonight* program. After a combative few minutes the pre-recorded segment ended and McNiven, who was in a Queensland studio, said to the film crew, 'If I were married to Rebecca Peters I'd probably commit domestic violence too.' The recording had officially ended, but Peters and the program's host, Helen Wellings, heard the remark clearly down their lines. Most of his words were still being recorded on sound tape. Several weeks later, after McNiven's notoriety ballooned due to his 'purchase freedom back [with] blood' remark, the program brought Rebecca back to the studio and replayed the sound tape of McNiven's remark.

In a truly remarkable incident, McNiven poured petrol on the fire of community speculation that some gun lovers were sublimating some form of sexual inadequacy or anxiety into their love of guns. In June two Federal Police visited him at his home. Afterwards, live on Sky TV, he said he believed the police were trespassing and that he was entitled to use his gun 'to defend my family'. Asked if he was armed, he replied:

No – I was in my pyjamas. The only weapon I had with me was my short arm, which was my stalk, and the gentlemen said to me that they would tell everyone that they'd seen me in my pyjamas. So that incensed me somewhat. So I climbed up on the verandah rail and dropped my pyjamas and shouted at them, 'I don't care if you tell everyone in the world I've got a small dick.' It was pretty small at the time because all the fear and harassment had shrunk it back to nothing.

66 Glover R. 'Unhinged and unbelievable', *SMH*, 18 May 1996: 30.

Other media reported the story,[67] which was repeated widely by bemused Australians.

McNiven's bizarre theories – delivered in interviews without a hint of leg-pulling – included his belief that Australians had a right to bear arms 'guaranteed to us in law by the English Bill of Rights 1688 that's part of Queensland's law.' He also urged shooters to refuse to accept Australian currency when handing in their guns, and accept only gold. He argued that Australian currency was somehow not legal tender. These crackpot views just kept on coming.

There was considerable debate over the way the media's fascination with people like McNiven gave them exposure completely out of proportion to their numbers in the community. McNiven and his type were obviously seen by many journalists as wonderful copy – people who unselfconsciously linked gun control advocacy with every silly theory about homosexuals, Zionist world conspiracies, Asian invaders, and the British monarchy. All that was missing was defence against UFOs.

Many people urged the NCGC to try to persuade journalists to stop covering these extremist views. Others wrote to newspapers urging them to show 'moral responsibility' by refusing to give them coverage.[68]

> The intense media debate . . . has unintentionally provided the gun lobby with a credibility it neither deserves nor has. While breath-taking to see in print, the impertinent nonsense incanted by Messrs Drane and Tingle, none of which bears repeating, their mere reportage in a journal of record delivers a status and forum not otherwise available . . .[69]

To some extent we shared this concern. The continuing media focus on McNiven and his ilk certainly created extra work for us, and for the politicians and public servants who were trying to make the new gun laws happen. In addition, the NCGC has always opposed fear-mongering, and several members of the public told us they felt afraid

---

67 Anon. 'Stay in touch', *SMH*, 17 June 1996: 24.
68 Walsh G. 'Postscript', *SMH*, 20 May 1996: 14.
69 Watson B. (Letter), *SMH*, 9 May 1996: 14.

to speak out in support of gun control lest they attract the attention of unhinged gun-nuts like those they had seen on television. We were also conscious that somewhere in Australia there could be an individual who might take McNiven's call to arms too much to heart, and might fantasise about being the hero in a real-life violent tableau. On the other hand, McNiven and his friends had greatly boosted the cause of gun control by becoming the gun lobby's public faces. McNiven's foot-in-mouth disease caused more outrage about the gun lobby than we might ever have hoped to generate ourselves.

Others in the gun lobby were plainly horrified at the damage McNiven was inflicting on their efforts to portray gun owners as decent, moderate people. John Tingle referred to the FOAA as the 'fulminating fruitcakes from the North'. A Queensland politician said the publicity surrounding the Gympie meeting had 'knocked the stuffing out of our case' (to water down the new gun laws). The SSAA stated: 'We completely dissociate ourselves from these people. They are doing a great deal of damage to our cause.'[70] Bob Katter Jr, who strongly opposed the new gun control proposals, said the 'extremist right-wing' views of McNiven and Owen 'make me sick . . . That fellow is . . . part of a disruptive element that does not reflect mainstream views.'[71]

Other extreme groups such as the Christian Patriots Association, Christians Speaking Out, the Home Security Association, the Australian Right to Bear Arms Association (all from the Queensland Sunshine Coast area), the Confederate Action Party, the Canberra-based Loyal Regiment of Australian Guardians and the AUSI (Australians United for Survival of Individual) Freedom Scouts were covered in articles about extremist gun groups in Australia,[72] as were the gun lobby's links with far right-wing anti-Semitic and anti-immigration groups.[73] On 4 June the Deputy Prime Minister, Tim Fischer, asserted that sections of the Australian gun lobby had been infiltrated by supporters of the

---

70 Roberts G. 'Pineapple extremists arm for freedom', *SMH*, 25 May 1996: 37.

71 Lamperd R. 'Fortress Katter', *Daily Telegraph*, 7 June 1996.

72 Roberts G. 'Pineapple extremists arm for freedom', *SMH*, 25 May 1996: 37.

73 Button J. 'Gun ho', *The Age*, 11 June 1996: A11.

anti-Semitic, anti-British, pro-gun American Lyndon H. LaRouche.[74] A *Sydney Morning Herald* report was captioned 'America's best-known political psychopath'.

Letter bombs and threats

In June 1996, several anonymous threats were made to at least four politicians in the form of letters, crude 'letter bombs' (a parcel containing pre-detonated cartridges) and white feathers marked with black dots – wartime symbols for cowardice.[75] The Federal Member for the Queensland seat of Groom told Parliament: 'I had two meetings in my electorate last week involving over a thousand people . . . After one of the meetings I was physically threatened and told, 'We would like to shoot you, Mr Taylor.'[76] These incidents dug the gun lobby further into the deep hole that McNiven had opened with his 'blood in the streets' remark.

Gun dealers

Gun dealers have always been a central part of the gun lobby. It is they, along with the importers, who stand to profit most from the free availability of firearms. Before the Police Ministers' agreement, some gun dealers proclaimed that a ban on semi-automatic weapons would be disastrous for their businesses. The usual hyperbole was paraded with one shop owner proclaiming: 'Come Monday morning gun shops will be left with only 10 per cent of their business.'[77] Another said: 'If we go

---

74 Wright T. 'Extremist plants in gun lobby: Fischer', *SMH*, 4 June 1996: 1; Attwood A. 'Poisoned political seed finds its ground', *SMH*, 5 June 1996: 9; Hogarth M. 'Fischer fingers bizarre world of conspiracies', *SMH*, 5 June 1996: 9.

75 English B. 'Gun fanatics send "letter bomb" to MP', *Daily Telegraph*, 15 June 1996; Loane S. 'Extremists white feather taunts fail to intimidate MPs', *SMH*, 15 June 1996.

76 Australian House of Representatives *Hansard* for 17 June 1996. Grievance debate: gun control.

77 Delvecchio J, Lamont L, Byrne A. 'Traders fear they may go broke', *SMH*,

on what John Howard said last night, he has banned every single rifle in this shop.'[78]

But some dealers took a radically different line. Serge Zampatti, a Sydney suburban dealer, told the *Sydney Morning Herald* he believed the ban on semi-automatics was 'long overdue' and would have 'little economic effect on the industry'. He claimed the industry had 'been in decline for at least 30 years, and most shops in NSW sell very few of the weapons which will be banned'. Zampatti stated that 'you would be lucky if you get two dealers who would agree on anything' and that the industry's decline was partly because 'kids tend to play computer games nowadays, which is probably a lot safer'.[79]

In fact, once the buyback of prohibited weapons began, the media carried stories of dealers crowing about a boom in business, claiming that shooters surrendering semi-automatics were replacing them with bolt-action rifles. The dealers claimed these extra sales proved the new gun laws were a failure, since the total number of guns in the community would not decrease. Like most gun lobby claims, this one was not backed up by the evidence. For example, the Victorian buyback brought in 130,000 semi-automatics in its first six months. In that period, some 23,000 new guns of all types were sold. However, since normal sales in that period would have been around 15,000, it seems that about 8,000 additional non-semi-automatic guns had been bought, making the net reduction of rapid-fire weapons more like 122,000. It was difficult to see this as anything other than a huge success. In any case, the APMC agreement included provision for compensating dealers for loss of business, and there was no shortage of dealers queuing up for their cheques.

---

10 May 1996.

78 Creer K. 'Clampdown "may shut gunshop doors"', *Sunday Telegraph*, 12 May 1996.

79 Wainwright R. 'Fading trade to lose little from ban', *SMH*, 13 May 1996.

Divide and rule

An old Australian expression says 'if it walks like a duck, sounds like a duck and looks like a duck, it must be a duck.' In other words, loudly proclaimed differences between similar interest groups or individuals are usually unimportant. This became a strategic axiom in the gun control debate. Like most areas of right and left wing politics, the gun lobby in Australia consists of several sometimes bitterly opposed factions. In several cases, the animosity between these groups severely reduced their ability to cooperate during the Port Arthur campaign.

Few Australians would be interested in the often technical policy difference between groups who were nevertheless united in their opposition to the core elements of the Police Ministers' agreement. The NCGC sought to exploit the public's indifference to such technical disparities, and many times various gun lobbyists wasted media opportunities by spending time attempting to differentiate themselves from the other groups. The public probably couldn't have cared less: a gun lobbyist was a gun lobbyist.

Shooters' Party leader John Tingle, in two letters published in the Sydney *Daily Telegraph*, protested at being 'unfairly blamed' for Port Arthur: 'If I am demonised, I ask only that it be for what I might have done, not for what somebody beyond my control has done.' In these letters he disavowed the NRA's slogan 'Guns don't kill people. People kill people.' Declaring the slogan 'ludicrous and offensive', he wrote that it had been 'taken up by a large shooting organisation in Australia. Not by us . . . We have a resolution on our books, directing our committee to decline any involvement with the NRA.'[80] He was referring to the SSAA.

Graeme Campbell

The right-wing Independent member for the Western Australian mining town of Kalgoorlie, Graeme Campbell, was the only federal politician who spoke out publicly against the proposed gun laws before the 10 May Police Ministers' meeting. Campbell blasted away at the

---

80 Tingle J. 'Targeting semi-automatics' (letter), *Daily Telegraph*, 8 May 1996.

'smug, sickening bipartisanship', calling the move a 'populist, knee-jerk reaction'. He added: 'That rifle hanging on the wall of the working-class flat or labourer's cottage is a symbol of democracy. It is our job to see that it stays there.'[81] Campbell became for the gun lobby 'their man in Canberra'. The *Sydney Morning Herald* prophesied: 'Do not imagine Graeme Campbell is alone among Federal MPs prepared to rationalise the means of mass murder. He is just the only one prepared, for the moment, to do so aloud.'[82]

The media put the spotlight on MPs who were known to be gun lobby supporters – who were 'sleeping with the enemy'. On the weekend after the Police Ministers' meeting, Queensland National Party MP De-Anne Kelly was questioned about officiating at the opening of a shooting competition for weapons 'similar to those used in the Port Arthur massacre'.[83] Mrs Kelly responded that the event's organisers 'had arranged for flags to fly half-mast in memory of the Port Arthur victims'.

Queensland National Party backbencher Bob Katter Jr. – constantly described as a 'maverick' – openly supported the gun lobby and became the subject of intense criticism from his party's leaders, who alluded to disciplinary action.[84] Katter described his home to journalists:

> If you come to see my house it's built like a fortress. You retreat through one set of locked doors and another set of locked doors and another set of locked doors and there's a siren and three locks on the door and every bed has a rifle, so if we're out and the kids are at home they can protect themselves. To leave my wife and kids unprotected because I'm away is absolutely appalling. I believe in it as an article of religious faith . . . I'm just the epitome of people who feel strongly about guns.[85]

---

81 Australian House of Representatives *Hansard* for 9 May 1996.

82 Anon. 'Campbell's lone stand in the Parliament', *SMH*, 11 May 1996: 37.

83 Roberts G. 'MP to open shooting contest', *SMH*, 10 May 1996.

84 Nason D, Taylor L, Emerson S. 'Whelan casts doubt on quick gun agreement', *The Australian*, 12 June 1996.

85 Lamperd R. 'Fortress Katter', *Daily Telegraph*, 7 June 1996.

Since Katter's son-in-law was the manager of Queensland's largest firearms importer, Nioa Trading, Katter's participation in public debate on gun control was somewhat compromised.

New political parties

With the unanimous endorsement of the proposed laws by the Police Ministers and the national bipartisanship immediately proclaimed on the issue, the gun lobby's much-flaunted political power disintegrated suddenly and unceremoniously. At the time, I commented that 'the gun lobby have been reduced to political eunuchs'.[86] The lobby's main form of political leverage – threatening candidates supporting gun control by urging shooters to votes for other candidates – was made obsolete by the bipartisan support for gun control which Port Arthur had established. No longer could one candidate be played off against another. Henceforth, the gun lobby's only political hopes lay in breaking down the bipartisan agreement, or in directly entering the political process by establishing its own political parties. This had been the Shooters' Party's strategy since its formation. After the parliamentary vote in NSW, John Tingle admitted in his column in *Guns Australia*, 'The Shooters' Party cannot make any headway in making any changes to this legislation while anti-gun proposals have bipartisan support.'[87]

Two political parties overtly sympathetic to guns were formed just after Port Arthur. At a pro-gun rally in Hobart on 23 June, the formation of the Australia First Reform Party was announced, with the SSAA's Ted Drane and the Western Australian Independent MP Graeme Campbell as its co-founders.[88] Whether coincidentally or otherwise, 'Australia First' had also been the name of an anti-Semitic, white supremacist group during World War II. One journalist wondered

---

86 Delvecchio J. 'Violation of civil rights, claims shooters' group', *SMH*, 11 May 1996.

87 Tingle J. 'An act of betrayal', *Guns Australia* September/October 1996: 65.

88 Grattan M, Watkins S. 'Pro-gun party accused of following US path', *The Age*, 24 June 1996: A2.

whether Campbell had chosen the same name in the hope that 'a whole lot of cranks and nuts and bigots and eccentrics will be attracted to his new organisation'.[89] Drane visited Pauline Hanson – the Queensland Independent MP who had drawn controversy over her views on immigration and Aborigines and whose party, in June 1998, was to attract nearly one in four votes throughout Queensland in the state election – in an unsuccessful attempt to convince her to join him and Campbell in the new party.[90]

The first branch of the new party was launched at Victoria's Rowville Football Club near Dandenong on 1 July 1996. An ABC radio *Background Briefing* program revealed the political sophistication of the new party officials: [91]

> *Emma Martin:* I'm Emma Martin. I have been recently elected by the committee, the Knox branch committee, as the spokesperson for the Australia First Reform Party, Knox branch.
>
> *Andrew Dodd (interviewer):* And what will that entail?
>
> *Emma Martin:* Secretarial duties I imagine, and you know, being up front and answering any questions that people may have about the group.
>
> *Andrew Dodd:* I notice here you have some notes in front of you where it says very clearly that you're not a racist, you wanted to get that across to the media.
>
> *Emma Martin:* Well I come from a multicultural background and I know one of the issues is immigration, and I mean my background is both English and southern European, and I just think it's very important that we're not seen as being a racist group. Employment is one of our main concerns, and

89 Oakes L. 'Campbell cranks up his separatist bandwagon', *The Bulletin*, 11 June 1996: 35.

90 'Stalking Ted', *Background Briefing* transcript. ABC Radio National, 21 July 1996.

91 Ibid.

we believe that once we've got employment under control, well then immigration will not be a problem.

Andrew Dodd: But there's no difference between that policy and the policy that is espoused by Australians Against Further Immigration, because that's exactly their line as well.

Emma Martin: Right. To begin with, I'm not strong on politics, I'm not strong on the policies of other groups. Ted is the best person you should speak to about our policies.

Andrew Dodd: But you're the spokesperson for the party.

Emma Martin: And I am learning.

But the unity in this new 'force' in Australian politics did not last long. Just over two weeks after the announcement of the new party, Drane was due to meet Campbell to discuss its development. Drane suspected that Campbell had invited members of the racist League of Rights to the meeting:

Andrew Dodd: This is the end of the alliance with Graeme Campbell then?

Ted Drane: Well it's looking that way, yes, it's looking that way. I won't have anything to do with the League of Rights at all. And I understand that this meeting that was planned for Canberra on Saturday has some members of the League of Rights at it, and I won't be involved in any way at all with the League of Rights.

In a speech at the National Press Club on 10 July, where he criticised Victorian Premier Jeff Kennett for 'shaking hands with the gay community', Drane confirmed that he was no longer planning to join with Campbell's Australia First Party because it was too racist and sought alliances with right-wing interests in the US.[92] Drane must have been the last person in Australia to become aware of Campbell's right-wing leanings. Campbell had openly teamed up with an anti-immigration group to contest the March 1996 federal election. His announcement

---

92 Middleton K. 'New party takes swipe at Kennett', *The Age*, 11 July 1996: A8.

that he planned to form the party was enthusiastically welcomed by the ultra-right-wing League of Rights.[93] John Tingle, who had shared a rally platform with Drane at the Sydney pro-gun rally, disassociated himself from both Campbell's and Drane's parties, saying they were 'too far to the right'.[94]

Within three months of Port Arthur, the gun lobby's much-vaunted 'new force' in politics had splintered into the old enmities, with no less than three political parties now on offer to disgruntled shooters: Tingle's Shooters' Party, Drane's Australian Reform Party and Campbell's Australia First Party. In mid July Drane claimed his as-yet-unregistered Australian Reform Party was receiving 'three or four hundred registrations a day'.[95] Campbell later estimated the total membership attracted to his new party at 'between 2,000 and 5,000'.[96]

Early electoral tests

What should we make of the movement to other gun lobby political parties? Before the Port Arthur shootings, the Shooters' Party had contested one state and two federal elections. At the March 1996 federal poll, confident after John Tingle's election in NSW, the Shooters' Party ran candidates in four states. But despite being organised for four years, having a formidable recruiting infrastructure through gun shops and clubs, and with the media-savvy Tingle as leader, the party polled just 114,724 votes across the country. In Queensland, home of the redoubtable Ian McNiven, it polled a resounding 0.63% of the primary vote. If we were to generously double this number, this would amount to 230,000 people who believed owning a weapon like those used by Martin Bryant was more important than all other political considerations when they voted. Across Australia, this would not give the Shooters' Party a squint at one Senate seat.

---

93 Savva N. 'Gun party gets rightist support', *The Age*, 4 June 1996: 3.

94 Middleton K. 'New party takes swipe at Kennett', *The Age*, 11 July 1996: A8.

95 Ibid.

96 Walsh K-A. 'Party unfaithful', *The Bulletin*, 17 September 1996: 16–17.

In late May, a month after the massacre, by-elections were held for two NSW state seats – the north coast seat of Clarence, and the central western seat of Orange. In both cases a 13% swing was recorded against the sitting National Party member. In Clarence this gave the seat to the Labor Party. The gun lobby attempted to capitalise on this, claiming that the swing against the National Party was a backlash against the party's 'betrayal' of shooters. But this was quickly revealed as arrant nonsense: editors of local newspapers told the media that guns had barely been mentioned in local debate and, in any case, attempts to punish the National Party electorally would only deliver votes to Labor – which also supported the new gun laws.[97]

The gun lobby's first real electoral test came in a by-election in Queensland in October 1996 in the suburban Brisbane seat of Lytton. Wendy Kelly ran for the Shooters' Party and received 750 votes, or 3.74%. Also in October, a by-election was held for the federal seat of Lindsay in Sydney's predominantly working-class Penrith area, said to be one of the heartlands of the Shooters' Party. The Liberal Party won comfortably with a swing of 6.1%. The Shooters' Party candidate received 1,865 votes, just 2.91%.[98] The party fared slightly better in the Port Macquarie by-election on 30 November 1996, when its candidate polled 2,528 votes (6.73%). State MLC John Tingle lives in the Port Macquarie area, on the NSW mid-north coast, and could have bolstered the vote for the local candidate.

In the West Gippsland Victorian state by-election in February 1997, candidates stood for the Shooters' Party and Ted Drane's Australian Reform Party. Together, both parties polled nearly 15% of the primary vote. This was not enough for either of them to win the seat, but their preferences directed to another independent candidate helped oust the sitting government member. Drane talked up the vote's importance to the shooting parties, claiming it bode well for a future attempt at a Senate

---

97 Goot M. 'Guns fail as election issue', *Australian Financial Review*, 11 June 1996.

98 Kitney G. 'Battered Labor must have finally got the message', *SMH*, 21 October 1996: 4.

seat. But if 15% was all the shooters could attract in their rural heartland, the hope of such a result statewide was pure fantasy. Support for shooting parties in the Melbourne area showed no signs of reaching this level. In May 1997, a Shooters' Party candidate obtained only 1.9% of the vote in the Queensland Kurwongbah by-election. In October 1997, the pro-gun Australia First Party polled only 7,764 votes out of 786,213 (0.99%) cast for seats in the South Australian Legislative Council.

The consistently poor electoral showing of Australian shooters was nothing compared to the fate of their equivalents in the UK. One of the UK's pro-gun leaders, Mike Yardley, ran a high-profile campaign against the anti-hand gun Tory MP David Mellor in the London seat of Putney in the UK's general election in May. Yardley, who had drawn huge publicity over his views in the wake of the Dunblane massacre and the British Government's subsequent introduction of tougher handgun laws, received only 90 votes, 11 less than the candidate from the anarchic Freedom to Party Party.[99]

One Nation in Queensland

The Queensland state elections held on 13 June 1998 saw nearly one in four voters voting for the ultra-nationalist, racist, anti-Aboriginal land claims, economic protectionist One Nation Party led by Pauline Hanson. Since the formation of the party in 1997, Hanson and her advisors had courted every disaffected, anti-government cause in the country. They wooed the shooting vote by promising to work to repeal the new gun laws, and parroting the SSAA line that 'Measures to control and apprehend those who illegally or irresponsibly use firearms are not to be used as tools to obstruct, harass or penalise legitimate, law-abiding firearm owners.' As the election neared, the SSAA declared its national backing for Hanson's policy on guns and vowed to spend 'thousands' backing her candidates at the upcoming Queensland state election[100].

---

99 http://www.bbc.co.uk/election97/constituencies/468.htm [no longer active, 2013].

100 Porteous C. 'Hanson sets sights on gun club support', *Melbourne Herald-Sun*, 19 May 1998.

One Nation's momentous vote was widely analysed as having attracted the support of many of Queensland's elderly, rural, proudly parochial, Royal Family loving and minimally educated voters who were attracted by Hanson's vacuous slogans and economically illiterate prescriptions – such as establishing a bank that would peg interest rates at 2%. Appropriately, one of the party's successful candidates, Ken Turner, was described as having made his claim to public office based 'on his nine-year reign as Santa Claus at a major local shopping centre.'[101] On the day after One Nation's victory, the harridan Hanson named pro-gun law reform as her party's first priority in the new Queensland government,[102] along with her ambition to replicate her support at the federal level. As I finish writing this book, this ambition remains to be tested, but such has been the success of Hanson's drive into the comfort zone of two party Australian politics, that it would be cavalier to predict her success.

What part did shooters play in One Nation's success in Queensland? Anyone wanting to argue that the pro-gun vote was a major factor in One Nation's showing needs to explain the abject failures of shooting candidates in all by-elections held in four states including in Queensland. All these were held closer to the passing of the new guns laws than the Queensland election. What coherent argument could explain lack of shooter electoral backlash lasting two years, and then its sudden revival? Were the nation's shooters somehow too stunned to vote for their representatives for two years? A far more plausible explanation is that Hanson's pro-gun policy was just one facet of her broad anti-government, Australia right-or-wrong sentiment that struck a chord with that section of the community hurting and disillusioned by the false gods of economic rationalism. The gun lobby will doubtless rush to translate her success as being largely a product of their efforts.

---

101 'One Nation winner', *SMH*, 15 June 1998: 4.

102 Kingston M. 'Fischer's nightmare sitting in a chintz chair', *SMH*, 15 June 1998: 4.

Talking up and talking down

After the historic agreement by the Police Ministers, gun lobby chest-beating predictably turned to talk of the vast sums that would be needed to buy back semi-automatics: 'We're talking about a billion dollars to buy them back,' said Ted Drane.[103] Throughout the gun control debate, the gun lobby made extravagant claims without any attempt to prove their veracity. Big figure cliams concerned:

- The number of gun owners in the community
- The number of guns in their possession
- The number of semi-automatics owned
- The dollar value of guns to be compensated
- The number of people the gun lobby claimed to represent and who would vote for it in an electoral showdown
- The number of supporters attending pro-gun rallies
- The amount of money the gun lobby would raise from its supporters to fight the new laws.

How many shooters?

It was plainly in the gun lobby's interest to promote the view that large numbers of Australians own guns. Gun owners can be licensed or unlicensed. Of course, there are no records of unlicensed shooters. Licensed shooters can be readily counted from the records of government licensing authorities. Table 5.1 shows a recent tally showing the approximate number licensed in each Australian state and territory.

The President of the Cessnock branch of the Shooters' Party claimed that 'only 36% of the town's gun owners were registered'[104] (presumably meaning licensed). How did he know this? We were never told.

---

103 Drane T. *7.30 Report*, ABC TV, 9 May 1996.
104 Hoy A. '7,000 shooters take aim at anti-gun plans', *SMH*, 27 May 1996: 2.

Table 5.1: Licensed shooters in Australia[105] (June 1995)

State	Shooters' licences	Population (million)	Licensing rate
NSW	150,000	6.115	1: 40.8
Vic	272,000	4.502	1: 17.3
Qld	302,000	3.277	1: 11.7
SA	125,000	1.474	1: 11.8
WA	110,000	1.732	1: 15.7
Tas	60,000	0.473	1: 7.9
NT	20,480	0.174	1: 8.5
ACT	7,451	0.304	1: 40.8
Total	1,046,931	18.051	1: 17.24

As of June 1995, there were an estimated 13,433,680 adults aged 18 and over in Australia, of whom about half were males. Most gun owners are men. A *Sporting Shooter* editorial titled 'A man and his gun', ruminated that gun owners 'are a peculiar mob. You see, most will quite contentedly plonk themselves down after dinner in their favourite chair and do one of four things: read hunting/gun magazines; play with his guns; watch hunting videos; or sit around with his like-minded mates and talk.'

The only comprehensive attempt to measure gun ownership in Australia was the 1978 General Social Survey (GSS), which found that only 1.1% of women aged over 15 reported owning a gun.[106] Everything about the representation of shooters in Australia suggests that men dominate this pursuit. The pool of potential gun owners is thus about half the adult population (ie men), plus the GSS estimate of 1.1% of women. This equates to around 6.79 million people in Australia. Discounting this figure by 10% to account for those who are very elderly (few of

---

105 Data on licensed shooters provided by Commonwealth Law Enforcement Board.

106 Harding R. *Firearms and violence in Australian life*. Perth: University of Western Australia Press, 1981.

whom would be shooters), we might then consider some 6.11 million adults as *potential* gun owners. During the debate Ted Drane repeatedly argued that 'two to three million' Australians owned guns. Drane was deliberately vague because, like everybody else, he had no way of actually knowing. Yet he claimed that two to three million of some 6.11 million adults, or between one-third and one-half of all Australian men, were gun owners.

How credible is this number? The most recent community survey on gun ownership was a 1994 NSW Health Department study. Out of a statewide survey of 16,165, a sub-sample of 2,251 people were asked questions on guns. This survey found that 11.7% of those interviewed reported a gun being in their home (6.6% urban, 26.3% rural).[107] Of course, some respondents may have known there were guns in their homes belonging to unlicensed owners and may not have admitted this to the interviewers. Also, the survey question asked about guns in homes, not numbers of owners. To account for these two complicating factors, we could generously lift the proportion from 11.7% to 20% – a figure almost matching the 19.6% reported in the 1989 International Crime Victimisation Survey (see Table 2.1).

If this proportion were extrapolated nationally, Australia would have 1.343 million gun owners – about 33% short of Drane's *lower* estimate of two million. As there are about 1,047,000 licensed shooters in Australia (see Table 5.1), this suggests 22% of Australia's gun owners (296,000) are unlicensed.

John Tingle offered an object lesson in the way the gun lobby talks up its numbers. Our files on Tingle's utterances on unlicensed shooters in NSW alone include 'half a million' (11 July 1995); 'as high as 700,000' (13 July 1995); 'as many as 750,000' (8 August 1995); and 'about 1 million gun owners', of whom only 150,000 were licensed, leaving 850,000 unlicensed (22 September 1995).[108] This 70% gain in less than three

---

107 National Centre for Health Promotion. *NSW Health Promotion Survey 1994*. Technical report. December 1995: 50–51.

108 Lagan B. 'Gun fee waived to tempt illicit owners', *SMH*, 22 September 1995: 3.

months would put Pinocchio's nose in the shade! Tingle's starting point of 500,000 unlicensed shooters in NSW compares to our national estimate of 296,000 unlicensed shooters.

How many guns?

And what about guns? Because there has been no national gun register, there is no reliable estimate even of legal guns in civilian hands. As John Tingle admitted in 1995: 'There could be anything up to three million [guns in NSW], but nobody knows for sure.'[109] Yet during the Port Arthur debate the gun lobby dramatically quoted everything from three million to 10 million guns. Nice round numbers. A statement signed by 12 officials from shooters' groups in the June 1996 issue of *Australian Gun Sports* claimed that, 'Registration of long-arms in Western Australia, Northern Territory, South Australia and Victoria has seen only around 50% of firearms actually registered.'

Richard Harding's 1978 surveys of gun ownership in NSW and South Australia for the Criminology Research Council[110] estimated that the average gun owner in NSW had 1.9 guns and in South Australia, 1.6. Acknowledging that 'moderate under-reporting' should be expected, Harding estimated that in Australia: [111]

– 1,220,000 people aged over 15 owned . . .
– 2,055,000 firearms (other than airguns) giving an average of . . .
– 1.68 guns per owner, or . . .
– 156 guns per 1000 population, that is . . .
– 478 guns per 1,000 households, with about . . .
– 25.3% of households having guns.

Harding has twice since updated his estimates from data on gun imports and population growth and from estimates of the proportion

109 Tingle J. 'The crossfire on gun legislation', *SMH*, 11 July 1995: 15.

110 Harding R. *Firearms and violence in Australian Life*. Perth: University of Western Australia Press, 1981: 47–48.

111 Ibid, 50.

of imports put to military and police uses. In 1983 he estimated that there were 2.8 million guns of all types in civilian hands. In June 1996, he estimated the following figure:

2,800,000 (the 1983 figure), plus
375,000 imports from 1982–88, plus
330,000 imports from 1988–1996, for a total of . . .
3,505,000 firearms in private ownership in a population of 18 million. [112]

The NCGC lampooned the gun lobby's dubious figures: 'Without registration, no one knows how many guns are in the community. If the gun lobby claims to know the size of this group, and claims to represent law-abiding shooters, why doesn't it report them?'[113]

How many semi-automatics and other banned guns?

So how many semi-automatics are out there? Ted Drane's highest bid for the buyback cost was $1 billion. Assuming an average price of $500 per gun, Drane was asking us to believe there were two million semi-automatics and pump-action shotguns owned by our 1.343 million shooters.

Table 5.2 shows data collated by the Commonwealth Law Enforcement Board for the Police Ministers, from information and estimates provided by firearms registries in each state and territory.

The estimate of almost 1.5 million prohibited weapons presented in this table is a worst-case scenario, almost certainly exaggerated, yet it was still 25% below Drane's estimate of two million.

---

112 Harding R. *Numbers, types and distribution of firearms in Australia*, 1996. Crime Research Centre, University of Western Australia, June 1996.

113 Chapman S. 'Now, about those guns . . ', *SMH*, 9 May 1996: 15.

Table 5.2 Estimates of numbers of prohibited firearms in each jurisdiction (thousands).

State	Semi-auto shotguns rifles	Semi-auto centrefire rifles	Semi-auto rimfire firearms	Pump-action shotguns	Total prohibited
NSW	55.3	46.3	216		450
Vic	70.4	6	91	State by state estimates not available	400
Qld	47.4	39	185		386
SA	11.486	8.982	40.723		87
WA	4.342	0.562	25.578		43
Tas	12.3	10.3	48		100
NT	2.478	1.2	5.39		19
ACT	.808	0.119	1.916		3.793
Total	204.514	113.263	613.607	557,409	1,488.793

How many would refuse to surrender their guns?

After the buyback began, the gun lobby continued to claim that many shooters would refuse to hand in their guns. John Tingle said: 'My reading of the situation is that only 40–50% of private gun owners will hand the guns in.'[114] Not to be outdone, shooting official Ted Leong claimed to have 'met . . . over 5,000 shooters' in three months who 'because of their trust, have indicated to me they will be burying their rifles when the laws are implemented.' He claimed that 96% said they would bury their rifles, but all would hand in a 'sacrifice' rifle to appease the authorities.[115] Leong's precision here is interesting: 96%, not 95% or 97%.

Despite the gun lobby's bluster, opinion polls indicated that support for the new gun laws was high even among gun owners. This was to be expected – after all, as both sides in the gun debate agreed, most

114 Passey D. 'Guns head for smelter as Tingle fires warning', *SMH*, 2 October 1996: 9.

115 Humphries D. 'PM over a barrel on gun buy-back funds', *SMH*, 30 September 1996: 5.

gun owners were no more inclined to break the law than other citizens. The large number of guns brought in for buyback also confounded the predictions of mass non-compliance. When the buyback began, accompanied by advertisements highlighting the financial compensation payable, shooters mobbed the collection centres, even though they had a year to hand in their semi-automatics.

Plainly, the gun lobby was now desperate to talk up its support base. Graeme Campbell predicted his new party would quickly attract 50,000 members.[116] In September, Campbell openly admitted that his support was nowhere near that number: 'I really don't know what the numbers are, but that was wildly optimistic.'[117] To register a federal political party with the Electoral Commission, a minimum of members in each state are required, with 300 members required in the least populated state. Campbell was reported as saying he 'thought' he had this number.[118] One claim was that membership inquiries were coming in to the Shooters' Party at the rate of '200 a day', but this was just one of many fantastic claims about the party's support. Soon after its formation, John Tingle bragged that a membership drive would attract 'more than 250,000' supporters.[119] Five months later, Tingle claimed his party had 'more than 20,000' members.[120] Clearly the other 230,000 were taking their time joining up. The SSAA claimed in early June that more than 10,000 members had joined in the past month.[121] Needless to say, none of these claims were accompanied by any proof.

One of the gun lobby's most common tactics was to claim that it spoke for all gun owners. For example, a statement released by ten firearms groups on the day after the Police Ministers' agreement claimed

---

116 Savva N. 'I won't buckle, PM pledges', *The Age*, 3 June 1996: 1.

117 Walsh K-A. 'Party unfaithful', *The Bulletin*, 17 September 1996: 16–17.

118 Ibid.

119 Fitzpatrick E. 'Shooters Party to fight new gun laws', *SMH*, 18 May 1992: 2.

120 Macey R. 'Govt may link mental health to gun ownership', *SMH*, 29 October 1992: 2.

121 Milburn C. 'How the gun lobby marshals its troops', *The Age*, 8 June 1996: A6.

they represented '1.8 million [gun] owners'.[122] But the largest group of the ten was the SSAA, which had only 45,000 members nationally (often expressed as 'up to 50,000').[123] If we included all 114,724 people who voted for the Shooters' Party at the March 1996 federal election, the total could reach 165,000. The other eight groups included the Greek Hunting and Fishing Clubs – together unlikely to muster even 20,000 members. In aggregate, these numbers were hardly 10% of the 1.8 million gun owners these groups claimed to represent.

Interesting, too, are the circulation figures for two Australian gun magazines monitored by the Audit Bureau of Circulations. In the period 1 July–21 December 1995, *Australian Sporting Shooter* had an average circulation of 19,830 per month and *Guns Australia* 9,865. These magazines are among the main vehicles promoting gun lobby propaganda in Australia, yet these figures suggest that only a fraction of shooters buy them.

How many at their pro-gun rallies?

Rallies and mass meetings both supporting and opposing the new gun control laws were held around Australia, all covered prominently by the media.[124] Judging from television coverage, men appeared to outnumber women at pro-gun rallies by perhaps 200 to one. The gun lobby organised buses to take its supporters to their rallies. The Federal Member for Groom in Queensland told Parliament: 'To give you an extreme example, last Wednesday evening there was a meeting in Toowoomba involving something like 700 or 800 people from outside my electorate;

---

122 Lawnham P, McGarry A. 'Shooters will defy news laws, MP warns', *The Australian*, 11 May 1996.

123 Grattan M, Farouque F. 'National ban on weapons', *The Age*, 11 May 1996: 1.

124 Ryan R. 'A 'silent' majority', *Daily Telegraph*, 3 June 1996: 5; Anon. 'Gun control: for and against', *The Age*, 7 June 1996: A11; Passey D. 'Gun-law protest to draw 85,000', *SMH*, 15 June 1996; Passey D. 'Even softly spoken Wilf says it's time to march', *SMH*, 15 June 1996; Millett M, Wright T. 'Under fire', *SMH*, 22 June 1996: 35.

a lot of these people are being bussed and driven in to beat the whole thing up.'[125]

All the rallies in support of gun control attracted much smaller numbers than those organised by the gun lobby. Many supporters told us they would not attend gun control rallies, fearing confrontations with the sort of aggressive shooters they had seen on television at pro-gun rallies. A rally organised by the Federal Liberal MP for North Sydney, Joe Hockey, had a smaller attendance than expected. People delivering leaflets in the area told us they had been followed by people, presumed to be from the gun lobby, who removed thousands of leaflets from letterboxes. A report of a rally held in Sydney on 28 July described the attendance as 'several thousand . . . by far the biggest anti-gun gathering yet'.[126] The day was wet, but the attendance at this extensively advertised event was estimated at only 5,000–6,000. In fact the biggest anti-gun rally took place in Melbourne on 2 June, when 30,000 people marched to Parliament House.

Gun lobby supporters sought solace from the onslaught of the new laws by pointing to the far larger crowds they were able to attract to their rallies.[127] They believed this disproved their opponents' claim that the community was firmly behind gun control. But media commentators saw through the vocal and self-interested minority: 'The amount of noise and placard-waving, and even substantial numbers, is no indication of public opinion . . . In the case of the gun lobby, there is no doubt that strict gun control and uniform legislation is supported by an overwhelming majority.'[128]

The largest pro-gun rally took place in Melbourne on 1 June. Organisers estimated the crowd at 150,000, but the official police

125 Australian House of Representatives *Hansard* for 17 June 1996. Grievance debate: gun control.

126 Macey R. 'Sydney takes to the streets in anger', *SMH*, 29 July 1996: 2.

127 Krivanek JF. 'Well done' (letter), *SMH*, 1 August 1996: 14.

128 McGuinness PP. 'Fanatics cause discomfort for the Nationals', *The Age*, 8 June 1996: A23.

estimate was 60,000;[129] in any case, it was the largest demonstration in Melbourne since the anti-Vietnam war rallies in the early 1970s. The organisers of the Sydney pro-gun rally on 15 June predicted that 85,000 would attend,[130] and another boast went as high as 100,000.[131] The official police estimate was 35,000,[132] but the organisers afterwards insisted that 100,000 had attended. 'The anti-gun lobby could only draw 1,500 but we've pulled in 100,000, so who is the real minority?' asked John Tingle.[133] In messianic style, Tingle told the 35,000 they had the power to overthrow the Government,[134] declaring: 'We are not going to end the campaign we started until they listen to us and they give us our way.'

One shooter sent us the following message via email:

> The official count of relative numbers at pro and anti firearms rights rallies (1/2 Jun 96) were initial figures by manual estimation; not known for their precision. We now have an official (but officially not released) count from the Police spy cameras installed on buildings within the Melbourne CBD. The official numbers are: 170,000+ for the pro side and 3,000–3,500 for the anti! Note: these figures were confirmed by an independent authority count using overhead photos taken by helicopter followed by an accurate grid by grid count.

Needless to say these 'official' figures were never released, nor did the media run any stories about a police 'cover-up' of attendance figures.

---

129 Anon. 'Thousands march against gun laws', *Sunday Telegraph*, 2 June 1996: 4.

130 Passey D. 'Gun-law protest to draw 85,000', *SMH*, 15 June 1996.

131 Gora B. 'Protesters vow to keep fighting', *Sunday Telegraph*, 16 June 1996.

132 Scott L, Stapleton J. 'Attorney-General targets state gun ads', *The Australian*, 17 June 1996.

133 Warnock S. 'Shooters storm city', *Sun Herald*, 16 June 1996: 3.

134 Gora B. 'Protesters vow to keep fighting', *Sunday Telegraph*, 16 June 1996.

How much money in their fighting funds?

There was much posturing, too, about the amount of money the gun lobby would throw at its campaign to overturn the laws. The Shooting Sports Council of Victoria suggested that a 'multi-million dollar fund' could be raised.[135] Ted Drane declared the day after the Police Ministers' agreement that the SSAA's national executive would commit 'up to $1 million' to fight the laws.[136]

The SSAA's internet site stated: 'The media has refused since the Port Arthur murders to run any PAID advertising to put the pro-gun viewpoint before the public.' This was arrant nonsense. The SSAA had run full-page advertisements in several newspapers before the 10 May Police Ministers' meeting, calling for shooters to donate money. The *Sydney Morning Herald* also noted that the organisers of the 15 June pro-gun rally in Sydney had run 'saturation advertising' . . . throughout NSW that week.[137] The SSAA's ads calling for donations appeared in the newspapers only once; surely, if they had succeeded in attracting large donations, they would have been repeated.

---

135 Gibson R, Chamberlain P. 'Wheeling out the big guns', *The Age*, 11 May 1996: A20–21.

136 Farouque F, McKay S. 'Angry shooters plan a $1 million protest', *The Age*, 11 May 1996: A6.

137 Passey D. 'Gun-law protest to draw 85,000', *SMH*, 15 June 1996.

6

The gun lobby's arguments . . . and the responses

Gun lobbies the world over have developed an extensive repertoire of arguments against gun control. For years, these have been repeated in their magazines, newsletters and on the Internet. The aftermath of the Port Arthur massacre produced an unprecedented daily media campaign run by a lobby desperate to defend its position. This chapter considers each of the arguments advanced by the gun lobby to reduce support for the proposed new gun control laws.

I summarise each argument, showing how these were used, and then describe how the NCGC, other gun control groups, journalists and the public responded. In particular, I'll highlight the vital role played by analogies in the debate. Along with personalisation – attaching a real person's experience to debate about issues – analogy and simile are probably the single most powerful rhetorical devices in public health advocacy. In essence, they allow links or parallels to be drawn between the issue under discussion and other issues or discourses with which an audience might be expected to readily concur. Analogy allows readers and audiences to draw parallels between events, policies or lines of reasoning that they accept in one circumstance, with the issue in question.

'We have not been consulted'

The gun lobby argued that the Police Ministers' resolutions 'struck a blow against democracy and justice in Australia . . . the new draconian gun laws are undemocratic because the firearm fraternity was not consulted. The new gun laws are unjust because they punish innocent people who have obeyed the law . . .'[1] The 'undemocratic' bluster was empty rhetoric, for the gun lobby knew every recent opinion poll showed overwhelming public support for gun law reform (see Table 3.1). Nobody took this argument seriously.

The calm face of reason

Gun lobbyists recognised that the law reforms had been born out of the immensity of the carnage at Port Arthur. An entire nation had been horrified by the killings there and more than 90% of the community endorsed the view that government should respond with appropriately serious reforms. While many in the gun lobby were apoplectic at the turn of events in gun law reform, some forlornly tried to call for calm, counselling that politicians and the community were acting emotionally because the 'anti-gun lobby . . . fills the public's heads with many uninformed inaccuracies and sometimes blatant lies based on emotion rather than fact'.[2] Predictably, the gun lobby fell back on the cliché that new demands for tough gun laws were a 'knee-jerk reaction'. Independent MP Graeme Campbell told Federal Parliament:

> It is quite clear what the House is going to do, but I want it on record that this is a knee-jerk reaction and one that will not address the problem. Neither the Government nor the Opposition will ever look at issues that do address the problem. We have been party to letting people out of institutions because it became politically correct to release people from institutions onto the street.[3]

Martin Bryant had never been in an institution.

---

1 Tingle J, Shelton B, Borsak R, Kounaris G et al. 'Shooters' response', *Australian Gun Sports*, June 1996: 21.

2 Roudenko A. 'One in 10,000' (letter), *SMH*, 8 May 1996: 16.

3 Australian House of Representatives *Hansard* for 9 May 1996.

The SSAA's Sebastian Ziccone wrote an article for *The Age* in which he promised readers 'the facts' and 'a rational approach.'[4] A Shooters' Party official said arguments for gun registration were 'high on emotion and sensationalism but lacking in reason and logic.'[5] This discourse sought to position shooters as people who could rise above the base emotionalism engendered by massacres. Its corollary was that those advocating gun control had let emotions cloud their judgment and that shooting representatives were the ones who should be heard amid this irrationality. Unfortunately for the gun lobby, as we saw in Chapter 5, people like Ian McNiven were presenting the media with rather different images of 'rational approaches'. These people belied any hope of a calm, unified and dispassionate voice from the gun lobby. They were easily provoked and little strategic thinking was required to cause them to further damage the gun lobby's reputation.

'These laws will turn law-abiding citizens into criminals'

The new gun laws would require all current gun owners to demonstrate that they had a legitimate 'reason' to own a gun; to register all guns which they were deemed eligible to own; and to surrender for compensation any guns now declared illegal. Anyone refusing to take out a shooter's licence, to have guns registered or to surrender banned guns would be breaking the law. This sudden change in the gun regulations seemed all wrong to some: 'I get up this morning as an unfair [sic] person to keep a gun that I've had for 20 years,' a shooter told *Channel 7 News* on 11 May 1996.

'My guns have suddenly become dangerous'

Ted Drane told the *7.30 Report* on the night before the first Police Ministers' meeting:

---

4 Ziccone S. 'In defence of arms', *The Age*, 10 May 1996: A15.

5 Howden J. 'Shooting from the hip on gun debate', *Newcastle Herald*, 3 April 1996.

> You're dealing with private property. In my case it's a firearm that is considered being banned – it's a .22 rim-fire, self-loader. I've had it for 36 years. And you tell me today that it's a danger to public safety and that if I keep it, I'll go to jail. That's pretty hard for people to comprehend, as why they can have something for so long and all of a sudden it's illegal . . . it's a danger to public safety.[6]

On the same night Drane told *ABC News*:

> The fact is that there are hundreds and hundreds of thousands of these firearms out there and they've been there since 1904. And all of a sudden they've become a danger to public safety. And I'd like to know how. I'd like to know why.[7]

The gun lobby thus sought to frame the changes as the Government 'criminalising' people who had previously possessed guns totally within the law. It would turn 'ordinary, law-abiding shooters into criminals', they claimed. But this claim failed to recognise that it would be only those shooters who deliberately chose to break the law who would become 'criminals'.

The argument was that there were hundreds of thousands, if not millions of shooters who did not pose a threat to anyone and who were being forced to obey new, stupid, politically inspired laws. The implication was that it would be entirely reasonable for such people to ignore these new laws, thereby turning themselves into criminals'.

- 'We're being punished for one man's crime . . . They wouldn't treat any other group with such disdain. We'll never give up, even if it takes years . . . It's natural to look for someone to strike out at. But we didn't do it.'[8]

- 'I absolutely refuse to be held responsible for something somebody else did. I didn't do it, you didn't do it, and I'm not going to pay the

6 Drane T. *7.30 Report*, ABC TV, 9 May 1996.
7 Ted Drane on *ABC News*, 10 May 1996.
8 Condon M. 'On the bus with the diehards', *Sun Herald*, 16 June 1996: 2.

price for it.' (Ted Drane at a gun rally.)[9]

- 'Laws that make criminals of decent people are dangerous laws, and they threaten the very fabric of our society.' (Graeme Campbell at the same rally.)[10]

The gun lobby and its political supporters sought repeatedly to present gun owners with impeccable backgrounds who challenged interviewers to say why they should suddenly be 'made into a criminal' by the new laws. NSW MP Peter Blackmore described himself as 'a perfect example of a responsible shooter who would be disadvantaged by the ban', going on to describe his 25-year-old Remington 1100 self-loading shotgun.[11]

Responses: The gun lobby considered this was perhaps their most compelling argument: they had not pulled the trigger on Martin Bryant's gun, and the great majority of them would never use a gun irresponsibly or in anger. So why should they be restricted by tougher gun laws? This presented a classic instance of a problem public health and community safety advocates face: selling impositions on whole communities or on large parts of the population to reduce the probability of harm to others.

The NCGC and many among the public pointed to instances of impositions and outlays we are all obliged to endure to make life in our communities safer. In Federal Parliament on 17 June, Michael Cobb, National Party Member for Parkes, said:

> If I may deal with some of the objections, they say that these proposals 'brand innocent people as criminals'. I think this was best answered by Associate Professor Simon Chapman, who, in the *Sydney Morning Herald*, said: 'This is rather like feeling insulted at being required to open your bag at the supermarket checkout, at having to walk through a metal detector at an airport, at being pulled over for random

---

9 Ibid.

10 Anon. 'Thousands march against gun laws', *Sunday Telegraph*, 2 June 1996: 4.

11 Aubert E. 'Blackmore digs in over weapons decision', *Newcastle Herald*, 11 May 1996.

breath-testing.' I remind these people that you cannot identify who will offend. Only 15% of those who do offend have a
previous history of mental instability.

We argued that anyone claiming to be insulted at the implication
that they were a potential terrorist by airport inspections should be
taken as seriously as those in the gun lobby who claimed to be insulted
because they were being branded as potential murderers.

An interesting comparison was made about the decision in the
1980s to ban radar scanners used by motorists to detect police speed
radar traps. These scanners were heavily advertised when legal, and
many thousands were sold to motorists who, after their ban, would be
'criminalised' if found using one. Unlike the ban on semi-automatics,
no compensation was paid to radar scanner owners. No one could recall
any community outrage from scanner owners.

Similarly, changes in consumer product technology frequently left
people with redundant products for which they were not compensated.
For example, the gradual abandonment in the 1980s of the video beta
system in favour of the VHS system left many beta owners with a com-
ponent that often cost more than $500 and which was now useless.
One letter writer told how his Ping golf clubs, worth $1,800, had been
declared illegal for competition use by the sport's governing bureau-
cracy, forcing him to buy new ones. He wasn't compensated, despite
being willing to use them 'for peaceful, recreational purposes'![12]

One gun lobby supporter displayed an intriguing degree of understanding of the arguments by urging gun control lobbyists to 'lobby for
the prohibition of automatic cars and set severe restrictions on the possession and use of manual cars', arguing that cars killed people too.[13]

'Gun violence is committed by criminals or madmen'

The core argument of the gun lobby's opposition to the new gun laws
was that gun violence is committed by criminals and the mentally

---

12 Wong B. 'Compo club' (letter), *SMH*, 18 June 1996.
13 Chiswell JC. 'Killer motor cars' (letter), *SMH*, 18 June 1996: 16.

unstable who are capable of being identified, and so it is wrong that people who had never committed or threatened an act of violence with a gun should be controlled, blamed or 'punished'[14] by stricter gun laws. From the very start of the debate that followed the Port Arthur massacre, the gun lobby argued that gun laws would do nothing to stop such incidents. 'Tighter gun laws are not the answer – laws become irrelevant in situations like this . . . Laws don't affect people who are going mad with guns,' said John Tingle.[15] Then demonstrating an ability to contradict himself within two sentences, Tingle went on: 'The NSW Shooters' Party thinks the Tasmanian laws are a disgrace.'

Banners at pro-gun rallies read: 'Madmen get trials. We get penalties'. A statement signed by the leaders of 12 shooting groups embodied this argument. It spoke of the Police Ministers' resolutions having 'cast a serious stigma on law-abiding citizens, especially legitimate firearm owners' and that 'legitimate gun owners are now being made to pay the price for what criminals and the mentally unstable have done . . . Declaring war on the law-abiding, and doing nothing to address the vast armoury of firearms held by unlicensed people – including criminals – the Police Ministers have attacked the wrong people!'[16]

This theme of being insulted and made to feel guilty, of being denied natural justice, of being convicted before being tried, and of all gun owners being considered potential mass murderers, was expressed by many gun owners contacting the media. One letter writer rebuffed this claim in a reply to a shooter who had written that ordinary shooters should not be judged by the actions of a madman: 'And he is right. They should be judged by the large number of gun suicides . . . the children accidentally injured or killed by unsecured loaded guns . . . and the senseless murder suicides perpetrated by estranged husbands . . . the

---

14 Lawson JB. 'Punished just for being a gun owner' (letter), *The Age*, 15 May 1996: A16.

15 Pitt H. 'Atrocity sparks gun law plea', *SMH*, 29 April 1996: 4.

16 Tingle J, Shelton B, Borsak R, Kounaris G et al. 'Shooters' response', *Australian Gun Sports*, June 1996: 21.

522 guns deaths recorded in 1994 . . . were mostly the actions of men who were angry, miserable and depressed – not mad, just human.'[17]

'The gun lobby has clean hands'

Before Port Arthur, the gun lobby had regularly boasted about the way it had derailed gun law reform in Australia. John Tingle crowed in the May/June 1996 issue of *Guns Australia* (presumably printed before Port Arthur) that the Shooters Party had 'helped persuade the NSW Police Minister to refuse to take part in Uniform National Firearms Laws proposed by the Federal Government. These laws would have meant universal firearm registration. NSW staying out has made national laws impossible.'[18] Yet in a letter to the *Daily Telegraph* on 8 May 1996 Tingle wrote: 'I have expressed my support for uniform gun laws, applied by the States.'[19] Tingle seemed prepared to express his full support for 'uniform gun laws' if these were weak and did not include gun registration.[20]

Responses: The NCGC sought to show that the gun lobby should take a large part of the responsibility for what happened at Port Arthur – to take some of the blame. An article in *The Age* argued that part of the gun lobby's proud record of 'success' was to keep the Tasmanian Government from changing the very laws that allowed Martin Bryant to gain access to the sort of weapons he used. Yet now it was arguing that its decent, law-abiding members were being 'blamed' for the massacre. 'What other word is there for it?'[21] The lobby's highly strategised opposition to national uniform gun laws had been at the heart of the failure of Tasmania to fall in line with tougher legislation in other states,

---

17 Worth C. 'Guns the link in so many deaths' (letter), *The Age*, 10 May 1996.

18 Tingle J. 'The great Australian guilt industry', *Guns Australia*, May/June 1996: 64–65.

19 Tingle J. 'Targeting semi-automatics' (letter), *Daily Telegraph*, 8 May 1996.

20 Morris R. 'I've become the whipping boy, says Tingle', *Daily Telegraph*, 1 May 1996.

21 Chapman S. 'Hit 'n' myth of the gun lobby', *The Age*, 12 June 1996: 15.

and yet Tingle argued: 'I was not responsible for [the massacre], nor have I done anything to make it more likely to happen.'[22]

The gun lobby's constant habit of describing perpetrators like Bryant as 'criminals' was a self-serving piece of sophistry. All murderers are by definition criminal after they commit their crimes. Yet to the gun lobby, all shooters with no criminal records and who haven't yet committed murder are 'honest, hard-working, tax-paying and law-abiding citizens'[23]. The moment one of these commits a gun crime they instantly are described as 'criminals', with the implication that they were always different to ordinary shooters.

Just as Philip Alpers had shown in the case of mass killings, a NSW Bureau of Crime Statistics study of 1,393 homicide offenders had shown that only 16% (223) were known to have some kind of mental disorder at the time or at some time before the offence, and only 17% (246) had any previous history of violent crime such as assault.[24]

'Guns don't kill people . . . people kill people'

The NRA's favourite slogan was widely aired during the debate. Two victims of shootings spoke out against the new gun laws. Kay Nesbitt, who had been shot in the face eleven years before, was pictured on the front page of *The Age* with a story in which she argued that gun owners were being unfairly blamed, and that Howard's response was 'emotional'. She voiced the argument that 'mad buggers out there . . . someone loopy' would always be able to get hold of a gun.[25] If she was right, loose gun laws just made it all so much easier. At a Sydney pro-gun rally on 15 June a former security guard who had been shot six years previously in an armed holdup and had since been confined to a wheelchair was invited onstage. He told the crowd: 'Unlike this Government, I possess

---

22 Tingle J. 'Don't blame me' (letter), *SMH*, 9 May 1996.

23 Bostock I. 'From the editor's desk', *Guns Australia*, July/August 1996: 4–5.

24 Wallace A. *Homicide: the social reality*. Bureau of Crime Statistics and Research, Sydney 1986.

25 Watkins S. 'Ban guns? Kay Nesbit has her say', *The Age*, 6 June 1996: 1.

common sense – common sense enough to know that a gun did not put me in this wheelchair. A person did. Guns don't kill. People kill people.'[26]

Responses: There were obvious retorts to this asinine slogan. Three of the more powerful included:

- 'This is the same as saying . . . bare wires don't kill, electricians do.'[27]
- 'The point is that people who, for whatever reason, are inclined to kill will be able to kill more, according to how efficient as killing machines their weapons are and how readily available they are.'[28]
- 'People kill – guns make it possible.'[29]

John Tingle, to his credit, realised what a silly statement the NRA slogan was. He explicitly repudiated the slogan several times, claiming he never used it.[30] This was a jibe at the SSAA, who were very enamoured with their US counterparts' anthem.

'They should set up prohibited persons registers'

Hand-in-glove with the gun lobby's position that people who are violent with guns are 'madmen' was their belief that it was possible to identify such people in advance and to place them on a 'prohibited persons register' for gun licences. Doctors, psychiatrists and social workers, they argued, would come across many people in their work who they could predict were likely to become violent. They should have a duty to report such people, whose names would then be placed on a register.

The trouble with this solution was that no one with any credibility in medicine, psychiatry or social work gave it a shred of credence. The

---

26 Gora B. 'Protesters vow to keep fighting', *Sunday Telegraph*, 16 June 1996.

27 Flanagan M. 'Why the gun lobby's rhetoric misses its mark', *The Age*, 8 May 1996: A15.

28 Anon. 'A cool look at gun laws', *SMH*, 30 April 1996.

29 Monteith A. Letter, *SMH*, 21 March 1996.

30 J. Tingle. 'Don't blame me' (letter), *SMH*, 7 May 1996.

vast majority of people with mental disorders are not violent. Most violent people do not have identified mental disorders,[31] and 88% of people shot in massacres in Australia and New Zealand in the past decade were *not* killed by anyone with a history of mental illness.[32]

Tellingly, the gun lobby's enthusiasm for these registers did not cause them to apply the same arguments that they used to attack the folly of banning semi-automatics: that criminals and those intent on getting these guns would get hold of them regardless of registration. Prohibited persons registers would somehow stop people on the registers from illegally getting guns; but the ban on semi-automatics was stupid because everyone knew these guns could still be obtained on the black market.

Again, to its credit, the Shooters' Party had been on record as supporting gun control groups' criticisms of prohibited persons registers. But the registers were never far from the minds of the SSAA.

> A prohibited persons register is what the SSA has been suggesting for years . . . It is obvious that the hundreds of millions of pounds spent in Britain on cracking down on semi-automatic rifles would have been better spent on mental health in an effort to identify such a murderer before the event.[33]

John Tingle's wife wrote in his defence after Tingle had been attacked in a letter to the *Sydney Morning Herald*. Discussing the Dunblane killer, she asked why her husband's critics had not done something to stop Thomas Hamilton before he shot the children:

> People . . . who appoint themselves as society's conscience, after the fact, did not have the moral fortitude to do something about this man. All the signs were there . . . If Thomas Hamilton had walked the streets with a neon sign around his

---

31 Dudley M, Gale F. 'Fewer arms, fewer deaths', *SMH*, 9 May 1996: 15.

32 http: //www.health.usyd.edu.au/cgc/fp_6_2_2.htm [no longer active, 2013].

33 Ziccone S. 'In defence of arms', *The Age*, 10 May 1996: A15.

neck flashing 'one day I am going to self-destruct, and take some of you with me, to punish you', it could not have been more obvious.'[34]

Responses: Twelve crown prosecutors and public defenders jointly responded to Tingle's wife in this way:

> If we understand correctly, Gail Tingle has the capacity to identify prospective perpetrators of horrific crimes such as that committed in Dunblane. She is able by reference to a certain profile to predict such offenders . . . Is she suggesting that all persons who fit this profile be arrested/detained; subjected to medical/psychiatric treatment against their will merely so that others might possess firearms?[35]

On registers, we retorted:

> The AMA's code of ethics already allows doctors to report those who endanger the community, whether it be the poorly sighted who refuse to stop driving or the shooter who exhibits violent intent. However, prior to Port Arthur, in Australia and New Zealand's thirteen gun massacres where five or more died, resulting in 92 deaths, 71 (88%) of the victims in these incidents were killed by someone with no record of mental illness. Besides further stigmatising the mentally ill, a register of the mentally suspect would still allow the majority of potential killers to get guns.[36]

The Institute of Australian Psychiatrists noted that:

> Most people who are dangerous are not mentally ill and in fact, the record for prediction of dangerousness by psychiatrists, let alone doctors, is poor. The predictors of dangerousness are such things as being male, previous history of dangerousness, being young, etc and mental illness is low on the list.

34 Tingle G. 'Everyone's an expert on killers' (letter), *SMH*, 21 March 1996.

35 Nicolson J et al. 'Stand up to the gun lobbyists' (letter), *SMH*, 23 March 1996: 36.

36 Chapman S. 'Now, about those guns . . ', *SMH*, 9 May 1996: 15.

Their representative pointed out: 'Psychiatrists already had a duty to warn those who might suffer as a consequence of recognised dangerousness in a patient.'[37] One psychiatrist wrote:

> The risk of people becoming mentally ill increases over the decades. Being mentally stable when obtaining a gun licence means little when the psychotic or depressive episode occurs 10 years later. Moreover . . . even if the gun owner and licensee is mentally stable, others with access to the gun may not be.[38]

Many writers were quick to point out that any register should start by listing members of the gun lobby. 'This same gun-toting group claims that its own members, on the other hand, act "responsibly" at all times. Really? Who gave them the all clear?'[39] One letter writer from the Humanist Society of Victoria defined sport as 'a contest between equal opponents' and argued that semi-automatic weapons were therefore unsporting.[40]. Others argued that anyone who enjoyed shooting animals for 'sport' had suspect mental health.

Finally, a writer in the *Australian and New Zealand Journal of Psychiatry* made the following calculation:

> If the annual rate of serious violence in the community is 20 per 100,000 [persons], then with a predictor with a sensitivity [detecting true positive cases] and a sensitivity [detecting true negative cases] of 95% for a society the size of New Zealand (3 million), you will be able to prevent in each year 570 assaults, will miss 30, but the price will be confining 150,000 innocent Kiwis. If you insist, as a matter of social justice, on not locking up more than one innocent man for each three potential assaulters, for the same base rate of violence, you would require a predictor with a level of accuracy of 99.99993%.[41]

---

37 Boettcher B. 'Alarming suggestion' (letter), *SMH*, 11 May 1996: 36.

38 Murphy R. 'The danger in a "sleeping gun"' (letter), *The Age*, 8 June 1996: 22.

39 Brownlee E. 'The hills are alive with them' (letter), *SMH*, 20 May 1996: 14.

40 Strand H. 'Wary of freedom, jungle-style' (letter), *The Age*, 21 June 1996: 12.

41 Mullen P. 'Mental disorder and dangerousness', *Aust NZ J Psychiatry* 1984,

Stigmatisation of the mentally ill

The widespread speculation that Martin Bryant had a history of mental illness fuelled the gun lobby's argument. A SSAA advertisement stated: 'The Port Arthur perpetrator['s] . . . mental condition has been widely reported on.'[42] The implication here was that press reports on Bryant's mental health were to be believed.

The assumption that Bryant was mentally ill and that this was pivotal to both understanding what had occurred and preventing future massacres angered advocates for people with mental disabilities.[43] The directors of the Victorian Schizophrenia Fellowship wrote: 'To the best of our knowledge, the man charged has not had a psychiatric assessment. If he has, no diagnosis has been made public.'[44] Their concerns were that the event would fuel calls for blanket isolationist policies, noting that callers to radio were bellowing, 'Lock them up and throw away the key!'[45] One person wrote: 'Behind all the labels used so far, stand tens of thousands of Australian citizens with disabilities waiting to see if they too are on trial, merely because they live with their disability.'[46] In Hobart alone, at least three cases have been documented of schizophrenics committing suicide following the allegation that Bryant had that condition.

Significantly, the Secretary of the Tasmanian Department of Community and Health Services wrote about 'unsubstantiated allegations about past contact between community service and health authorities in this State and Martin Bryant . . . This Department would

18: 8–17.

42 SSAA. 'An urgent message to all gun owners' (advertisement), *Daily Telegraph*, 10 May 1996.

43 Nicholls R. 'Why the stigma on the ill has to stop' (letter), *The Age*, 6 May 1996: A14.

44 Crowther E, Burger J. 'Targeting more innocent victims' (letter), *The Age*, 6 May 1996: A14.

45 Ibid.

46 Green D. 'Mentally ill should not be stigmatised', *The Age*, 10 May 1996.

wish to counter the allegations . . . but because of the pending proceedings against Mr Bryant, is not free to do so.'[47] This letter all but indicated that stories about Bryant having a history of mental health problems known to authorities were unsubstantiated. The following excerpts from the assessment provided to the court show that while Bryant had been assessed by a psychiatrist who considered him to be 'intellectually handicapped and personality disordered', he had never been diagnosed as having schizophrenia:

> In February 1984 Mr Bryant was assessed by a very experienced clinical psychiatrist, Dr Cunningham-Dax. This assessment was initiated to consider Mr Bryant's eligibility for a disability pension. Dr Cunningham-Dax stated that Mr Bryant was intellectually handicapped and personality disordered. He also raised the possibility that he might be developing an illness of a schizophrenic type. On the basis of this report and subsequent assessments which relied upon it, Mr Bryant was granted a disability pension. There are subsequent references to Mr Bryant having a schizophrenic illness and of being a paranoid schizophrenic in the records of Dr Mather (December 1991) and Dr PM McCartney (December 1991). These diagnostic formulations, it transpired, were not the results of the doctors own conclusions, but based on the report of Mr Bryant's mother that he had been diagnosed by Dr Cunningham-Dax as suffering from this illness. This was a misunderstanding on Mrs Bryant's part and it is this misunderstanding which lead to an opinion by Dr Cunningham-Dax that Mr Bryant might develop schizophrenia being transmuted into a diagnosis of this severe mental illness. Mr Bryant has had no contact with the psychiatric services since this time.

When Bryant changed his plea to guilty before the trial set to begin on 19 November, the *Sydney Morning Herald* reported that his counsel and his mother had worked for weeks to help him understand that his denials of guilt were not defensible. 'Most particularly, no psychiatric

---

47 Biscoe G. 'Bryant concern' (letter), *Sun Herald*, 12 May 1196: 43.

evidence could be found by the defence to argue Bryant was not guilty on the grounds of diminished responsibility – or insane.'[48] Psychiatrists who had interviewed Bryant in prison concluded that he had a low IQ of 65, a mental age of 11 and that if any diagnosis could be applied to him at all, it was possible that he had Asperger's syndrome – a form of autism characterised by emotional disengagement, lack of affect and empathy.[49] The trial judge, Justice William Cox, described Bryant as 'a pathetic social misfit'. A defence of insanity was not available to Bryant.

John Wyche, range captain of the NSW SSAA, implied that only cheap guns would be used in massacres, arguing for a form of income-based link between 'madmen' and the purchase of such weapons: 'The bulk of licensed sporting shooters would have quality guns worth more than $4,000 each. You don't buy those sorts of weapons to kill people. It's the madmen who buy the cheaper variety.'[50] Ironically, it emerged that Bryant had purchased his AR–15 for $5,000.

'This won't prevent another Port Arthur'

The gun lobby became fond of arguing that the new gun laws would not prevent 'another Port Arthur'. 'It will not stop the likes of Martin Bryant,' said Roy Smith of the SSAA;[51] 'Focussing on the semi-automatic style of arm as a solution to a possible mass murder is pathetic political tokenism. In England, there were already extremely restrictive gun laws before the Hungerford shootings . . . Yet some years later came the Dunblane killings. Restriction did not work.'[52]

Responses: As discussed in Chapter 2, no regime of gun control promises to *eliminate* all gun violence. Reduction is a realistic goal. Many

48 Darby A. 'Why Bryant changed plea', *SMH*, 9 November 1996: 9.

49 Montgomery B. 'Inside the mind of Martin Bryant', *Weekend Australian*, 23–24 November 1996: 25.

50 Wainwright R. 'Fading trade to lose little from ban', *SMH*, 13 May 1996.

51 Wainwright R. 'We'll take to streets, say sporting shooters', *SMH*, 13 May 1996.

52 Ziccone S. 'In defence of arms', *The Age*, 10 May 1996: A15.

commentators accepted this argument, but re-framed the importance of the laws in terms of reducing the chances of future massacres, not preventing them. 'The agreement will not ensure that there can never be another Port Arthur–style massacre. No legislation can ever do that. But the legislation . . . will make Australia a safer place . . . The news laws will not prevent future tragedies but they might make them less likely.'[53]

The Dunblane massacre was not proof that gun laws are ineffective. It was evidence that insufficiently tight laws will permit the wrong person to have access to a rapid-fire weapon. Semi-automatic pistols were not restricted in the UK after the Hungerford massacre; nor was the British licensing system sufficiently rigorous or properly enforced. That Thomas Hamilton had a gun licence demonstrates evidence of poor screening of shooters.

One commentator argued that 'acts of theft have been committed for millennia and no one suggests that we scrap the crime of stealing. Very few laws, if any, succeed in eliminating crimes. Their aim is to minimise them and express a community standard.'[54]

'Guns are vital for self-defence'

Before Port Arthur, self or family defence was not officially recognised as a justifiable reason for being granted a firearms licence in any jurisdiction in Australia. But it was certainly the case that many applicants for licences acquired them with this reason in mind and simply ticked a box on gun licensing forms indicating that they wanted a gun for other purposes, like hunting.

The debate about the right to use a gun in repelling or defending oneself against the new nomenclature of the 'home invader' had greatly amplified this aspect of the gun debate. In 1993, the SSAA set up a fighting fund to contribute $60,000 to the legal defence of Laurie Morris, a former executive of the SSAA who had hidden in wait for the return of

---

53 Anon. 'A worthwhile victory on guns' (editorial), *The Age*, 24 July 1996: A12.

54 Flanagan M. 'Why the gun lobby's rhetoric misses its mark', *The Age*, 8 May 1996: A15.

a housebreaker and then shot and permanently crippled the man with a military rifle.[55] Morris was charged with attempted murder and various firearms offences including possessing 15 unregistered rifles. He was subsequently acquitted of the attempted murder charge.[56] The 1995 shootings of 16-year-old Matthew Easdale in Brisbane and of another intruder by an 84-year-old disabled man in Adelaide – in both cases those firing were subsequently acquitted by courts – galvanised the gun lobby's infatuation with self-defence even further.[57] As Queensland gun lobbyist Ian McNiven said – when discussing a previous incident where a trespasser was shot dead in a Brisbane house – such acts were the regrettable 'blood price' the community had to pay from time to time to allow citizens to be freely armed.[58]

The Shooters' Party's Mike Ascher located the issue in terms of his ideas on masculinity: 'I would use whatever force was necessary and take the consequences afterwards . . . Whether I would be legally entitled to do so or not would make no difference . . . Anyone who is half a man would do the same.'[59] Commenting on the Easdale shooting, John Tingle said: 'It's time to put all potential intruders on notice that they leave their rights at the door when they invade someone's home.'[60] In 1995, Tingle gained publicity for his plan to introduce a bill allowing home occupants to avoid criminal liability if they used 'deadly force' against home intruders.[61]

---

55 Catalano A. 'Gun lobby aids householder in intruder case', *The Age*, 16 April 1993: 6; Lewis J. 'Shooters seek cash to defend gunman', *SMH*, 17 April 1993: 9.

56 Greene G. 'Shooters defend the right to use guns', *The Sunday Age*, 20 August 1995: 5.

57 Zdenkowski G. 'Coroner must decide in home invasion killings', *SMH*, 18 May 1995: 17.

58 Roberts G. 'Break, enter and die', *The Bulletin*, 9 May 1995: 15, 17–19.

59 Ibid.

60 Ibid.

61 Lagan B. 'Tingle's gun law aimed at home intruders', *SMH*, 17 November 1995: 1.

Less than a week before the Port Arthur massacre, a Shooters' Party official wrote: 'Yesterday, I read with disgust how yet another family . . . was forced to endure a home invasion that resulted in, among other things, the repeated rape of the family's adolescent daughter.'[62] A shooter wrote: 'As a father, my primary duty is to protect my wife and family. The Government is planning to force me to surrender my gun, the only means by which I can defend them.' After explaining that he would refuse to hand in his gun he continued, 'I am certainly no extremist. I am a middle-of-the-road Australian, a law-abiding citizen.'[63]

Such arguments raised the spectre of those opposed to liberalising access to guns preferring to stand by and let one's family be assaulted, raped and murdered rather than act to defend them. Support for access to guns was thus a sign of bravery, decency and coming to the defence of victims being attacked by vicious criminals. By implication, anyone questioning open access to guns stood – as the NRA's Bob Corbin had said on TCN 9's *A Current Affair* in 1992 – for a spineless set of values that said: 'If you're going to be raped, lay down and be raped . . . if you're going to be robbed – hand over your money!' This was powerful rhetoric.

One *Age* letter writer cited the case of the suburb of Kennesaw, Atlanta. He wrote that the local government had enacted a law 'requiring every household to own a firearm', except for religious conscientious objectors and those with criminal records. He claimed that 'in the first seven months of the law's enactment the burglary rate fell by 89%. This result was not unexpected because it had been assumed that criminals would avoid these homes for fear of being apprehended by an armed owner.'[64]

---

62 Guest M. Letter, *SMH*, 22 April 1996.

63 Reitze RN. 'How will I protect my family?' (letter), *The Australian*, 18–19 May 1996: 20.

64 Brimblecombe CJ. 'Guns: what is the American path?' (letter), *The Age*, 8 July 1996: 10.

In this context, the work of the gun lobby's favourite criminologist, Gary Kleck, was championed by several people.[65] Kleck's US research purports to show that, in the US, armed communities with liberal gun laws have less gun violence than less armed communities with tighter gun laws. Kleck argues that when criminals and violent people expect there is a good chance that a victim is armed, they will think twice about committing the crime. While Kleck's research is the subject of serious debate in the US, its bottom line is that even the US states and cities which have the most liberal gun laws have levels of gun violence that are generally much higher than those in nations with tougher gun laws. Applying Kleck's arguments to Australia is like saying to people living in peace time 'let's start a war, but make sure everyone is properly armed . . . that way we can minimise the killing'.

Some in the gun lobby smugly pointed to instances of people who previously favoured gun control arming themselves during the Rodney King–inspired riots in Los Angeles in 1992. At the time, Ted Drane stated that if everyone in the city had been armed 'I don't think there would have been any toll at all'.[66] To this, one commentator replied: 'I dare say that many an otherwise peaceful man caught up in the madness of the Bosnian war sought to arm himself to defend his family. But Australia is not Bosnia'.[67]

Responses: The NCGC sought to deflate this argument as nonsense perpetrated by people overwhelmed by unrealistic fears imported from America. We repeatedly emphasised that by far the most probable victims of a gun kept in any house were the gun owner (from suicide), followed by members of the gun owner's immediate family (through suicide, domestic homicide or unintentional firearm discharge), followed by neighbours or other persons known to the gun owner (through homicide by the gun owner). In Australia, taking up a distant last place

65 Stanfield S. Letter, *SMH*, 20 June 1996: 16.

66 Offord J. 'Guns would have made riots "safe"', *Daily Telegraph*, 9 May 1992; Anon. 'Guns would have saved LA: shooter', *SMH*, 9 May 1992: 6.

67 Flanagan M. 'Why the gun lobby's rhetoric misses its mark', *The Age*, 8 May 1996: A15.

on this list of victims, came intruders shot in some act of self-defence by the gun owner or another family member. In this analysis, we drew on a study of all firearm deaths recorded by the Brisbane coroner from 1980 to 1989.[68] In this period, 587 deaths were recorded and of these only *one* involved the killing of someone who was involved in a crime at the time of the incident.

One person wrote a tongue-in-cheek letter saying that he and his wife planned to travel to Queensland and had been disturbed by reports about the need to have guns for self-defence. He asked: 'Should we endeavour to purchase automatic shotguns, automatic rifles of a heavy calibre, or would repeating rifles, 12-gauge single-shot shotguns or rifles of only .22 calibre be sufficient?' He also asked if it would be sensible to 'advertise for other like-minded people who are travelling [to Queensland] to join us and travel in convoy'.[69]

The issue of repelling armed home invaders was not prominent during the post Port Arthur debate, but in the past the NCGC had always responded by adding to the above arguments and saying that 'Australia had not yet introduced the Iranian system of summary execution for people involved in break and entering houses and theft of video-recorders'.

'We have the right to own guns'

One of the most significant statements to emerge from the Police Ministers' agreement was the reaffirmation that: 'The ownership, possession and use of firearms is a conditional privilege, not a right.'[70] The gun lobby in Australia had long claimed, like its US counterparts, that there was some sort of constitutionally defined or guaranteed 'right' to own a gun. There was not and never had been any such right in the Australian constitution, nor in Australian law.

---

68 Cantor CH, Brodie J, McMillen J. 'Firearm victims – who were they?', *Med J Aust* 1991, 155: 442–46.

69 Ringland DW. 'Packing to travel' (letter), *SMH*, 13 June 1996: 14.

70 Howard J. 'We must act now or lose the chance', *SMH*, 10 May 1996.

Response: Attorney General Daryl Williams appropriated the word 'right' by saying: 'I am more attracted to an argument that all Australians have a right to exist in a society where they are not subject to the needless risk of being injured or killed as a consequence of the widespread availability and irresponsible use of firearms.' He went on to use a variation of the analogy with car registration that the NCGC had promoted for years:

> Citizens are subject to regulation with respect to other, less inherently dangerous activities such as driving motor vehicles ... Moreover, persons are not allowed to drive any vehicle on roads simply because they want to. It would be ludicrous to suggest that a person has a right to drive Formula One cars simply because of their performance.[71]

In a similar vein, one writer cleverly appropriated the usual claim on the word 'right', inverting it to make the powerful point: 'The "right" to life must outweigh the "privilege" of gun ownership.'[72] The fact that fireworks had long been banned without the emergence of a Fireworks Users Rights Party[73] was used many times as an example of the way that concern for public safety had overridden the right of some to have fun with those dangerous goods. Even Tasmania had limited public access to fireworks by 1993.

'This is a violation of our civil rights'

After the 10 May APMC announcement, Ted Drane went into hyperbolic overdrive claiming: 'This amounts to one of the greatest infringements on the liberties of individuals in Australia's history. It is a draconian penalty against thousands of law-abiding Australians.'[74] A SSAA press

71 Anon. 'Ownership not a right', *SMH*, 11 May 1996.

72 Phelps G. 'Ban guns and give the world a lead' (letter), *The Age*, 7 May 1996: A14.

73 Armstrong H. Letter. *SMH*, 23 March 1996: 36.

74 Delvecchio J. 'Violation of civil rights, claims shooters' group', *SMH*, 11 May 1996.

release described the new South Australian firearms legislation as 'the most infamous legislation ever passed by an Australian Parliament and an outright abuse of civil rights . . . a contemptuous assault on the rights of law-abiding shooters.'[75]

Responses: This caused the editor of *The Age*, Michelle Grattan, to comment: 'The shooters' lobby which, judging from its over-the-top reaction alleging liberties are being dramatically threatened, borders on the fanatical.'[76] The public response produced dozens of examples of curtailments on the freedoms of citizens with which they taunted the gun lobby:

> Since our democratic right to throw dwarfs was taken away, it has removed our strong possibility of producing a future Olympic gold medal winner . . . Don't the bleating gun lobby realise how pathetic it sounds when it sings a similar tune?'[77]

> Our rights are similarly taken away when we are 'unjustly' forced to sit for a licence to drive a car, take out third party insurance, observe the speed limit, or drive with our headlights on after sunset.[78]

'We're going to lose all our guns'

After the initial announcement about which guns were to be banned, the gun lobby sought to incite its followers into believing that just about all guns were implicated. Kel Vickers, a former Commonwealth Games silver medallist in pistol shooting, told a gun rally in Sydney that Howard's policy was the thin edge of a much wider agenda.[79] They tried to put the view abroad that the new laws were but a prelude for what was to come. This was said by the editor of a gun magazine to

---

75 http://www.tnet.com.au/~ssaa/ [no longer active, 2013].

76 Grattan M. 'Howard shows mettle', *The Age*, 11 May 1996: A6.

77 Perry C. 'Sound pathetic' (letter), *SMH*, 13 May 1996.

78 Ibid.

79 Gora B. 'Protesters vow to keep fighting', *Sunday Telegraph*, 16 June 1996.

be 'a hidden agenda which will ultimately result in completely disarm-ing all Australians. This is a view reinforced by the previous Keating Government being a signatory to a UN treaty which promises to disarm all Australians by the year 2000.'[80] This claim was made on the basis of a Japanese UN resolution which called in general terms for the global control of firearms!

One National Party member sympathetic to the gun lobby even tried to get publicity for a technical argument that the rusted, inop-erable memorial cannons and Bofors guns that can be found in many Australian country town parks would now be illegal under the wording of the new laws. His efforts were mocked by appearing in a column known for its lampooning of political idiocy.[81]

Responses: It was simply not the case that all guns were to be banned. It was very easy to point this out. Several writers knocked this nonsense on the head by listing, at great length, the wide range of guns that would still be available to shooters:

> Anyway, Australian's *can* bear arms. Here are some of the guns you can own under the new laws: bolt action centre-fire military rifles; lever action centre-fire sporting rifles; pump-action centre-fire sporting rifles; rimfile rifles with bolt, level or pump actions; double-barrel shotguns. If you can't knock down a fox with one of the above, the solution is perhaps not a semi-automatic but an ophthalmologist with a centre-fire laser.[82]

The Federal National Party Member for Parkes, Michael Cobb, told Federal Parliament:

> I condemn the misinformation that is going around on this matter and which has been whipped up by some groups. The Sporting Shooters Association of Australia (New South Wales) Inc. has written something that has been put on my

---

80 Harvey N. Letter. *Guns Australia*, July/August 1996: 8.

81 Anon. 'Gossip', *SMH*, 2 August 1996: 20.

82 Carlyon L. 'A half-cocked debate on guns', *SMH*, 1996: 17.

desk today. I am disappointed to see what they say because my own 13-year-old son is a junior member of this Association. They say that 80% of Australian target shooting will be banned. On another page of the document, they say that about 80% of gun owners will be banned with no compensation. That is absolute, ridiculous nonsense. Indeed, if they cared to read what is being put out, some of it is quite reasonable indeed. I am pleased to say that I am now receiving letters from the farming community around my electorate in particular saying, 'Hang in there. We support what is being proposed. It is quite reasonable and it will help make Australia a safer place for our children.'[83]

'Hitler tried to disarm the Germans'

Internationally, the gun lobby is fond of comparing gun control agenda with that of Hitler in pre–World War II Germany. Hitler, they argued knowingly, also sought to disarm the population. Queensland's Ian McNiven argued: 'Once they're disarmed, as we saw with Hitler when he disarmed the Jewish people, the Government can basically do whatever they like with those people.' An editor of *Guns Australia* wrote: 'Once the Government has complete records of who owns what guns, what's to stop them from instructing police and the military to confiscate all privately owned firearms? This was the strategy used by dictators like Hitler and Stalin to disarm the populace of Russia and Germany and turn them into police states.

And there was still more: 'We are ruled by politicians who would have no compunction about asking help from foreign governments to enforce these bans if all else fails.'[84] Those who promoted these perspectives wanted the community to understand that they were enemies of tyranny, sympathisers with oppressed groups and armed to the teeth prepared to resist any neo-Hitlerian pretenders.

---

83 Cobb M. Federal *Hansard*, 17 June 1996.
84 Harvey N. Letter, *Guns Australia*, July/August 1996: 8.

Others argued that the community needed to be armed to defend itself against the Government. They insisted that Howard's agenda was to disarm the population while simultaneously increasing the armed capacity of the police to establish a totalitarian state: 'Are you not even curious as to why our police force is being issued with outrageously powerful handguns and military-style bullet-proof vests, while the rest of us are slowly being disarmed?'[85] This writer offered to buy me and Rebecca Peters a one-way ticket to Romania, China or North Korea where 'civilians do not own firearms', and hoped that police would soon raid our houses so we could experience the sort of 'peace and freedom you will no doubt find when you migrate to a country where civilians do not own firearms.'

Responses: The columnist Mike Carlton ridiculed this claim by specifying the sort of consequence McNiven's rhetoric was presumably alluding to: 'Uh huh. Possibly fearful of being trucked off to a gas chamber by the Liberal-National Coalition.'[86] Carlton then guffawed about how McNiven had lodged a rejected complaint with the Australian Federal Police accusing the Prime Minister of having prejudiced 'the safety or defence of Australia by disarming its citizens'.

Another writer suggested that 'the chances of disarmed Australian citizens being gassed by their Government is somewhat less than that of being shot by an armed fellow Australian',[87] while another put it that the 'more valid comparison is between the cunning propaganda practised by the shooters and the Nazis'.[88] Significantly, the Jewish Board of Deputies attacked the Hitler analogy, claiming that 'the Jewish community finds [it] repugnant and offensive, and totally rejects the comparison'.[89]

One writer challenged the very notion that in modern societies, tyrannies were overthrown with guns. He pointed to the examples of

---

85 Eyre C. 'Can't you see what's happening?' (letter), *SMH*, 6 June 1996: 14.

86 Carlton M. 'Mike Carlton' (column), *SMH*, 11 May 1996.

87 MacAdam T. 'No comparison' (letter), *SMH*, 21 May 1996: 10.

88 Simmons A. 'No comparison' (letter), *SMH*, 21 May 1996: 10.

89 Anon. 'Row over gun rally remarks', *SMH*, 27 July 1996: 6.

the unarmed 'people power' revolutions in the Philippines, Russia, Poland and East Germany and contrasted this with chaotic nations where armed civilian militias roamed the country (Somalia, Rwanda, Cambodia, Afghanistan).[90]

'We want to defend the nation'

Those who wanted to defend themselves against a future tyrannical government nearly always believed that they had big roles to play in a para-military citizens' army that would defend the nation against external attack. These people argued that 'disarming the population' would make the nation defenceless if Australia was invaded by a foreign power. This was nearly always said to be Indonesia. Indonesia's expansionism into the former West New Guinea (now Irian Jaya) and into East Timor were given as evidence of the threat Australia faced.

The Federal Member for Herbert told Parliament:

> I received a mock media release dated the year 2000 in the mail just this week and I will read two paragraphs from it. It states: 'Last Sunday night Northern Australia was invaded by up to 1,000,000 Asian soldiers and militias using thousands of new plastic landing craft deployed from high speed aluminium supercats . . . The invading forces are concentrating on every outlying community and isolated station owners and mining sites. They are shooting the males from long range then dismembering them, raping the women and shooting or slashing the kids and babies to death.'[91]

Some of the anti-Asian propaganda being circulated was particularly sick. Tony Pitt, national chairman of 'The Australians', widely distributed an article at gun rallies which described Indonesians as 'those gentlemen [who] would cut out your genitals, sew them into your mouth and prod your bum with a bayonet, driving you through the streets as a spectacle, making la-la noises with your new tongue.

90 Gillin T. 'Rule of law over .303' (letter), *SMH*, 17 June 1996: 16.
91 Australian House of Representatives *Hansard* for 24 June 1996.

This game would last until your blood supply ran out and you could no longer respond to the stabbing pain in the bum'.[92] In 1997 Pitt joined Pauline Hanson's One Nation Party.

Responses: This argument mixed xenophobia, racism and folk memories of citizens' defence forces belonging to eras of warfare long before the contemporary warfare of the Gulf War era. To people who subscribed to these sort of values, no amount of argument about it being unrealistic and plain silly was likely to make any impact. Whenever we could, we ridiculed those advocating an armed population as proponents of a 'Dad's Army' view of Australian defence (a reference to the former BBC TV comedy series about a bumbling group of aged and eccentric home guardsmen in England during World War II).[93]

One press story reported the views of 63-year-old Vietnam War Victoria Cross winner, Keith Payne. The story pictured a crusty and grim-faced Payne cradling his gun, together with an archival photo of him receiving his Victoria Cross from the British Queen in 1970. Payne, speaking from 'his home in the gun lobby stronghold of Mackay, Queensland' was said to be 'blast[ing] gun lobby elements who claim an armed population is vital for Australia's safety against an invading Indonesian army'. Payne pilloried these elements as 'cowboys' saying that 'the idea of them defending Australia is ridiculous' and urging them 'to try to join the military reserve, that is if they are psychologically fit to join and were admitted'.[94]

'Why don't you ban knives and clubs?'

A perennial gun lobby argument is that restricting access to guns is folly, because those who want to kill themselves or others can chose from a variety of lethal weapons. 'People hang themselves . . . are you going to ban ropes?' they argue. In dozens of letters and emails sent

---

92 Steketee M. 'Backlash: targeting the gun vote', *The Australian*, 8 June 1996.
93 *7 Days*. SBS Television.
94 Warnock S. 'Gun lobby claim "stupid"', *Sun-Herald*, 14 July 1996: 25.

during the debate, people supporting the gun lobby declared gun control supporters (especially people who worked in public health) were hypocrites for not simultaneously trying to 'ban' every other cause of death in the community. The logic behind this argument ran: 'There are many public health problems in the world. If you aren't willing to instantly fix all of them, it is hypocritical to try and fix any of them!' One erudite writer told *Age* readers:

> If they were genuine about lowering the suicide rate, they'd advocate the immediate banning of cigarettes . . . they would argue that the only ones who should have cars are taxi drivers, truck drivers and bus drivers . . . cars, which weren't even designed to kill, are killing 2,000 Australians a year.[95]

We formed the view that letters editors at newspapers published such inanity as 'all in their own words' examples of gun lobby reasoning.

The SSAA's Sebastian Ziccone argued: 'Anyone giving the matter a moment's thought would realise that the Dunblane murderer . . . could have easily achieved his deranged ends by other means, such as flame accelerant.'[96] We took this challenge, gave it a moment's thought, but searched for a long time to find any examples of mass killings by flame accelerant. Mass killing with guns were far easier to locate. A pro-gun American letter writer pointed out that tyre levers, bottles, kitchen knives, scissors, chemicals and many other 'weapons' had been used in murders.[97]

Responses: A barrage of replies to this letter included:

> Twenty-five people massacred by a bottle-wielding bottleman? The bottleman owned a large arsenal of bottles? Do they make semi-automatic bottles?[98]

---

95 Wegman J. 'Zealots miss out on the big killers' (letter), *The Age*, 4 June 1996: A12.

96 Ziccone S. 'In defence of arms', *The Age*, 10 May 1996: A15.

97 Shyne M. 'Blaming the guns instead of killers' (letter), *The Age*, 21 June 1996: 12.

98 Bond J. 'Risks compared' (letter), *The Age*, 22 June 1996: A22.

Once again the word 'mass' has been followed by the word 'shooting'. Not stabbing, clubbing, choking or bashing, but shooting.[99]

The NCGC emphasised the difference between guns and other weapons by arguing: 'Fists and knives leave people hurt, but the problem with firearms is that they are a permanent solution to what is often a temporary problem.'[100]

A machete attack on children attending a picnic in Wolverhampton, England – where the assailant was found to have kept files on the Port Arthur killings – was reported in Australia in July.[101] Again, one letter writer put it simply: 'Gun plus criminal intent equals 17 dead (Dunblane). Gun plus criminal intent equals 35 dead (Port Arthur). Machete and criminal intent equals seven injured (Wolverhampton). Guns do kill people.'[102]

The research evidence on the lethality of weapons was also useful here. Police records from Atlanta in the US found that assaults on family members and intimates using guns were three times more likely to result in death than assaults with knives and 23.4 times more than assaults involving other weapons or bodily force.[103] The gun lobby has retorted here that people intent on killing choose guns, while those less determined might choose less lethal weapons.[104] This assertion is contradicted by research which examined the location and number of knife wounds as a basis for judging the assailants' intent to kill. More attackers

---

99 Alvaro F. 'Something must be done, now' (letter), *SMH*, 1 May 1996: 14.

100 Sutton C, Gilmore H. 'Ban these games and toys of war', *Sun Herald*, 5 May 1996: 3.

101 Reuter. 'Briton held after machete attack "kept file on Port Arthur killings"', *The Age*, 11 July 1996: 9.

102 Neyle DA. 'Irrefutable' (letter), *SMH*, 12 July 1996: 10.

103 Saltzman L, Mercy J, O'Carroll P, Rosenberg M, Rhodes P. 'Weapon involvement and injury outcomes in family and intimate assaults', *JAMA*, 1993, 267: 3043–47.

104 Kleck G. *Point blank: guns and violence in America.* New York: Aldine de Gruyter, 1992.

with knives than those using guns appeared intent on killing.[105]

Two writers described killing with guns as a way of allowing the perpetrator to put some distance between him and his victims, allowing for a psychologically 'easier' act of killing to occur: 'Killing with a gun is easy, instant: it allows for 'remote control' death where the reality of the victims' terror and agony are minimised compared with 'hands-on' killing';[106] and 'Murder by remote control must stop now.'[107]

Our reply to the 'why are you picking on guns . . . cars kill many more people' argument was to produce it in parallel in the form of a question: 'Isn't your argument like accusing a cancer specialist of being a hypocrite for helping people with cancer because people also are dying of heart disease? Or a road safety advocate of being a scoundrel because children are also drowning in backyard pools?'

'This will only cause a black market to thrive'

The gun lobby, which opposed the ban on semi-automatics, warned that a black market in the banned guns would develop with 'an endless supply of illegal guns.'[108]

Response: Black markets have always existed for guns and doubtless, the new laws would cause many guns to go underground and be sold illegally that would otherwise have been traded openly. Those very intent on getting them would be able to buy these guns in the future as they had in the past. But yet again, this argument sought to dichotomise gun users into the unproblematic, simplistic categories of good and bad. The new laws would make it very much more difficult for the ordinary shooter, unfamiliar with ways of acquiring illegal guns, to get such a

---

105 Zimring F. Is gun control likely to reduce violent killings? *University of Chicago Law Review*, 1968, 35: 721–37.

106 Monteith A. Letter, *SMH*, 21 March 1996.

107 Nissen P. Letter, *SMH*, 1 May 1996: 14.

108 Dunlevy S. 'Lobby warns of black market', *Daily Telegraph*, 11 May 1996; Rees P. 'Shooters call crisis talks', *Sunday Telegraph*, 12 May 1996: 8.

weapon. Anyone wanting such a gun would henceforth have to deal with criminals, break the law themselves and live with concern about being apprehended and being charged with a serious offence. Such a distribution system contrasted with any shooter being able to walk into any gun shop and buy a semi-automatic weapon.

'Many shooters will disregard these stupid laws'

On the announcement of the Police Ministers' resolutions, the gun lobby began to emphasise that many shooters would disregard the new laws: they would not surrender their banned guns and they would not register those deemed legal.[109] This allowed them to wallow in ambiguity about whether they were predicting lawlessness or actually urging it. With their association with other historical examples of principled civil disobedience, Tingle sought to infer that the laws that would be broken were objects of understandable contempt in the eyes of sensible, knowledgeable people ('laws made by people who understand absolutely nothing about guns'[110]). He stated: 'You can keep a gun forever and no one would know. Many shooters are saying they will not hand in or register their guns.'[111] Ted Drane joined in the chorus, prefacing his remarks with the obligatory: 'I would never advocate that people break the law. But shooters are bitter . . .'[112] A previously unknown group calling itself 'The Gun Lobby' dispensed with the ambiguities and openly advised gun owners to break the law, saying its aim was to create 'a nation of more than one million passive criminals'.[113]

The day before the 10 May Police Ministers' meeting, Drane was publicly stating that he would obey the law if it required him to surrender his guns:

109 Passey D. 'Owners of guns will resist, say lobbyists', *SMH*, 24 July 1996: 7.

110 Lawnham P, McGarry A. 'Shooters will defy new laws, MP warns', *The Australian*, 11 May 1996.

111 Vass N. 'Owners won't give up weapons: Tingle', *SMH*, 13 May 1996.

112 Passey D. 'Owners of guns will resist, say lobbyists', *SMH*, 24 July 1996: 7.

113 Hayes B, Patty A. 'Shooters plan gun law revolt', *Sun Herald*, 12 May 1996: 3.

Interviewer: Mr Drane, would you hand your weapons in?

Drane: Yes, I would, that's right.[114]

But by the time of the Sydney pro-gun rally on 15 June Drane was telling the crowd: 'And I'm not gunna give up any guns that they're going to take off me! Are you gunna give yours up?'[115]

Others in the gun-owning community were more candid about the proportion of shooters who would not merely actively disobey the law, but who would try to offload their guns to criminals rather than hand them in for market value compensation. A writer to a gun magazine said:

> Howard is hopelessly naive to think that any more than 10% of the total number of semi-automatic weapons will be handed in under the Howard ban. The vast majority are just going to disappear until they resurface again in the hands of criminals. There are many people not wanting to be caught with the weapons but they are unwilling to hand them in. They are going to sell them.[116]

Tony Warner, of the Western Australian division of the SSAA, wrote in July to WA Premier Richard Court arguing that shooters who would refuse to obey the new laws would be somehow compelled to break them:

> I urge your Cabinet and Government to reject the Prime Minister's intractability and enact laws in this State that reflect the sovereignty of the State and to enact laws that all normal law-abiding people see as reasonable. To do otherwise *is to invite involuntary lawlessness* by otherwise law-abiding citizens. (my emphasis)[117]

---

114 *Lateline*, ABC TV, 9 May 1996.

115 Drane T. *Channel 9 TV News*, 15 June 1996.

116 Ellis M. Letter, *Guns Australia*, September/October 1996: 18

117 SSAA website, July 1996.

The gun lobby wanted it both ways on the question of how many shooters would surrender their guns. It expediently argued that few gun owners would hand in their banned guns; and that so many would be handed in that the estimated costs of the compensatory buyback were ludicrously low. It argued: 'The new gun laws will not significantly reduce overall gun numbers . . . Banning self-loading long-arms and pump-action shotguns will remove *only the few* held by people who comply with the law.' (my emphasis)[118]

'Where will the surrendered guns go?'

In mid June 1996, claims surfaced that Victorian police had re-sold semi-automatics surrendered during a 1987–88 amnesty to a Victorian gun dealer.[119] The guns were to be sold overseas by the dealer. Another claim was that a gun Bryant used at Port Arthur had previously been surrendered to police in another state.[120] A gun collector claimed he 'believed' an AR–15 rifle he had surrendered in 1993 was the weapon used at Port Arthur. He was reported as saying: 'I hope and pray it wasn't my rifle which was used . . . but in my heart I believe it was.' This was enough for some media to report his claims, despite noting that 'police claim records show that Mr Drysdale's gun was destroyed'.[121] It was revealed at Bryant's sentencing that he had bought his gun brand new from a Hobart gun dealer.

A by-now desperate gun lobby milked these stories for all they were worth,[122] trying to build a spectre of mistrust in the bureaucratic

---

118 Tingle J, Shelton B, Borsak R, Kounaris G et al. 'Shooters' response', *Australian Gun Sports*, June 1996: 21.

119 Anon. 'Anger over police amnesty rifle sale', *SMH*, 17 June 1996: 4; Green S, Adams D. 'Outcry sparks gun destruction order', *The Age*, 18 June 1996: 1.

120 McGuire P, Jones W. 'Port Arthur rifle came from police', *Sunday Telegraph*, 9 June 1996.

121 Anon. 'My gun killed 35 – farmer', *Sunday Mail* (Adelaide), 23 June 1996: 2.

122 McGuire P, Jones W. 'Port Arthur rifle came from police', *Sunday Telegraph*, 9 June 1996.

process by arguing that guns handed in following Port Arthur could similarly find their way back into the community after police sold them. This argument was baseless, relying on the assumption that surrendered semi-automatics could be sold in states that did not ban them. Because the ban would be nationwide, the speculation would not hold up, but the gun lobby believed the claim would nonetheless fuel its supporters' mistrust of police.

Responses: NCGC members were interviewed many times on our reaction to the gun lobby's claims that the ban would be futile and establish a black market. We responded by painting the gun lobby as a group that was inciting law breaking.[123] We challenged them to act responsibly, and linked the accusation of irresponsibility with one of self-interest and naked opportunism: 'They should voluntarily hand in excess arms, cooperate with the new laws, and most importantly abandon their spurious campaign for funds and direct that money towards the victims of the massacre.'[124]

This was an important definitional exercise. The gun lobby had sought to define the ban as a futile exercise that would fail because it was *unjust*. They thus sought to speak using a voice of principled civil disobedience, and we saw it as our task to re-frame this voice into one seen to be coming from people who were not just dispassionately predicting lawlessness, but actively encouraging it.

Another core NCGC response to talk of mass lawlessness over registration was to advocate a mechanism whereby people in the community should be encouraged to alert police to people who owned illegal guns.

> Registration will only work if it is accompanied by a high profile confidential hotline, like Operation Noah for drugs, where people can report those they know who are keeping illegal guns. Penalties for possession of unregistered guns after the amnesty period must also be spectacular and police

---

123 Wainwright R. 'We'll take to streets, say sporting shooters', *SMH*, 13 May 1996.

124 Dunlevy S. 'Lobby warns of black market', *Daily Telegraph*, 11 May 1996.

directed to take all reports seriously. Anything less will be an abject failure.'[125]

This idea was supported by trenchant critics of current state-based firearms registration systems, who argued that without a 'dob in' scheme and harsh penalties, many guns would continue to be held unregistered.[126] Describing the Police Ministers' resolutions, Attorney General Daryl Williams said of penalties 'the adjective we used was "severe".'[127]

Accusations about police selling guns back to the community were never heard again when television news reports began to show film of guns being crushed and smelted down.

Arguments for exemptions

In the run-up to the Police Ministers' meeting and from the time its terms were announced, the gun lobby and sections of the National Party argued the case for categories of shooters to be exempt from the ban. These arguments focused on:

- the need for farmers to have semi-automatics
- endangered and hungry pilots being forced down in the Australian outback
- rural women
- competitive target shooters
- collectors and heirlooms.

'Farmers need semi-automatics'

Much publicity was given to a public apology made by the Prime Minister to 'tens of thousands of law-abiding Australians, particularly

---

125 Chapman S. 'Now, about those guns . . .', *SMH*, 9 May 1996: 15.

126 Fife-Yeomans J. 'Call to dob in, imprison illegal firearm owners', *The Australian*, 11 June 1996.

127 Daryl Williams. *7.30 Report*, ABC TV, 10 May 1996.

in the country areas' for being inconvenienced by the new gun laws.[128] But as the debate unfolded, it became doubtful that there would in fact be widespread demand for such an apology. Many farmers called radio programs to express their support for the reforms. Typically, they stressed five arguments: that it was a myth that farmers needed an arsenal of guns; that semi-automatics were largely unnecessary on the average farm; that they had experienced drunken and drugged aggressive shooters coming onto their properties and shooting stock and equipment; that they wanted to make it clear they fully supported the proposed new laws; and that the 'gun lobby' was not speaking for them.

When the gun lobby insisted that farmers needed semi-automatics to cull wild and feral animals and destroy sick or drought-stricken stock, it was difficult for anyone without first-hand experience to refute this with authenticity and plausibility. The gun lobby had no shortage of farmers willing to insist that city people knew nothing about the rigours of country life and shooting.

Media advocacy for gun control during the debate was voiced by five groups: politicians, editorial writers, gun control advocates, gun victims and their families, and the general public. Between these groups, there was a huge depth of experience, authority and perspective that allowed powerful, compelling statements to be made in support of gun control. However, a sixth category of gun control advocate – who might be termed the responsible shooter – also received considerable and often invaluable news coverage.

Letters were published from ordinary gun owners who quietly explained that, 'I realised that there was a more important issue than any love of the sport – the safety of the community and the obvious fact that fewer guns means fewer deaths.'[129]

Professional shooters also often supported the new laws. The Queensland representative of the Association of Professional Shooters,

---

128 Grattan M, Savva N. 'Howard to tour rural areas to sell gun laws', *The Age*, 6 June 1996: A5.

129 Anderson B. 'Why I handed in the 12 gauge' (letter), *The Age*, 6 June 1996: 16.

Greg Carlsson, was among several who stated doubts about whether farmers needed semi-automatics. His comments were picked up by the media as a standard refutation of the claim.

Carlsson, a professional kangaroo shooter from western Queensland with 22 years experience, pilloried claims about shooters needing semi-automatics, saying such statements applied only to amateurs from the city: 'The basic people who own semi-automatic firearms come from the city and are more interested in blowing away anything that moves ... The common terminology out here for them are weekend shooters – that's when we are being nice about them . . .'[130] Carlsson went on to describe the need to use more than one bullet on an animal as 'inhumane, unprofessional and a breach of the wildlife harvesters' code of practice' and said semi-automatics were 'too inaccurate to be humane'.

A similar story featured a professional kangaroo shooter who described semi-automatics as inaccurate saying: 'I can drop five roos in 15 seconds [with his single-shot, bolt-action rifle] if everything is running right and still get another crack at the mob after reloading.'[131] A similar letter came from a country man who had previously operated a hunting safari business and had abandoned the enterprise as too dangerous, having seen 'too many fools with firearms to believe that anyone has an ordained right to possess such a weapon ... a percentage of clients would arrive travelling high on various drugs'.[132]

The Land newspaper featured an article on archetypal farmers, father and son Garth and Scott Dutfield, who told how single-shot rifles were adequate for their needs to cull kangaroos, rabbits and foxes. They had banned shooters from their property after complaining about 'city hunters coming up on weekends and 'shooting everything on sight', including sheep.[133]

130 Collins C. 'Single-shot Greg takes aim at the semi-automatics lobby', *The Australian*, 11 May 1996.

131 Bearup G. 'Son of a gun town', *SMH*, July 6 1996: S5.

132 Rhoades B. 'Too many fools with firearms' (letter), *The Australian*, 17 June 1996: 10.

133 Johnson P. 'Single shot's fine at Mumbil', *The Land*, 9 May 1996.

A *Sydney Morning Herald* journalist who had grown up in the country wrote a long piece describing how most people on the land would be either untroubled or openly welcome the ban on semi-automatics, and how deeply they resented being lumped together with what she described as

> this sub-species of rural hoodlum . . . [who] live in country towns and may or may not lease a few hectares. They wear flannel shirts and American baseball hats. And they love guns. On weekends . . . they blast the daylights out of road signs, mailboxes and native birds. If you have stock in the paddock beside the highway, they'll take pot-shots at hapless sheep or steer. They call it hunting.[134]

One writer wrote a lengthy article where many of the gun lobby's arguments about farmers needing semi-automatics were addressed. These are worth quoting at length: [135]

> The true feelings of farmers towards guns and gun control are being manipulated and misrepresented by the fierce vested interests of the arms dealers and their pro-shooter lobby groups.
>
> The farmer's single shot rifle is occasionally dusted off for the unpleasant but effective task of destroying injured livestock or the occasional rogue sheep dog. The average farmer today simply does not have a need for an armoury of rifles, let alone high-powered semi-automatics – that is a myth promoted by the arms dealers and recreational shooters.
>
> Modern pest control on the Australian farm has seen guns replaced in the main by safer and more cost-effective poison, trapping and biological control methods. Shooting, except for professional contract shooting of pigs and kangaroos, is time-consuming, ineffective . . . and expensive.

---

134 Loane S. 'Real farmers a long shot from gun-ho marchers', *SMH*, 5 June 1996.

135 Cocky. 'Farmers, too, fear a belly full of beer and a magazine full of lead', *The Bulletin*, 28 May 1996: 95.

What the farmer knows – but the sporting shooter ignores – is that if you miss the rabbit or kangaroo with your first shot, your target takes off. To respond by spraying the paddock with lead, which the semi-automatic allows, does nothing but threaten livestock, signs, water tanks and farming families.

Displaying an ignorance of basic livestock management, the NSW National Party leader Ian Armstrong, this month said [on radio] that graziers might need semi-automatic rifles to shoot crows at lambing time. Perhaps Armstrong should talk quietly to a real lamb breeder, who would almost certainly be appalled at the thought of automatic rifle fire anywhere near lambing ewes . . . Who is feeding Armstrong such misinformation?

The National Farmers Federation 'applauded' the new laws after 'extensive talks had produced unanimous agreement on tightening the rules'.[136] This was despite, as one journalist noted, 'being one of the groups most disadvantaged by them'.[137]

While much publicity was given to dissent over the new laws within the rural-based National Party, it soon became apparent that many women in the party strongly supported the reforms. 'Women, the National Party has discovered, overwhelmingly support the Prime Minister's proposals on guns.' One delegate to a meeting said: 'We need to take a broader view and look at how this affects the community as a whole . . . To not support tighter gun controls is to condone the action of the gunman at Port Arthur.'[138]

A great deal of attention was given to the feelings about the new laws among people living in the bush and in country towns. One feature article, for example, profiled the views of people living in the New England town of Guyra, population 2,000.[139] The article began with a

---

136 Dunlevy S. 'Lobby warns of black market', *Daily Telegraph*, 11 May 1996.

137 Ibid.

138 Loane S. 'Extremists' white feather taunts fail to intimidate MPs', *SMH*, 15 June 1996.

139 Bearup G. 'Son of a gun town', *SMH*, July 6 1996: S5.

description of the gun murder-suicide 11 years ago of a local family of four, and its impact on the town. It ended with the story of a youth who had committed suicide after a split with his girlfriend. Most of the story covered the different reactions of shooters in the community, from those who said they would not surrender their guns, to those who planned to willingly do so, concluding that the town was 'divided'.

The head of the Anglican Parish of Broken Hill, the Venerable Dr Edwin Byford, wrote to the NCGC describing a meeting of the Synod of the Diocese of Riverina, which covers about one third of the state of NSW. A motion supporting the new gun controls was put to the meeting.

> The debate was characterised by speaker after speaker getting up and saying that they were land owners and that the last thing they wanted was people on their properties or in their districts with automatic or semi-automatic guns. This was very passionately put by one grazier from near Wilcannia. When he got up to speak most of us had expected that he would oppose the resolution, but he was one of the strongest speakers in favour.

Earlier he had written to the press:

> Only 1 to 2% of the [Broken Hill] population had turned out for the free barbecue that the gun lobby put on to attract people to its Sunday meeting. The 98 to 99% of the population that stayed away clearly demonstrated that the gun lobby . . . [is] out of step with the sentiments of the people of this city.[140]

Because of the notoriety that Ian McNiven and Ron Owen had brought to the gun debate, their hometown of Gympie in South Queensland became shorthand for the 'unofficial redneck capital of Australia'. Many locals deeply resented the reputation a few had brought to the town of 14,000, and several stories were written about their efforts to restore the town's good name, their support for gun law reform and

---

140 Byford E. 'Broken Hill: an oasis on the edge' (letter), *SMH*, 13 June 1996.

the anonymous death threats they had received.[141] In late August 1996 the town was back in the news when a local gun enthusiast shot dead three of his family before fleeing into the bush.

In Tasmania, the Firearm Owners Association argued that semi-automatics were needed to cull sheep as 'recommended by the RSPCA (Royal Society for Prevention of Cruelty to Animals)'. No source for this assertion was ever provided.

'How are we to keep wild beasts at bay?'

The notion that parts of the outback were crawling with predatory wild beasts intent on attacking defenceless humans developed into another favourite gun lobby argument for availability of semi-automatics. Talk of crocodiles, charging water buffaloes[142] and wounded wild pigs turning on shooters ('With wild pigs, you need one . . . because one shot might not stop them'[143]) was typical. Perhaps the most remarkable claim was made by Queensland National Party MP Mrs De-Anne Kelly, who argued that semi-automatics were necessary for killing snakes: 'I live in taipan [a highly venomous snake] country and you only get one chance if you have a small child and a taipan.'[144] Given the slender and highly mobile nature of snakes, and the usual way of killing them in the bush – with a stick or shovel – the scenario of a parent fetching the semi-automatic to blast away at such a small and elusive target in Mrs Kelly's 'one chance' was worth some reflection. Presumably, a bazooka or flame thrower would serve this purpose even better, yet Mrs Kelly did not argue for the liberalisation of laws allowing the public in taipan country to have access to these.

---

141 Roberts G. 'Town cringes at its gun-happy image', *SMH*, 25 May 1996: 37.

142 Farr M. 'Rednecks, whingers unite for greater good', *Daily Telegraph*, 11 May 1996.

143 Chapman S. 'For the Howard plan' (vox pops), *SMH*, 10 May 1996; McNicoll DD. 'Urban cowboys take shot in the dark on gun control', *The Australian*, 9 May 1995.

144 Roberts G. 'MP to open shooting contest', *SMH*, 10 May 1996.

Response: Former NSW Labor Premier Barrie Unsworth said: 'They argue they need them for wild pigs – that's bullshit. There is more trouble with pit bull terriers in Sydney suburbs than with wild pigs in the country.'[145]

'What about pilots forced down in the outback?'

A rather bizarre variation of this argument asked us to consider pilots forced down in the outback: 'Pilots who serve Australia's remote Gulf region should have a semi-automatic for protection against wildlife – and to kill for food – if the aircraft is forced down.'[146] This suggestion had also been supported by the Northern Territory's Chief Minister Shane Stone.[147] But neither Stone nor the reporter of this story ventured into the questions of how many pilots are ever 'forced down' in the Gulf region (few, if any); how many so forced down have been threatened by wildlife (again, none to speak of); and why single shot weapons would not suffice in such (wildly improbable) situations anyway.

A Northern Territory Department of Primary Industries officer provided a more sobering consideration. He expressed concern that a blanket ban on high-powered semi-automatics would preclude his department from contracting aerial shooters armed with such weapons in helicopters to efficiently destroy tubercular cattle and buffalo in the vast outback expanses.[148] But in the course of this news report, it was revealed that a mere 23 D-class shooting licences were currently issued in the Northern Territory for such purposes. This figure placed in perspective generalised claims being made by the gun lobby and its political supporters that 'people in the outback' required high-powered semi-automatics. The reality was that only 23 professional shooters in the Northern Territory needed to apply for a licence to use such weapons.

---

145 Byrne A. 'Unsworth gloomy on summit', *SMH*, 3 May 1996.

146 Warnock S. 'Gun lobby claim "stupid"', *Sun Herald*, 14 July 1996: 25.

147 *Lateline*, ABC TV, 9 May 1996.

148 Alcorn G. 'Flying shooters need fast power', *SMH*, 10 May 1996.

'How will isolated rural women defend themselves?'

Some chivalrous types in the gun lobby were very concerned about women on isolated rural properties. These women would often be alone with their men away, so the argument ran. So they would need semi-automatics to defend against escaped criminals, rapists and other undesirables. Woe betides any anti-gun advocate from the city who might imply that these rural women should be left defenceless.

Response: Several women were scathing in their rebuttal of this argument. One, who had lived for ten years alone in isolated remote Aboriginal communities in the Northern Territory asked:

> Who does Mr Stone wish to arm in these communities? Does he want Aboriginal people to have greater ability to slaughter their families, when upset, than the rest of the community? Or does he want to give whites the ability to slaughter Aboriginal people?[149]

Sara Henderson, a bestselling author whose books tell of her life in the Australian outback, declared her support for tougher gun controls.[150] The Country Women's Association also supported the changes. Its NSW state president declared: 'It's sad it takes such a public tragedy to get action, but we need some sort of register so we know who has these guns. It's amazing to think someone can just walk into a shop and buy one.'[151]

'The laws discriminate against the aged and frail'

The gun lobby argued that the bans on self-loading shotguns would severely disadvantage 'women, young people, the elderly and disabled' who participated in clay target shooting.[152] The recoil or kickback from

---

149 Roberts R. 'Offensive' (letter), *SMH*, 11 May 1996: 36.

150 Anon. 'Gun lobby silenced by poll reality', *Daily Telegraph*, 9 May 1996.

151 Dick A. 'Reforms needed: survey', *The Land*, 9 May 1996.

152 Bearup G. 'Son of a gun town', *SMH*, 6 July1996: S5; Savva N, Farouque F,

self-loading shotguns is often appreciably less than that from dou-
ble-barrelled shotguns, so the gun lobby argued that frail members of
the community would deeply resent the ban. Said the Federal Member
for Riverina:

> I had a phone call today from some elderly shooters. They
> were saying that they need automatic [sic] shotguns because
> of the recoil on their shoulder. The women who shoot in
> clubs would prefer to use that type of firearm also, because it
> is less restrictive and does not hurt their shoulders.[153]

Response: We made no attempt to respond to this claim, judging it
as one of the more desperate appeals that would be seen by most as
plain silly. The idea that politicians would consider placing the shoulder comfort of perhaps a few hundred elderly shooters above the
reasons for one of the central platforms of the new reforms was not
worth any effort at response. But we were proved wrong on this when
the NSW Government passed amendments to its *Firearms Act* to allow
exemptions in this regard and the Tasmanian Government adopted the
exemption as well.

'Our Olympic shooters will be disadvantaged'

1996 was the year of the Atlanta Olympic Games and we expected that
this would provide an extra pretext for the gun lobby to claim that
Australia would be severely disadvantaged in Olympic shooting if the
ban on semi-automatics went ahead. With support for Olympians being
a virtual sign of patriotism, the shooters probably felt they held a powerful card. We did not have to wait long. Roy Smith of the SSAA said on
13 May: 'How do you compensate someone for removing their sport;
people who have spent years becoming an elite athlete?'[154] A former

Graham D. 'Hard-liners buckling on uniform gun laws', *The Age*, 19 July 1996:
A7.

153 Federal Parliament House of Representatives *Hansard*.

154 Wainwright R. 'We'll take to streets, say sporting shooters', *SMH*, 13 May
1996.

Olympic shooter said he was 'outraged' at the decision and that the 'changes seemed to mean sporting shooters would not have sufficient reason to own and fire guns'.[155]

With huge irony, Australia's first gold medal at Atlanta was won by Michael Diamond in the trap shoot on the same day (22 July) that Prime Minister Howard forced the states to abandon their calls for crimping. Shooters' Party head John Tingle climbed aboard the victory to try to portray government and media criticism of shooters as unsportsman-like: 'They had to compete knowing that an opportunist Prime Minister had labelled them and their fellow shooters as threats to society.'[156]

The gun lobby argued that restrictions placed on shooting by children would disadvantage Australians in future Olympic competition because the children would not have enough years to build the experience needed to compete at the highest level. They also argued that the new laws would reduce the pool of shooters needed to produce Olympic champions.[157]

In Tasmania the gun lobby suffered a major setback when the Tasmanian Rifle Association publicly agreed with the Tasmanian CGC to support the Howard gun law proposals. Representing competitive shooters, the TRA did not hesitate to support bans on self-loading rifles, a policy it adopted in 1991 after the Strathfield massacre. As a result of that policy the TRA was expelled from the Firearm Owners Association of Tasmania.

Response: An editorial stated that the argument about disadvantaging Australian children from becoming future Olympic champions was akin to arguing that having legal limits on driving age disadvantaged potential race car champions.[158]

---

155 Creer K. 'Clampdown "may shut gunshop doors"', *Sunday Telegraph*, 12 May 1996.

156 Savva N. 'Gun laws will not stop Olympic gold: ministers', *The Age*, 23 July 1996: A2.

157 Ibid.

158 Anon. 'Gold shot' (editorial), *SMH*, 28 July 1996: 34.

Whatever advantage the gun lobby sought from these remarks was rapidly extinguished when the Attorney General pointed out that no Australian shooter in Atlanta was using a gun that would be banned under the new laws, and that target shooting was explicitly included as a legitimate reason to own a gun.[159]

'You're snatching back family heirlooms'

Another angle used by the gun lobby to attack the resolutions concerned what they chose to refer to as guns that were 'family heirlooms'.[160] This description sought to evoke sentimental notions of doting fathers on their deathbeds handing their prized guns onto loving sons. One story profiled a Bathurst man shown holding his recently deceased father's photograph and the gun he had bequeathed to his son. 'My father had this gun for 40 years . . . It's worth $500. But to me it's worth a million. I could never give it up. My father died of cancer a few weeks ago. It's something I could never hand over,' he said.[161] Guns were thus positioned as symbols of rites of passage or the continuity between generations of decent men. The Government, the gun lobby now argued, would become engaged in 'raiding homes to seize banned weapons',[162] evoking notions of police and bureaucrats wrestling grandfather's antique semi-automatic out of the hands of the owner who had gazed at it lovingly on its wall mount for the last 20 years. Others sought to draw a contrast with cultural concerns to preserve historic buildings and 'governmental cultural vandalism at its very worst' in destroying guns, 'which are equally important as our buildings'.[163]

---

159 Savva N. 'Gun laws will not stop Olympic gold: ministers', *The Age*, 23 July 1996: A2.

160 Hayes B, Patty A. 'Shooters plan gun law revolt', *Sun Herald*, 12 May 1996.

161 Condon M. 'On the bus with the diehards', *Sun Herald*, 16 June 1996: 2.

162 Dunlevy S. 'Lobby warns of black market', *Daily Telegraph*, 11 May 1996.

163 Thurgar S. 'Historic guns to be destroyed' (letter), *The Australian*, 11 June 1996.

Response: The NCGC elected not to engage with this argument. Had we chosen to, the obvious retort would have been to draw an analogy between the way war souvenirs such as mortar bombs and grenades are frequently confiscated by the police from home mantelpieces and garages despite protests from their owners claiming sentimental attachments. When the laws were passed throughout Australia, those wishing to retain firearm heirlooms were able to do so if the guns were made permanently inoperative before the heirloom licence was issued.

'This does not address the "real" causes of violence'

The gun lobby's stock explanation about violence in the community was that guns were merely one means through which violent individuals expressed their anger. Controlling guns, they argued, would not work for many reasons, but even assuming that it did, violent individuals would simply choose other means of inflicting violence. Violent people had underlying psychosocial problems that were the real cause of their violence. If society was sincere in wanting to reduce violence, it would commit resources to address these *real* causes of violence. 'What we should be asking ourselves is why we have seen this upsurge of violence in the community in the last 15 years or so. Firearms have been in the Australian community since 1788, but until very recently they were never the cause of the sort of problems we see now,' wrote John Tingle, sweeping over 200 years of violence against Aborigines under the convenient historical carpet. 'Isn't it time we started asking what's changed in the behaviour of some of our citizens that they really believe that an act of outrageous violence can in some way resolve their problems?'[164]

Plainly there is much sense in any analysis of community violence that seeks to move beyond controlling the weapons used in violent acts. But the gun lobby's argument about real causes always goes one step further: it argues 'go ahead and address these "real" causes, but do little or nothing to restrict access to guns'.

---

164 Tingle J. 'The crossfire on gun legislation', *SMH*, 11 July 1995: 15.

Response: The NCGC tried to expose the poverty of this argument with an analogy developed by psychiatrist and youth suicide prevention specialist Dr Michael Dudley, who argued that 'patients bleeding to death may suffer from any number of underlying problems, but doctors looking for causes do not ignore the immediate threat to life – they first stop the bleeding'.[165]

'. . . which are violent videos, movies and games'

Almost immediately after the news of Port Arthur broke, the issue of the role of violence in the media as an influence on violence in the community resurfaced. Calls began for further restrictions on these films and games. The American actor Dustin Hoffman's comments were widely reported when he attacked Hollywood's obsession with violence, saying this was directly linked to massacres like Port Arthur and Dunblane.[166]

A report in two News Ltd newspapers (the *Herald-Sun* and the *Daily Telegraph*) on 14 May stated that police had removed from Bryant's house 2,000 'violent and pornographic' videos that included 'violence and explicit sex acts including bestiality'. A former girlfriend and a video storeowner confirmed that he liked violent videos. These 'facts' rapidly entered the national folklore that circulated about Bryant until the Chief Censor, John Dickie, rapidly deflated the story at an Australian Medical Association conference on 28 June. Dickie contacted the Tasmanian Department of Justice and Trustees that was holding all Bryant's assets. The person who removed the videos told Dickie the collection consisted mostly of early musicals and classics with stars such as Clark Gable, Myrna Loy and Bette Davis. These belonged to the elderly woman who owned the house in which Bryant lived.[167]

The gun lobby were enthusiastic members of the chorus about movie violence, arguing that violent films and games were the issues

---

165 Dudley M, Gale F. 'Fewer arms, fewer deaths', *SMH*, 9 May 1996: 15.

166 Lusetich R. 'Stars lash Hollywood over violence', *The Australian*, 13 May 1996: 1; Cumming F, Abbott G. 'Killer videos on sale', *Sun Herald*, 12 May 1996.

167 Riley M. 'Censor slams tabloids over Bryant stories', *SMH*, 29 June 1996: 2.

on which governments should take action, while leaving guns alone. SSAA advertising stated: 'The public must realise that the problem is not simply about guns. We must look carefully at the impact of violent videos and movies, drugs, alcohol and our mental health system.'[168]

A parliamentary committee was rapidly convened to examine questions of media depictions of violence. Despite there having been 12 largely inconclusive inquiries into media depictions of violence since 1987,[169] the official revisiting of this issue largely diffused the gun lob-

---

168 SSAA. 'An urgent message to all gun owners' (advertisement), *Daily Telegraph*, 10 May 1996.

169 Australian Institute of Criminology. *Video viewing behaviour and attitudes towards explicit material: a preliminary investigation*. Joint project by The Australian Institute of Criminology and the Attorney-General's Department, Australian Institute of Criminology 1987; Australia. Parliament. Report of the Joint Select Committee on Video Material, (R.Klugman, Chair). Canberra: AGPS, 1988; Victoria. Parliament. Social Development Committee. Third and Final Report, Inquiry into Strategies to Deal with the Issue of Community Violence, with Particular Reference to the Mass Media and Entertainment Industries, Government Printer 1989; Australian Broadcasting Tribunal. TV Violence in Australia, Report to the Minister for Transport and Communications, Vols I–IV, Parliamentary Papers Nos. 131–34, 1990; Australian Institute of Criminology. National Committee on Violence. Violence: Directions for Australia (Duncan Chappell, Chair). Canberra: Australian Institute of Criminology, 1990; Australia. Parliament. Senate Select Committee on Community Standards Relevant to the Supply of Services Using Electronic Technologies. Report on video and computer games classification issues. (Margaret Reynolds, Chair). Parliamentary Paper, Canberra 1993; Australia. Parliament. Senate Select Committee on Community Standards Relevant to the Supply of Services Using Electronic Technologies. Report on Overseas Sourced Audiotex Services, Videos and Computer Games, R-Rated Material on Pay TV (Margaret Reynolds, Chair) Parliamentary Paper 131, Canberra 1994; Australia. Parliament. Senate Select Committee on Community Standards Relevant to the Supply of Services Using Electronic Technologies. Report on R-Rated Material on Pay TV Part 1 (Margaret Reynolds, Chair). Parliamentary Paper 9, Canberra 1995; Australia. Parliament. Senate Select Committee on Community Standards Relevant to the Supply of Services Using Electronic Technologies. Report on R-Rated Material on Pay TV, Regulation of Bulletin Board Systems, Codes of Practice in the Television Industry (Margaret Reynolds, Chair)

by's argument. The new inquiry allowed the Government to point to a comprehensive concern about violence in the community and thus avoid gun lobby accusations that only one element in gun violence – guns – was being addressed. The focus on media violence created a substantial parallel debate that ran simultaneously for many weeks of the gun control debate.[170]

'Doctors kill more people than guns'

There has been a long antipathy between sections of the gun lobby and the medical profession. The reasons for this are obvious. Doctors have been prominent among those who have advocated gun law reform. Doctors became the targets of three attacks from the gun lobby during the debate. In their advertising, the SSAA suggested that 'the medical profession has a major role to play and, after Port Arthur, may see their responsibilities more clearly'[171] – plainly an allusion to their call for doctors to set up registers of those unfit to have gun licences.

Sections of the gun lobby are also preoccupied with a convoluted theory that there is an international conspiracy by doctors and pharmaceutical companies to medicate the community with psychoactive 'control' drugs like Prozac. When Joe Wesbecker, who had been

---

Parliamentary Paper 153, Canberra 1995; Australia. Parliament. Senate Select Committee on Community Standards Relevant to the Supply of Services Using Electronic Technologies. Report on Operations of Codes of Practice in the Television Industry part 1 (Margaret Reynolds, Chair) Parliamentary Paper 463, Canberra 1994; Australia. Parliament. Senate Select Committee on Community Standards Relevant to the Supply of Services Using Electronic Technologies. Report on Regulation of Computer On-Line Services part 2 (Margaret Reynolds, Chair) Parliamentary Paper 464, Canberra 1995; Australia. Parliament. House of Representatives Standing Committee on Employment, Education and Training. Sticks and Stines: Report on Violence in Australian Schools (Mary Crawford, Chair) Canberra: AGPS, 1994.

170 Wright T, Humphries D. 'All-out attack on film violence', *SMH*, 10 July 1996: 1; Savva N. 'Crackdown on violent TV films', *The Age*, 10 July 1996: 1.

171 SSAA. 'An urgent message to all gun owners' (advertisement), *Daily Telegraph*, 10 May 1996.

prescribed Prozac three weeks previously, shot and killed eight workers, seriously wounded 12 others and then shot himself at his workplace in Kentucky in 1989,[172] the advocates of this theory became obsessed with the notion that nearly all mass killers were people on psychoactive medication, and that it was doctors who were to blame for prescribing these drugs which caused otherwise peaceful gun owners to go berserk.

In Australia, this theory is routinely circulated in gun lobby circles and was perpetuated by the Federal Member for Kalgoorlie, Graeme Campbell:

> Any pharmacist will tell you that a lot of the mind-altering drugs, such as Prozac, which are used to calm people down, in 3% of cases have exactly the opposite effect. No one is looking at this factor and nobody will look at it. While the Government, supported by the Opposition, is prepared to hammer ordinary Australians, it will not pull on the multi-national drug companies.[173]

On several occasions at the height of the Port Arthur debate, when explaining to journalists (usually from rural areas) that few mass killers had histories of mental illness, we would be asked meaningfully, 'Yes, maybe, but how many of them were on drugs like Prozac?'

Response: We judged this conspiracy theory to be so bizarre that most hearing it would immediately reflect on the motives and bona fides of those spreading it about. We felt that many would immediately wonder about the implicit message contained in this accusation – presumably that many people on such psychoactive medication should be taken off it. No one with any credibility advanced this argument in Australia, so we pointed this out whenever asked by journalists.

One of the gun lobby's more recent arguments has been that the number of deaths from medical malpractice and misadventure far exceeds those caused by guns:

---

172 Cornwall J. *Power to harm: mind, medicine and murder*. Ringwood: Penguin, 1996.

173 Australian House of Representatives *Hansard* for 9 May 1996.

> I suggest doctors look at the statistics on surgical accidents
> before becoming concerned with gun control. In New South
> Wales in 1992/93, there were 27,337 hospital admissions
> resulting from medical 'accidents', abnormal reactions
> or complications. There were only 144 firearm-related
> admissions.[174]

Another writer cited the same source but put the number of people 'injured by surgical procedures' at 31,701.[175] And another: 'You have 70 times more chance of dying from a doctor's malpractice than from a gun'[176] which suggested a figure of 10,080 deaths from medical negligence. Despite the slight problem of the fluid magnitude of these numbers, this argument sought to paint gun deaths as a relatively minor problem compared to medical malpractice, and thereby to discredit medical voices from participating in calls for gun control.

Response: We were intrigued about the doctor-consulting habits of principals within the gun lobby and waited in vain for an opportunity for one leading voice – who had made it known that he was a diabetic under medical care[177] – to use this argument. We also were ready to ask advocates of this position where they believed the injured taken from Port Arthur should have been taken for care if not to the Royal Hobart Hospital's doctors and nursing staff.

The AMA's Dr Keith Woollard told a Sydney rally that doctors had been told to 'butt out' of the gun debate. He said: 'It is absolutely and unequivocally our business. It is the doctors who are left to clean up the mess. It is the doctors who are faced with healing the ripped flesh, the ruptured organs and the splintered bones.'[178] Another said: 'The harm done to people from medical procedures is at best accidental and at

---

174 Gould I. 'Physicians need to heal themselves' (letter), *The Age*, 13 June 1996: 18.

175 Brown B. 'Guns and damned statistics' (letter), *SMH*, 27 March 1996.

176 Roudenko A. 'One in 10,000' (letter), *SMH*, 8 May 1996: 16.

177 Aiton D. 'Out for a duck', *The Sunday Age*, 21 March 1993: 4.

178 Harvey A. 'Sydney takes to the streets in anger', *SMH*, 29 July 1996: 2.

worst negligent; it is not wilful murder. It is ridiculous to use such a comparison.'[179]

Dr Brian Walpole was head of emergency medicine at the Royal Hobart Hospital and was in charge of the team that attended the injured brought in on the afternoon of the massacre. His face had become one of the most publicised symbols of the community's outrage at the incident, when he was shown on TV and in the press throughout Australia in a tearful embrace with an equally distraught Prime Minister outside the hospital.[180] Brain Walpole, who had been an active supporter of the Tasmanian CGC, was to become a vitally important voice in the advocacy work that followed the massacre.

Walpole's most obvious interest to the news media lay in his 'doctor in the front line' role, and in the way that, as one who had tried desperately to save the lives of those critically injured and experienced the grief and anger of relatives and friends of the dead and injured, he now stood as a passionate advocate for gun law reform. Here was someone whose experience could not be denied or somehow argued away by those seeking to make light of the massacre and to prevent it from translating into law reform. Here was someone who – in the face of argument from the gun lobby about semi-automatics being safe in responsible hands and so on – could describe what happens to human flesh when bullets from these weapons hit a shoulder, a chest or a stomach.

Walpole understood this very well, and chose to repeatedly emphasise the parallel between a quiet Sunday afternoon in Tasmania and a war zone: 'We went to war for a day in Tasmania and we saw on the bodies of all those people the havoc the weapons of war can wreak.'[181] Outside Tasmania's Parliament House, Walpole told a gun control rally that Australians should 'stiffen the spines of those politicians behind us who shilly-shallied with this issue for 20 years, to just get it fixed'.

179 Phillips H. Letter, *SMH*, 30 March 1996: 36.
180 Lee S. 'Prime Minister on verge of tears', *Daily Telegraph*, 2 May 1996: 2.
181 Wright T. 'A doctor can look forward with hope', *SMH*, 11 May 1996.

7

The future tasks for gun control

The 10 May 1996 Police Ministers' meeting marked the end of a major first stage of the gun control advocacy response that Port Arthur had unleashed. From then on, the goal became one of safeguarding the agreement and preventing backsliding in the weeks and months before each state would eventually pass its individual legislation and accompanying regulations reflecting the APMC agreement. Michael Gordon, political editor of the *Australian* suggested that Howard's policy victory owed much to his having 'seized the moment' before the 'shock, pain and outrage of the massacre [had been allowed] to recede.'[1] With every day that passed, the potential for the resolve caused by Port Arthur to fade and for the gun lobby to exploit the incoming tide of apathy increased.

There was widespread concern that as time went by without the states implementing their agreed law reforms, and that as the memory of Port Arthur receded, with it would go any passionate conviction among the community and politicians that urgent law reform was required. Gun lobby definitions of the episode as one-off and as something impervious to policy reform risked gaining ascendency. One commentator wrote 'Recent history . . . suggests that as time passes, the political pressure of the gun lobbies intensifies, the fervour of community support for gun control wanes the interest of the media diminishes, the nervousness of the politicians grows and in the end little gets done.'[2]

---

1 Gordon M. 'Savagery unites an unlikely Coalition', *The Australian*, 11 May 1996.
2 Richards M. 'Keeping guns and mental illness apart from violence', *The Age*, 6 May 1996: 15

The gun lobby organised many public meetings and rallies to oppose the new laws. During the period between the first and the second Police Ministers' meetings (10 May–17 July 1996) these meetings were reported regularly in the media. Most reports framed these as signs that the initial resolve was on the edge of fragmenting, particularly in rural seats held by National Party members.[3]

As Rebecca Peters put it on the evening of the agreement, the task was to become one of 'put[ting] the pressure on state governments to make sure they don't try to squirm out of this under pressure from the gun lobby'.[4]

The gun debate presented a dilemma to many rural politicians who perceived that they – far more than their city colleagues – were most at risk of backlash from angry shooters. On 19 June 1996, two rural Labor members of the NSW Government walked out of a party room meeting in protest at what they described as a lack of time to consult their constituents about the planned new laws.[5] The publicised walk-out bore all the signs of a ritualistic display to signal to the gun lobby in their electorates that they had not passively accepted the process of law reform. The protest came to nothing, as did the support of 12 NSW rural National Party members for a parliamentary amendment moved by an independent rural politician opposed to gun registration.[6] Knowing that their combined vote would go nowhere near to defeating the votes in favour of registration, these men may have been seeking to appease their gun lobby constituents while knowing that their votes would do nothing to upset the NSW Liberal-National Opposition's broad support for the package of reforms. Such gestures allowed them to run with the gun control pack and while hunting with the gun lobby hounds.

3 Emerson S, Taylor L, Meade K. 'Cracks widen in Nats' gun resolve', *The Australian*, 5 June 1996: 1.

4 Lawnham P, McGarry A. 'Shooters will defy new laws, MP warns', *The Australian*, 11 May 1996.

5 Lagan B, Millett M. Country 'MPs walk out over State's laws', *SMH*, 20 June 1996: 1.

6 Chulov M. 'Nats split over vote', *Sun Herald*, 23 June 1996: 13.

The list of agreements reached at the Police Ministers' meeting represented, in one swoop, more promise of gun law reform than had ever been achieved in Australia's entire legal history. Despite the breadth of the reform, many concerns remained. There was particular worry about the gap between the spirit of the new agreement and its translation into state and territory law and especially about the extent to which its various provisions would be actually implemented. There was also concern whether the clause providing exemptions for primary producers who could demonstrate 'genuine need' to possess low calibre semi-automatics would allow wholesale abuse when implemented. Police were to be given authority to assess applications about whether the guidelines on 'genuine need' were satisfied, and despite the Prime Minister's assurances that 'you're not dealing with a group of people who are going to lightly tick off applicants',[7] there was concern that in many cases, personal friendships with police or cases of police who personally regarded the guidelines as being too tough, might lead to easy access to semi-automatics. In the months to come, data on the number of licensed shooters will become available that will resolve whether or not government policy and practice has allowed *carte blanche* rubber stamping of existing shooter's licences, or whether the new criteria have been conscientiously applied causing many gun owners to be refused a license.

In the months that followed the APMC agreement, all states and territories passed legislative acts that embodied the core platforms of the agreement. However, along the way to the final passage of these acts, many amendments were introduced which fell well short of the spirit of gun law reform embodied in the initial APMC agreement. Those interested in scrutinising the detail of the new Acts can find them by searching AustLII Databases.[8]

---

7 Shanahan D. 'No blanket access for farmers', *The Australian*, 11 May 1996.

8 Available at: http: //www.austlii.edu.au/databases.html.

Two years on

As was feared, nearly two years after Port Arthur, there have been a number of disturbing cracks which opened up following amendments to the bills that were introduced following deals with the gun lobby in attempts to pacify rural electoral unrest, particularly in vulnerable seats. In March 1998, intense media debate on gun control erupted with the announcement that the Victorian government planned a series of amendments to its gun laws. The Queensland and South Australian governments also indicated dissatisfaction with aspects of the laws. While the media debate was concentrated on what seemed imminent in these states, it highlighted that slippage from the APMC had in fact already been occurring in all states. The proposed Victorian changes included:

- Allowing members of clay pigeon target shooting clubs to use semi-automatic and pump-action shotguns. The APMC agreement restricts access to semi-automatic (Category C) weapons to clay target shooters who are affiliated with the Australian Clay Target Association (ACTA). However Victoria, Queensland and the Northern Territory amended their legislation to allow licences to members of approved clay target clubs using an approved club range, regardless of whether they are affiliated with the ACTA. The Western Australian government estimates that less than 100 additional people are affected by this regulation

- Granting minors' permits to allow children to shoot. This is contrary to the APMC resolutions, in that the minimum specified age for a shooters licence is 18. There is no mention in the APMC resolutions of any procedure for children under that age to be granted 'junior licenses' to shoot. Several of the new state gun laws allow children as young as 11 to have gun licences if they are supervised by adults. As the Victorian changes were being publicaly debated, all other states and territories were already breaching the agreement by permitting children under 18 to shoot. NSW, South Australia, Tasmania, and the ACT permit children from 12 years to have legal access to guns via minor's permits, while in Queensland the minimum age is 11 years. Western and the Northern Territory set no minimum age for shooting. Under Australian laws, children aged under 18 are considered too young to smoke, purchase or be supplied with alcohol, watch violent movies, vote, consent to medical treatment, drive (if under 17), or have sex (if under 16). We don't for example, issue driving learning permits to children under 16, despite the requirement of a licensed adult driver to be present when a young driver of 16 is learning. If as was so often said, the national gun control agreement had turned Australia away from being a 'gun culture', the new laws were an acknowledgment of a sea change in community tolerance of casual gun laws. Part of taking a less casual approach to guns must be to state clearly that guns are not appropriate for children.

- Waiving the 28-day cooling off period for the purchase of second or subsequent weapons. This was a clear breach of resolution No. 7 which stated 'All jurisdictions to establish a 28-day waiting period prior to the issuing of *all* firearms permits.' Again, Western Australia and the Northern Territory were already breaching the agreement on this: police there are not required to wait 28 days to issue firearm permits.

As the debate increased about the Victorian government's intentions, on the second anniversary of the Dunblane massacre Walter Mikac wrote an impassioned plea in *The Age* to politicians to stop the slide. He wrote

> Have too many years passed since the Hoddle Street and Queen Street shootings? Maybe the politicians think it cannot happen here again. Has complacency set in so soon after Port Arthur? . . . In many ways I still feel shock that this issue has raised its head again. Like revisiting all those emotions . . . Surely it is up to our representatives to provide us with a safe community to live in . . . Despite the rhetoric of the Police Minister, Bill McGrath, people are perceptive enough to see that the amendments in Victoria must weaken the uniform national policy. The presentation of the amend-

ments to the public has been unprofessional, without enough consultation and definitely lacked sensitivity. When we met McGrath on Tuesday, he admitted that the Premier, Jeff Kennett, had said exactly that to him earlier that morning. These amendments are the first erosions to our national policy. They could open the floodgates for other states.[9]

As the drift toward ad hoc amendments appeared to be gaining momentum in March 1998, Prime Minister Howard re-entered the gun debate, using the occasion of a Premiers' conference on March 20 to bring his concerns to a head. The conference was called in the middle of sustained protests from all states about the poor funding promised to them for health care by the Federal Government. Howard's intransigence on this issue caused a walkout by all Premiers before the gun issue agenda item was even reached. As they left the room an angry Howard reportedly called out: 'So what you are saying is that you refuse to discuss guns? This is very important. What you are saying is that I am going to have to address this myself.' Commentators wrote 'The public wants service at hospitals. They blame both governments when they can't get it. Everyone loses on health, always. But on guns, John Howard is on a winner.'[10]

Days later, Howard acted to ensure that the watered down gun laws being passed by the states would henceforth be meaningless. From midnight on 24 March Howard banned imports of semi-automatic guns. Howard stated 'with effect from midnight tonight, there will be a ban introduced on weapons designated as Category C under the 1996 agreement'. Exemptions for farmers who could produce police guarantees they were primary producers, and clay target shooters with the written authority of the federal Attorney General were to be allowed. Howard's action meant that should any state liberalise access to Category C guns, a person thus newly licensed would have very few opportunities to legally

9 Mikac W. 'Heaven on earth is a place without guns', *The Age*, 13 March 1998.

10 Kingston M, Cleary P. 'They all came, they dined well, they walked out', *SMH*, 21 March 1998.

purchase such a gun unless obtaining authorisation from the federal Attorney General. Only those guns placed on the market by the limited number of persons authorised to have access to Category C guns would be legally available to such shooters.

The SSAA's website quoted correspondence received on this matter:

> On 25 March 1998, Statutory Rules 1998 No. 52 commenced operation. It amended the Customs (Prohibited Imports) Regulations to restrict the classes of people who are permitted to import self-loading rimfire rifles, self-loading shotguns or pump action repeating shotguns or parts) to primary producers who can pass the 'police authorisation' test and have permission from the Attorney-General to import the articles.

> Members of the Australian Clay Target Association who owned self-loading shotguns or pump action repeating shotguns as at 15 November 1996, or who, for reasons of lack of strength or dexterity need such weapons to compete in competition, and who can pass the 'police authorisation' test, and have permission of the Attorney-General to import either self loading shotguns or pump action repeating shotguns (or parts) may also import such weapons (or parts).

> Finally, licenced firearm dealers may, with the permission of the Attorney-General, import limited quantities of self-loading shotguns, pump action repeating shotguns or self loading rimfire rifles. Such weapons (and parts) are to be stored with customs, and will only be released if the importer can prove he or she has sold the weapon to a certified primary producer or sports shooter.

Safe storage

As described in Chapter 4, while the new laws specify minimum standards of storage for guns in homes, there is little evidence that these standards are being policed. A 1997 SSAA survey on the buyback reported that only 2% of its self-selected respondents had 'been subject to a search/visit/inspection at your business/home premises by members of your State Police in relation to the firearm buyback scheme'[11] Arguments that the sheer number of gun owners precludes any universal system of inspection prior to granting a licence contrasts with the way the state takes seriously building and motor vehicle inspection. Any building owner wishing to alter the structure of a building is required to allow (and pay for) an inspection of whether the alterations meet specifications. If as a community we can endorse the need for user-pays building and car inspections (often for reasons of safety), to deny this in the case of gun storage is to revert to the *laissez faire* attitude of the pre– Port Arthur days. With unsecure home storage of guns contributing to the frequency of gun theft from homes and the fortunately less common accidental discharges by children, the abject neglect of the implementation home storage regulations remains a major weakness in Australian gun law regulation.

Collector's licences

The APMC resolutions and the modifications of 17 July 1996, required collectors to prove they were 'bona fide'. Collector's licences were intended to be a very limited category of licence covering existing collectors whose guns had genuine historical value. Because collectors were to be allowed to own more guns than other licensees, the need to apply stringent tests for this type of licence is obvious. However, collectors provisions in all states and territories constitute loopholes that can be exploited by those intent on maintaining or building up large stocks of guns. The Queensland Act for example, has no criteria for determining whether someone is a bona fide collector. The term 'bona fide' is absent, and there are no requirements to join a collectors' club or furnish any proof of a history of collecting.

---

11 http://www.ssaa.org.au/Survey.htm [no longer active, 2013].

Variable buyback rates

As shown in Table 4.1, the final results of the gun buyback showed great per capita variation across the country, ranging from one gun surrendered per 41.7 head of adult (15–75 years) population in the A.C.T. to one gun per 10.9 adults in Tasmania, the site of the massacre and the state that along with Queensland, had previously had Australia's weakest gun laws. These figures though, present a very misleading picture. Recalling our argument in Chapter 5 of the domination of gun ownership by men, we might well divide the final adult per capita buyback figures by two to give a buyback rate per adult (15–75 years) *male* head of population. Nationally, this would result in one semi-automatic or pump-action shotgun being surrendered for every 10.4 adult males, and in Tasmania, one per 5.5 adult men. While I have been unable to obtain data on the mean number of guns surrendered by those coming forward, it is known that many handed in many more than one gun.

When the gun buyback ended there were 640,401 fewer semi-automatic and pump-action shotguns in the Australian community; a national system of gun registration had been established on 1 July 1997; and judging by the numbers of complaints on shooters' web pages, many people applying for shooters licences were being rejected as having insufficient reason to own a gun. Moreover, it seemed possible that many gun owners may well have decided that their gun ownership was at an end. In early 1997, the Victorian secretary of the Firearm Traders Association, Robert Brewer said 'Out of every 100 firearms handed in, only eight are being replaced. That means a massive drop in the number of firearms.'[12] By October, this pattern appeared to be well entrenched. In Victoria, only one in 12 shooters surrendering a gun purchased a new, legal replacement weapon. In Western Australia, the figure was one in six.[13] The buyback was the largest ever attempted anywhere in the world and by any standard has radically reduced the national gun arsenal.

---

12 *Herald Sun*, 13 December 1996: 1–2.

13 Wainwright R. 'Gun shy', *SMH*, 4 October 1997: 33.

In April 1998, Australia's biggest firearms distributor, Fuller Firearms, announced that it would close at the end of the 1998 financial year. Its owner claimed that national sales had fallen by 80% and that about only 10% of the money paid in compensation during the buyback had been reinvested in legal weapons.[14] The Fuller situation appears to reflect the national picture. In late April 1998, the *Sydney Morning Herald* reported data compiled by the Australian Bureau of Statistics showing that the number of firearms imported in the first nine months of the 1997–98 financial year fell almost 70%.

> The ABS statistics give weight to assertions by gun dealers that the buy-back scheme has forced many companies out of business and could result in the collapse of the industry. All of the weapons sold in Australia are imported. Between July last year and March this year, 20,493 rifles and shotguns, valued at $8.9million, were imported, 32 per cent of the importations from the comparable period the previous year. More than 83,000 rifles and shotguns, valued at $33 million, were imported for the 1996–97 year.[15]

But how many illegal guns remain in circulation? As detailed in Chapter 4, the Commonwealth Law Enforcement Board advised the Police Ministers prior to the buyback that there were probably 1,488,000 soon-to-be-illegal guns in circulation before the buyback commenced. That would mean that after the surrender of some 631,000 guns that 857,000 illegal guns remain in the community. True to form, John Tingle estimated that in NSW alone, there were 2.5 million illegal guns in circulation[16] – meaning that on average every adult male in the state would have had 1.1 semi-automatic weapons, not to mention legal guns as well! But even if the Commonwealth estimates are reliable, such differences speak of massive, widespread and deliberate illegal gun

---

14 Wainwright R. 'Sales drop forces gun company to close', *SMH*, 8 April 1998: 3.

15 Wainwright R. '300,000 banned firearms still in circulation', *SMH*, 27 April 1998: 3.

16 Ibid.

retention, particularly in NSW where rifles were not required to be registered. NSW's rate of 30.2 guns surrendered per adult is 1.65 times less than the national average (after removal of the NSW figures). So much for earnest gun lobby talk about law-abiding shooters.

Australia is now a country where anyone now owning an illegal gun or being an unlicensed shooter faces the prospect of large fines and/or jail sentences; where near universal awareness exists that semi-automatic weapons are illegal; and where community support for gun control remains higher than practically any other single issue in public affairs. Any shooter who has retained such a weapon will need to be constantly vigilant to the possibility that if it is being rapidly fired within earshot of others, that someone hearing the distinctive sequence may call the police. Those who have broken the law and kept these guns will also need to keep their mouths shut. It would seem highly likely that many neighbours, acquaintances, workmates and family members fearful of the potential for these weapons to be used in acts of violence may report these owners to the police (see below).

The NSW police have announced that they will commence checking gun dealer's sales records against the buyback details. This was the process used to trace the gun used by the backpacker murderer Ivan Milat to a suburban gun shop. In a letter sent to Philip Alpers the New Zealand gun control researcher, NSW Police Superintendent Clive Small confirmed that the Milat case has caused the police to 'collate importation details from various companies over a period of approximately 20 years in regard to all weapons of the type used in the murders and subsequent inquiries regarding ownership.' Such a database will be an invaluable tool in tracing many guns still in circulation, should governments direct police to take this issue seriously.

But – thanks to the previous absence of gun registration – there will be thousands of shooters who bought their guns from someone privately or down at the pub and will be feeling smug that there is little chance of a knock on the door from police checking. Unless Australian police are ordered to engage in active rather than passive policing of this issue, most of the illegal gun owners' complacency will be proven justified.

Gun control advocates have repeatedly called for the potential of community concern to be channelled into a highly publicised anonymous reporting or 'dob in' scheme whereby people pass information on such gun owners to police. Such strategies are used routinely and successfully in the areas of child abuse, paedophilia, drug dealing, and environmental pollution and are promoted as examples of civic mindedness. If we can give priority to organising anonymous community phone-ins for drugs, child abuse and even poor university teaching standards, a high profile dob-in campaign is surely an obvious means of locating many of these guns. Like Ted Drane who said publicly on 15 June 1996 'I'm not gunna give up any guns that they are going to take off me! Are you gunna give yours up?', many shooters openly declared their refusal to hand in their guns. With guns being so central to these men's lives, many will have boasted about their weapons to neighbours, workmates and ex-girlfriends. Numbered among these will be many who will share the community's concerns about the stability of people willing to risk a jail term to retain a rapid-fire weapon. The Tasmanian police have confirmed they will commence raiding homes following tip offs from gun owners who have obeyed the law and are resentful of those who have refused.[17]

Reforms welcomed by many sporting shooters

With the exception of the politically motivated end of the gun lobby, it seems that many shooters have come to realise that the law reforms may actually prove to be good for their sport. With membership of an established sports shooting or hunting club being one criterion for gun licensing, many clubs have seen booms in membership. Not only does this bring new membership fees, but also it holds the potential to bring some of the 'cowboy' element among shooters under the positive

---

17 'Tasmanian police to raid homes for guns', *The Advocate* (Hobart), 7 May 1997.

influence of the many responsible sections of the shooting fraternity. From the perspective of responsible shooters seeking to change the negative image of shooting, the new licensing laws hold promise of weeding out many 'weekend Rambos'.

Despite the efforts of many in the gun lobby to portray gun control advocacy groups like the NCGC as gun prohibitionists, there was nothing in the APMC package and nothing in any statement made by the NCGCs representatives that could justify this label. The NCGC has never advocated prohibition of all guns and fully recognises the importance of guns in feral animal control and in farming, and is not opposed to target shooting organised under proper controls. Here, it is worth quoting at length Philip Alpers' speech to the United Nations Commission on Crime Prevention and Criminal Justice meeting in Vienna in April 1998:

> I'm a licensed gun owner. I enjoy target shooting and I have no objection to the use of appropriate firearms in pest control, on the farm and in sport. Given the number of pests introduced to New Zealand by colonists, I have little option. But it's also my belief that the regulation of guns is an important human rights issue.
>
> While a small number of men do claim that they have the right to carry a gun, the vast majority of the people on this planet insist that they have the right to live in a society free of the fear of guns. Some will tell you that the more guns you have, the safer you are. If that were truly the case, the United States would be the safest nation on earth.
>
> Personally, I don't need study after study to tell me that the more guns you have in a community, the more people are likely to get shot. To many of us, it is simply self-evident that the availability of firearms is directly related to their subsequent use in crime and violence. I have yet to hear of a drive-by knifing.
>
> So, every nation has a duty to regulate guns. As you've seen from the excellent United Nations study on firearm regula-

tion, for many years it's been the norm in both industrialised and developing nations to employ two parallel registers in a system similar to that used for automobiles. We license the individual – that's the driver or the gun owner – as a fit and proper person, and we register the object – that's the car or the firearm – to make the owner more responsible and personally accountable for any damage done.

Gun registration in particular is recognised as the cornerstone of any effective tracking and tracing system for firearms. You will have seen the Secretary-General's report on the regional workshops on firearm regulation.

With regard to some issues, this document is a wish list. But on the central issue of licensing each gun owner, supplemented by the parallel registration of individual firearms, I can assure you that it was the view of the great majority of the 149 experts from 79 countries who attended, that these two measures together constitute our best chance – and perhaps our only chance before it's too late – to control the proliferation of firearms.

In promoting the regulation of firearms at these UN workshops, delegates deserve the thanks of millions of citizens who see it as their right to live without having to worry about someone else in the crowd carrying a gun . . . There is also a growing international recognition that most of the deaths in conflict since World War II have been effected, not by nuclear weapons, by tanks or by bombs, but by cheap, easily accessible, guns.

In coming months the efforts of the United Nations will be supported and encouraged by a wide range of NGOs and governments who are becoming just as concerned about guns as they have been about landmines.

Of course, the pro-gun lobby will oppose all of this. The National Rifle Association of America has already coined the phrase 'global gun grabbers' to describe you and your aims. The NRA has become openly distressed at the initiatives promoted by the Crime Commission . . .

Now you may think that the reason you're all here is to discuss illicit trafficking in firearms, the reduction of firearm-related crime and the public health of your nation.

But in her fund-raising letter Mrs Metaksa [of the US National Rifle Association] told millions of Americans that the Crime Commission process is the main thrust of what she calls 'the UN's world-wide anti-gun campaign which threatens the sovereignty of our nation, and [our] personal right to keep and bear arms.' According to the NRA, 'a multi-national cadre of gun-ban extremists is lobbying the United Nations,' demanding a declaration that would include a 'world-wide ban on private firearms ownership.'

That's worth repeating. Mrs Metaksa claims that you're here today to plot and to promote 'a world-wide ban on private firearms ownership.' As you know, this is far from the truth. You know that this initiative is part of a United Nations initiative which began in Cairo in 1995.

You know that 138 member nations voted unanimously to give this process its mandate. But the National Rifle Association campaign targets only one of those 138 countries. They single out 'the Japanese government . . . one of the most anti-gun in the world,' as being both the originator and financier of what the NRA calls the UN's 'global gun ban scheme.' The NRA letter continues: 'we can't give the Japanese and other UN gun-banners even half a chance to ban our guns and attack our US Constitution.'

Mrs Metaksa then went on to urge NRA members to send at least a million protest letters to United Nations headquarters in New York. That was last November. Since then, the NRA has refused to reveal the extent to which its members have – or have not – followed its instructions.

So you can see that your purpose here today has been blown out of all proportion by the US gun lobby. In a campaign with obvious overtones of racism, the gun lobby is doing its utmost to exploit anti-Japanese and anti-United Nations sentiment. They're making a cynical appeal to their own domestic audience at the cost of the rest of the world. And all of this to prop up the gun lobby's mythical, and dangerous notion that there is a so-called 'right' to possess unlimited guns.

Ladies and gentlemen, you came here to discuss the serious business of firearm regulation for the purpose of public safety. These antics may seem like a sideshow. And of course that's exactly what the NRA's campaign amounts to. It's a shameless beat-up of a very normal process. The United Nations Commission on Crime Prevention and Criminal Justice has every right – indeed it has an obligation – to discuss illicit trafficking in guns, just as it has to co-ordinate worldwide efforts against drug trafficking, money laundering and trans-national car theft.

Guns should not be treated any differently to any other tools of crime. The fact that firearms hold a special and romantic place in the hearts of a small minority of men in a handful of wealthy nations should in no way dissuade you from treating guns as just another hazardous consumer product. Guns and their owners should never be regarded as somehow exempt from regulation.

And now, having spoken at length about the gun lobby, I'm going to urge you to treat them as irrelevant. I suggest that you're here to co-operate in finding ways to improve the public safety of your nations. The peculiar attitudes of a small minority in the United States have little application or relevance outside that country's borders. Please, proceed with the important work of firearm regulation by sponsoring and promoting the work of the Crime Commission, and just ignore the sideshows.

I have every confidence that your citizens will thank you for doing so. Thank you.[18]

---

18 Seventh Session, Vienna, Austria, 27 April 1998, Item 5: Measures to Regulate Firearms Statement of Philip Alpers, gun policy researcher Auckland, New Zealand.

The current leadership of the gun lobby remains apoplectic over the new laws because of its leaders' political ambitions and because of the involvement in the lobby of importers and dealers who will lose money from the restrictions imposed by the new laws. As I showed in Chapter 4 where I reviewed electoral results since Port Arthur, this end of the gun lobby appears not to have the confidence of even a modest proportion of gun owners or indeed even members of the SSAA. Almost daily, the guest book on the SSAA's web site (www.ssaa.org.au) features statements from angry shooters saying they will never vote for again for either the Coalition or the Labor party, but will support minor candidates who advance shooters interests. The SSAA's home page has a web counter underscored with 'We are aware of [web site count number] who will not vote for John Howard'. Given that people many people working in gun control visit the site often more than once a day, this 'whistling in the dark', talking-up self-assurance is revealing of the insecurity the SSAA administration plainly feels.

On 30 September 1997, the final day of the gun buyback, the SSAA published an advertisement capital city newspapers highlighting 'Responses to an Australian Audit Office requested survey of 80,000 SSAA members.'[19] Such was the apathy among the SSAA's membership that it received 'more than 5000 responses' (say 6.3%) and chose to key in only 2,137 (2.7%) respondents from its 80,000 membership. Presumably the 93.7% of SSAA non-respondents had more on their minds.

Getting guns out of homes

Besides working to address some of the shortcomings of the new laws as outlined above, perhaps the Australian gun control's major policy challenge for the future is to lobby for laws that require gun owners in urban settings to store their guns outside of homes in community armouries. Ex-residential storage of all handguns was a key recommendation made by Lord Cullen after the Dunblane massacre, and was adopted by the

19 http://www.ssaa.org.au/ad.html [no longer active, 2013].

British government in the interim period before the Blair government banned all handguns. Curiously, Cullen's recommendation for ex-residential storage only applied to handguns, not to rifles and shotguns which of course are equally capable of causing the sort of carnage that occurred at Dunblane school.[20]

The main arguments for community armouries are:

- By law, guns cannot be fired in residential settings; hence there is no need to have guns in houses in towns and cities.
- Self-defence is not recognised as a legitimate reason to keep a gun. Therefore any reference to this reason as legitimising home storage can no longer apply in Australia.
- Guns are regularly stolen by thieves, with homes being the most common site for gun theft.[21]

  Removal of guns from homes would eliminate most accidental firearm discharges by children in the manner depicted in the NSW government's graphic pre–Port Arthur gun amnesty television advertisement.

  The gap between the impulse to suicide caused by the time required to go and check out a gun from an armoury may prevent many suicide deaths.

  During domestic violence episodes guns could not be grabbed and used to threaten family members.

  If guns were required to be stored in armouries, with a storage fee attached, this would act as a disincentive to many shooters to retain guns that they seldom used.

In Australia, ex-residential storage would only be practical for urban and town residents because of the distances that often exist between population centres. Rural gun owners and those in towns not served by a police station should be obliged to store their guns securely in locked

---

20 Chapman S. 'Getting guns out of homes', *British Medical Journal*, 1996, 313: 1030.

21 See http://www.medfacc.usyd.edu.au/medfac/GunControl/fp_3_2.htm for a detailed report on gun theft in New Zealand [no longer active, 2013].

cabinets as currently required under the new gun laws. As argued, these should be inspected at a cost borne by the shooter.

Advocates for community armouries typically suggest that the armouries could be licensed gun clubs or police stations. They argue that both of these locations are already or could easily be securely fortified so as to allow for very secure storage. The gun lobby typically responds that community armouries would provide criminals with golden opportunities to steal hundreds or even thousands of guns from one location. For example Neil Jenkins, a target shooter who is one of Australia's most reasonable spokespeople on guns argues:

> Rifle clubs typically operate on a non profit basis and carry only enough funds to pay the electricity bill and the occasional coat of paint. Also, most rifle ranges were built prior to World War II and are nothing more than well maintained weatherboard rooms with an office an alarm system sitting behind a barbed wire fence, hence would need to be rebuilt from the ground up to accommodate an armoury. The only way this could be financed would be through a second gun levy. My club is a typical one that opens one night a week. We have enough problems with amateur thieves who think we store guns at the club without having to worry about the professional ones aware that each rifle may be worth up to $5,000 each.[22]

In the UK after the passing of the Cullen recommendation on ex-residential storage, many gun clubs not solvent enough to upgrade their security facilities appear likely to close. It seems certain that Australia would see a similar scenario should such a policy be adopted here regarding storage in clubs. None but the more extreme ends of Australian gun control interests are in any way committed to using such a pretext to force the closure of target shooting clubs.

However, Danny Walsh from the Victorian Police Association offered an obvious solution to the very real points raised by Jenkins. On ABC-TV's *Lateline* on 9 May 1996 Walsh suggested that licensed

---

22 http://www.alphalink.com.au/~tonka/link4.htm [no longer active, 2013].

gun dealers could double as community armouries. Walsh argued compellingly that we already trust gun dealers to securely store guns. Many gun dealerships are open seven days a week to service shooters' needs. The argument that gun shops would become targets for thieves already applies now. Gun shops are always heavily secured and have not to date been frequent targets for robberies in Australia. Certainly, more guns are now stolen from homes than from occasional robberies of gun shops. Most tellingly, the gun lobby is not on record as arguing that they should be closed because they are accessible repositories of guns for criminals. Gun dealers would doubtless be strongly supportive of such a plan as it would provide them with extra income through storage fees as well as customer traffic (many shooters would probably purchase shooting accessories when collecting their guns).

The NSW Firearm Dealers' Association has 400 registered gun dealers and predicts that up to 75% of them will go out of business because of the tightening of gun laws causing an expected reduction in the number of licensed shooters and preventing sales to the many unlicensed gun owners in the community.[23] If governments were to arrange for gun shops to serve as armouries, the financial impact on gun dealers would be far less, and may well increase their business substantially.

The main problem remaining with gun storage in armouries concerns the duration and frequency that shooters would be permitted to check out their guns. Potential difficulties would arise with shooters who legitimately wanted to go on weeks' long hunting trips and with those who were determined to beat the system by claiming that they more or less continually needed to check their guns out from armouries in order to go on one such trip after another – all the time simply returning the gun to their home. Challenges in drafting reasonable guidelines to address this problem still remain but are not insurmountable.

---

23 Wainwright, 8 April, *op. cit.*

Banning semi-automatic handguns

Thomas Hamilton, the Dunblane killer, used a semi-automatic pistol to kill 16 children and their teacher. The sort of weapon used by Hamilton – who was a licensed pistol shooter – can be commonly found in the hands of licensed shooters in Australia today. As Hamilton demonstrated, these guns are capable of hideous, rapid and lethal firepower. It defies all logic to argue that Australia was justified removing semi-automatic long-arms from all but the few who could demonstrate genuine need for them, while continuing to allow handgun weaponry with the same rapid-fire capability to be available to shooters.

Compared to long arms (rifles and shotguns), Australian laws on handguns have long been much stricter. Handgun (pistol) licences are normally available only to members of handgun clubs and those employed in the security industry. Doubtless the gun lobby will argue passionately that there have been few incidents where semi-automatic handguns have been involved in gun violence and that therefore there is no need to place further restrictions on their availability. However, the facile nature of this argument can be seen by reflecting on what would have eventuated had Hamilton and Martin Bryant (respectively) used a rifle and a handgun, rather than the other way round. The carnage in both cases suggests that the myopia of the Australian law in only outlawing semi-automatic rifles and shotguns and not handguns as well may well return to haunt our legislators. While we can all hope and pray that such a prediction will never come to pass, the failure of even the Howard government to go the whole distance on gun law reform shows there remains much work to be done.

The lasting legacy of Port Arthur remains the way the tragedy all but destroyed the use of gun control as an expedient political bargaining chip that could be used to play one party off against the other. The outrage in the Australian community bound all major political parties in a common bond to move Australia more toward being a safer nation. The glue cementing this multi-party bond appears firm, although by no means permanent. For now, the gun lobby appears confined to the largely irrelevant political detritus status it shares with every conceivable shade of right wing extremism. We all must ensure it stays that way and keep alive the memory of the Port Arthur 35 by preserving and strengthening the laws their deaths finally allowed us to have.

Any man's death diminishes me because I am involved in mankind and therefore never seem to know for whom the bell tolls. It tolls for thee.
John Donne

Those killed at Port Arthur on 28th April 1996 were:

Winifred Aplin
Walter Bennett
Elva Gaylard
Zoe Hall
Elizabeth Howard
Mary Howard
Mervyn Howard
Ronald Jary
Tony Kirstan
Sarah Loughton
Chung Soo Leng
Dennis Lever
Pauline Masters
Allanah Mikac
Madeline Mikac
Nannette Mikac
David Martin
Sally Martin
Andrew Mills
Peter Nash
Gwenda Neander
Anthony Nightengale
Mary Nixon
Janet Quin
Glen Pears
Jim Pollard
Royce Thompson
Helene Salzmann
Robert Salzmann
Kate Scott
Kevin Sharp
Raymond Sharp

Over our dead bodies

Ng Moh Yee William
Jason Winter
Name unknown, India.[24]

---

24 '35 reasons why our leaders must act', *Daily Telegraph*, 2 May 1996: 1

Other books by Simon Chapman

Simon Chapman. *The lung goodbye: tactics for counteracting the tobacco industry in the 1980s.* Sydney: Consumer Interpol 1986.

Simon Chapman. *Great expectorations: advertising and the tobacco industry.* London: Comedia, 1986.

Simon Chapman & Wong Wai Leng. *Tobacco control in the Third World: a resource atlas.* Penang: International Organization of Consumers' Unions and the American Cancer Society, 1990.

Simon Chapman and Deborah Lupton. *The fight for public health: principles and practice of media advocacy.* London: British Medical Journal Books, 1994.

Simon Chapman & Stephen Leeder (eds). *The last right? Australians take sides on the right to die.* Sydney: Mandarin, 1995.

Simon Chapman, Alexandra Barratt & Martin Stockler. *Let sleeping dogs lie? What men should know before getting tested for prostate cancer.* Sydney: Sydney University Press, 2010; http://purl.library.usyd.edu.au/sup/9781920899684.

www.ingramcontent.com/pod-product-compliance
Lightning Source LLC
Chambersburg PA
CBHW071411090426
42737CB00011B/1427